Thank You Max,
for being the
inspiration
in writing
my first novel xx

# THANK YOU
# FOR THE KISS

BETH JORDAN

*Beth Jordan*
*07. 03. 2023*

First edition printed and published in the United Kingdom 2023.

A CIP catalogue record of this book is available from the British Library.

ISBN: 978-1-7392749-0-0 (Hardcover)
ISBN: 978-1-7392749-1-7 (Paperback)

Imprint: Independently published by Moultavie
Editor: Christine Beech
Purchased stock imagery credit to: Crystal Bolin Photography, Aurore Kervoern, Eloi_Omella & ilbusca - Via iStock
Cover design: Jenn Garside Illustration and Graphic Design
Typesetting: Matthew J Bird

For further information about this book, please contact the author at:
www.bethjordanwriterphotographer.life
thisisitamwriting@gmail.com

*To men and women who kiss and receive the unexpected*
*To my mother whose tender kiss healed me*
*To my child whose kiss I yearned for*

# MAP OF CUBA

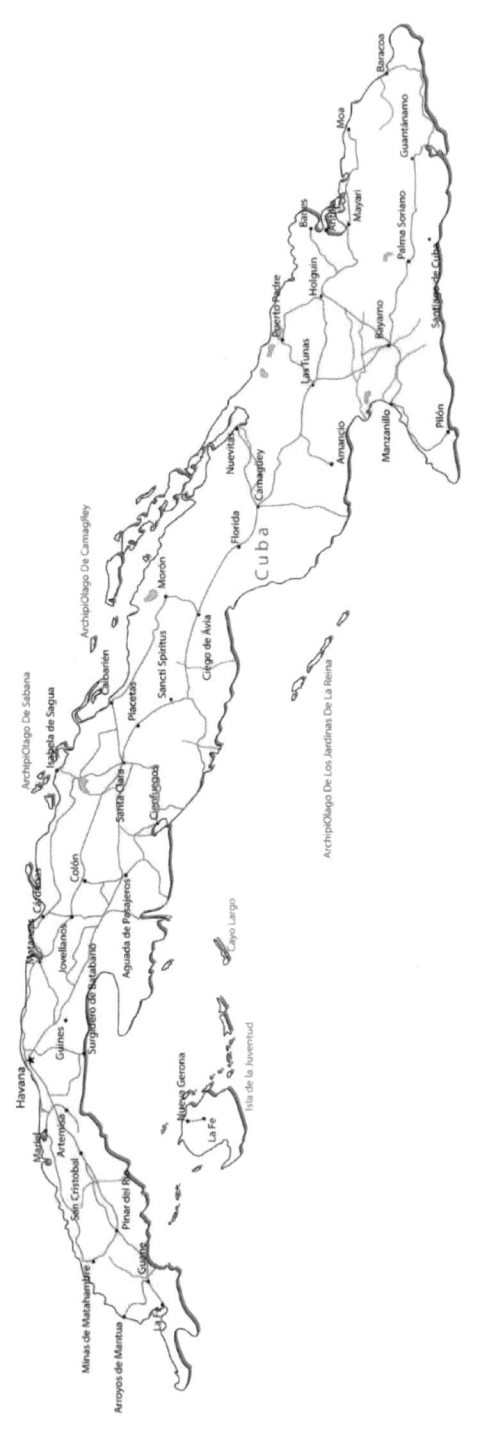

Archipiélago De Sabana

Archipiélago De Camagüey

Archipiélago De Los Jardines De La Reina

Cuba

Baracoa

Moa

Guantánamo

Mayarí

Palma Soriano

Santiago de Cuba

Holguín

Bayamo

Pilón

Manzanillo

Amarijio

Las Tunas

Puerto Padre

Bajas

Nuevitas

Camagüey

Florida

Ciego de Ávila

Moron

Sancti Spíritus

Placetas

Caibarién

Santa Clara

Cienfuegos

Colón

Isabela de Sagua

Aguada de Pasajeros

Jovellanos

Matanzas Cárdenas

Güines

Surgidero de Batabanó

Havana

Cayo Largo

Artemisa

Madi

Güira

Pinar del Río

Sen Cristobal

Soroa

Minas de Matahambre

Arroyos de Mantua

Isla de la Juventud

Nueva Gerona

La Fe

# 1

I walked across the expansive plaza filled with sunshine, with laughter and a smile; a breeze, its fingers brushing through my long brown hair. I felt carefree, alive. How could I know then that my curiosity, my vanity, my naivety, and my age, which should not have but did, lead me to a hell disguised as paradise? That seven months later, on a dark hot and humid night, I would be sitting on an old stone bench, under a watery-yellow lamp post, in anger and revenge. A black nemesis my new lover. That darkened corner of the square, edged with tall night-green trees, off-street lights picking their way through gaping branches had, in times past, seen streams of people filling this same place, with anger and revolution, hope and despair filling their hearts. Those same old emotions now filling my heart and twisting it to breaking point.

I sat waiting in Parque Central, Havana, as it reverberated to its old vibrant self. A place of brooding sensuality, pulsating to the sound of Latin rhythms. Its old worn cream flagstones, shiny from years of furious and hurried footfall of white-suited bronzed-skinned men, dark-haired, blond-haired, and dressed to kill many hearts and men. Slender, curvy women with shiny ink-black hair, glossy like the feathers of a crow, with high Afro-European cheekbones, eyes of liquid darkness, lazily looking around at all who walked through.

My head was abuzz as the sound of traffic whirled around this historic Spanish-style plaza steeped in antiquity, locked in an almost forgotten time. The low growl of brightly coloured long-tailed American Chevrolets and Buicks swam around the plaza or lay like exotic fish on a seabed of tarmac roads. Their leather upholstery, creased, scratched, repaired, with concave indentations of worn seats, held many stories, many memories of romance or escape. Those old cars left over from the 1950s, their bodies still shining, their inner parts a mix of hundreds of different bits and pieces, held together with another kind of hope and wish, much like the people of Cuba. And now, those low-slung sleek cars of Schiaparelli pink, limoncello yellow, acid turquoise blue, and pimento red, those primary colours of vibrancy and childhood drawings were offering tourists insights into the former glory of Havana for a ride around, $50, one hour, one person.

Sitting, crouched over, waiting, I too felt much like those old cars looked, eyes bright, chrome shiny on the outside, my emotions held together with pins of my determined self to never give way to hurt or remorse of any kind.

Throughout the day I had sat, not wanting to move in case I missed his arrival. Legs crossing and uncrossing, as the sun warmed the old stone bench, looking up and around at the ebb and flow of the plaza.

Parque Central, the heart of Old Havana, sparkled in the sunlight, surrounded by heavily overgrown Jacaranda trees, tall and stately. In each corner of the plaza, groves of white scented Mariposa flowers grew, delicate yet bold, and dried-up baptismal-shaped fountains sat idly, no longer playful. Old men sat closely together, waiting, some wearing discoloured ragged khaki jackets and Che Guevara berets, medals pinned to the brim. Their long knobbly fingers dangling across their crossed bony knees. They limply held or read a newspaper, some pulling on a thin papery roll-up, spittle stuck between yellowing teeth. Eyes, now cataractous and watery-blue peering out from beneath wisps of greying hair, bare-footed, grimy, with broken toenails, but still proud. Arturo (I had taken his photo on a previous happier trip), stood apart, leaning with one bare foot against a lamp post, proud and tall. Those old men held memories and postures of former soldiers, still fighting for their thread of life, as if still in that great revolutionary war, alongside the iconic Che Guevara. They sat hoping for a tiny handout given in exchange for a souvenir photo for some tourist to take home and pin up on a wall, somewhere.

My half-closed eyes took in the young men, redolent in different corners of the plaza, one leg propped up on a bench, the latest cotton canvas Converse on their feet, impeccably dressed. Their eyes roving, darting, looking unobtrusively or purposefully over tourists, all possible opportunities. A scene I saw repeated in every city I travelled to throughout Cuba.

I continued to sit, the waiting becoming a purgatory. How much longer would this continue?

I let time while away.

Following a movement in front of me, my eyes tracked the short flight of a bird as it flew to the top of a tall plinth, settling on the head of the white marble statue of Jose Marti, a young hero of the old Cuban Revolution. His marble memory surrounded by tall slender green Royal Palm trees bending gently from a sea breeze blowing off the Malecon, Havana's famous waterfront. Marti gave his young life for Cuba's independence, a revolution that would change Cuba from a rich sugar-producing country, with its capital Havana, built on borrowed lines of elegant Spanish architecture of cavernous proportions, to a run-down, worn-out city. Across from Marti, a golden-top cathedral, richly carved, a white stucco, and stone edifice, rose like a star. A shining blaze to the lofty offices of Tobacco Companies where one can buy the famous Cohiba cigars. But don't buy from their store, find a pretty boy to take you just round a backstreet where one can buy a box of 20 for $100, $30 for himself and $70 for the seller, always a helping hand around the corner.

I pressed the recall button on my phone endless times, but a long slow buzz told me he would not answer.

Throughout the day, a furious continuous round of vehicles circled the plaza. There were the droning sounds of cars, buses, honking, traffic lights on wires blinking, and pedicabs blaring out reggaeton and salsa music, making hips unconsciously wiggle and sway. From the shade of the old 1896 Hotel Inglaterra, a continuous humdrum of tourists and locals, eager and impatient, hurried in all directions of streets and alleyways, under a sun full of fury and fire but by late afternoon a sudden hush.

The frazzled heat had arrived, still and sticky and somnolence descended.

A passing ice cream vendor stopped near me. I pulled myself up and walked towards him, buying a moment of coolness, anything to bring down the rage inside me.

My senses had begun to drift across waves of the afternoon's suffocating heat as I tiredly looked at the old men still sitting in the plaza. The mood of the afternoon shifted slightly as elderly greying-haired ladies joined them wearing long faded floral dresses, fabric threadbare and worn, hair pinned back, cloth shopping bags hanging from loose fingers, dragging bodies wearied by an age of living tough, on meagre handouts.

Particles of thought stopped as I held her in my vision. She ambled on bent legs, an old pretty-faced wrinkled woman, her cheeks smooth and high, shining in the heat. A bunch of bright pink Bougainvillea was tucked in her hair, her dress was a brightly coloured assorted bundle of cloth. She found a solitary bench and sat down with the largest cigar one can imagine between pursed lips. She drew heavily on this tourist attraction, its end lighting up, her eyes closed. She let out a ring of smoke, a perfect 'O' and slowly opened her hard care-worn eyes to see who was taking a photo of her. Her lips turned upwards, as her deeply creased, worn brown hands extended outwards.

Throughout the relenting heat of the day, as passersby wove in and around and passed me by, I too felt a separation from myself as I crisscrossed shattered memories of times past, called his phone now at least thirty times, remembering promises of him coming.

*How much longer will you be before you come to Havana?*
*I'll be there soon.*

The day had begun to leave its shadow behind and slide into the late evening. Too late now to wait any longer. I slowly uncurled my spine, one memory at a time, straightening, allowing my back to ease its anxiety. I felt alone and angry under the streetlights as they suffused the dark night with a dull glow and only the lights from the surrounding buildings added pinpoints of sparkle. A few night-people wandered past. An old man with curiosity in his eyes ambled up to me and spoke a guttural Spanish which I ignored. He stood still in front of me for a few moments, uncertain, then shuffled away. The darkening plaza had begun to encroach upon me, its stickiness sickening. The daytime sounds were now silent, the night heat oppressive.

In the silence of the cicadas, I looked up at the statue of Jose Marti, and a tumble of memories of my first Cuba visit ran riot through my body, flashpoints pricking my skin.

It seemed to me that this story which slowly unfolded had started long before I found myself sitting on that warm stone seat in Jose Marti Plaza. A story of grief and loss which started before the loss and love of my mother and husband and never really knowing when a story begins and ends.

# 2

My story, with its beginning and end, creates events that simmer beneath the surface of our lives that mutter and murmur and whisper within our unconscious self, nudging us to behave or make decisions that in our conscious self we may never consider enacting.

We may begin to lead parallel lives, functioning in a conscious state of mind yet subliminal forces posit themselves in our psyche so that our usual decision-making processes are subverted.

I mused on all of this as I sat in my office, five years after the event that took place in Cuba that left me scarred, vulnerable, foolish, embarrassed, disgusted by my vanity, unable to believe that I had allowed myself to do what I had done and unable to control myself from continuing until events occurred and the madness, that had taken hold of me, stopped.

What type of craziness had inflicted my behaviour during my nine visits to Cuba in 2014/2015? It started as a new place to visit and discover, a holiday as a reward for working hard, a way to move forward from the painful and unexpected breakup of my twenty-three-year relationship, which had ended three years earlier.

Twenty-three years of living with someone is a long time, falling in and out of love with him, then loving him again and all the while talking about being with each other well into our eighties, growing old together. We still held hands while walking, sitting in bed on a Saturday morning chatting about books, philosophy, this and that, listening to the same jokes umpteen times and still laughing and he, astounded that I still laughed at his jokes. Lying in bed at night, reading science fantasy books by our favourite authors and giggling over our adult childish loves and passions. So much time spent together. For twenty-three years we shared the same bed until one day another joined us, a youngish woman, and the life we had had together was no longer that same shared life.

After the breakup, Jack took three months off work and travelled to Brazil, Peru, and the Galapagos to "get over his life with me" and "regain a sense of his former self". He visited a shaman in Peru who helped him reveal his inner struggles and eagerly told me on his return that I had been the cougar (the dangerous wild creature of his darkness) that leapt out of his body during one of his hallucinogenic experiences.

He was free of me!

I felt utterly broken and small, the pain knew no bounds. I never contemplated suicide, that was not a part of my character or soul. I loved life and lived it to the full. I was an adventurer at heart, bold enough and brave enough to withstand most adversaries throughout my life, but there was this vulnerable part that rarely showed itself. Instead, it was the warrior woman, the fighter, my Queen-self, the one who coped and looked after others, but rarely did I look after myself. If I had to look at the events as they unfolded, I would see how my deep, troubled broken and unconscious self steered me towards the decisions which I later made.

He was gone and I continued working, unable to change the way I lived my life, not knowing how, longing to find some answers, blaming myself, forgiving myself, trying to find closure, wracked in grief, burying that grief so deep that all light had been suffocated by the dark.

A year later in 2012, my mother died from the effects of Alzheimer's. This was too much, so soon after the breakup. I was totally heart broken. My chest ached, and the tears flowed. In the quiet of my home, in the darkness of the night, I curled up in bed and was inconsolable.

I tried various ways and found no solace. I shut myself in my internal room, telling myself innumerable stories, using mental flagellation to get rid of those doubting questions, being kind to myself, continuing to travel to escape. Looking into the hearts of other lives I found no comfort. I dwelt on every detail of our past life, analysing, picking, and poking at the way I had lived my life with Jack and seeing the glaring holes that were covered up with laughter and humour over the span of time we had been together.

How does one mend a broken heart and overcome grief? Family and friends advised me to seek grief counselling, but I resisted this. There was a part of me that knew I had to work through it and come to my own healing. I should have heeded the words of those who loved me.

The grief was unrelenting, but I hid it well, or so I thought, and never could I have imagined how it would unfold in the months ahead. It was a grief that I acknowledged but left unresolved. It was a shapeshifter, and it had no end. Its deepness could bend one in bewitching and dangerous ways. It was a player on a stage where the actors could continue to pretend that "all's well that ends well", yet the outcome was not written in that play until the end and, like the beginning of a story, when does that end?

Back in 2010, a South African architect friend of mine suggested we go to Cuba. We each booked our flights, excitement rising at the thought of going to Havana, a place I had seen in old 1950s movies, with those colourful American Cadillacs, the images of a place almost lost in time. But it did not happen and as my friend explained, one week before we were due to leave, that if she took time off work to go on holiday, she would lose her job. I cancelled my flight and I never saw my "friend" again.

In the Autumn of 2014, business had been good, and the idea of Cuba resurrected itself like a phoenix. It arose from a moment in time, a phone call, another person's deep longing, a forgotten thought and later, whenever that later had begun, the idea of Cuba was re-awakened.

A dear cousin of mine, who had been on her own for over ten years, was grappling with the idea of another unspectacular New Year's Eve in England. Amid innumerable conversations, glasses of wine and a desire to begin to move on to new chapters in our lives, new plans unveiled. We decided that New Year's Eve in Havana had to be a better thrill and adventure than sitting in our own backyards.

I already had a strong cinematic image of Cuba, of sugar plantations, rolled tobacco leaves, huge cigars protruding from pouting lips, rum, salsa, the evening warmth, Ernest Hemingway, an island in the sun, and the usual touristic images, but I knew nothing of its heart.

We booked our flights, flew Air France via Paris, and landed in Havana in the early evening of 27th December 2014.

As I stepped out of the plane and stood still on the upper metal platform of the disembarkation portable stairs, feeling the mid-evening warm moist air dampen my face, and walked down its steep rickety stairs, I was already in a story that had been written into another story.

# 3

Arriving in Cuba for the first time, with my cousin Ella, it held back its whispers of what would enfold from a chance meeting if I believed in chance meetings. Our girlish excitement and anticipation mounted as we stood side by side in the arrival hall of Havana International Airport. We found our senses open to the unknown of this exotic island and eager to allow ourselves to become receptive to new freedoms and explorations.

We felt at ease under its dimmed lights. It was not a Norman Foster-designed airport but shabby by international standards, but neither of us was surprised by this. It was mid-evening and through the tall glass windows, the sky was pitch black. There was a familiarity all around, as though we had landed in Delhi or Kolkata, which made us both smile. It was a feeling of unadornment and sophistication which we appreciated, having become jaded by the fast-paced vacuity of other countries visited, where so much of what we saw was of glitz and glamour and uniformity. We both already loved that here we would not be assailed by 21st-century commercialism.

I let my tight shoulders drop down to their natural equilibrium, felt my back uncurling and shook my hair loose, remembering back to a time in the 1980s when I first landed at the old Kai Tak Airport in Hong Kong, stepping out of the arrival terminal and breathing in that warm moist air, which tickled my nostrils, and feeling as though I had arrived back home in India.

Neither of us could stop smiling. Two grown women with children and young grandchildren grinning uncontrollably.

Our eyes took in every new sight as we waited for our travel guide to meet us. The local people standing around, mixtures of ancestral Spanish, dark brown and creamy coffee-coloured African origin, men and women, old and young. We identified with them, being of mixed-race (Eurasian) people of India, often called "chee-chee" or "half-caste". Ella, my cousin, was statuesque at 5'8", swarthy complexioned, with golden honey-coloured smiling eyes and a mop of brown curls kept short; while I at 5'5" was slender, fair skinned, with brown-hazel green eyes and straight shoulder-length-streaked caramel brown hair.

We were excited at arriving in Cuba, impatient to explore its island magic. A completely new country, a Caribbean Island, with visions of long white beaches, depicted in so many travel magazines and posters stuck in the windows of travel offices. Most of our travels had been to the Indian subcontinent, the Far East, and parts of Africa, with visits to Europe, North and South America, Canada, and Australia.

Arriving just after Christmas there was a festive feeling, a lightness in the air. A certain smell that neither of us could quite describe at that moment, or maybe it was just "that smell" and no need to think too deeply about it. Glad to have escaped the mundanity of New Year's Eve in England and looking forward to dancing salsa, wearing summer clothes, sitting out in the evenings at cafés, drinking coffee and wine, ice-cold mojitos, and chatting with whoever passed our way. Both of us were confident and well travelled women, bruised and adaptable. We understood and respected new cultures, forever embracing life. We had been dancing throughout our lives, starting when we were five-year olds. Ella had been dancing salsa for several years, while I had started a few months prior to my trip, as my main passion in dance was the Argentinian Tango, a dance which I later discovered had been introduced to Cuba in the last couple of years.

Used to being solo travellers, this was going to be our first trip together and, in the quiet of our minds, hoped it would work out. We would be sharing the same room, being in each other's company twenty-four hours a day for twelve days.

There was a genuine fondness between us as first cousins, growing up as neighbours in Gomoh, India, attending the same Loreto Convent School in Asansol. We had jived, jitterbugged, and danced rock 'n' roll at the local Institute, shared family picnics on moonlit nights and, on many a hot day and evening, sat out in our gardens, eating huge poly-mangoes with their warm juice, sweet and sticky, running down our arms as we buried our mouths into the soft orange flesh, laughter abounding. The time came when both families left India in the early 1960s and immigrated to England within one year of each other. Each family lived in different parts of the country. I was in the South and Ella was in the Midlands, but we remained close-knit and stayed in touch throughout our lives.

After waiting for about thirty minutes, with various men approaching very politely, asking in Spanish or English (none of the usual hustling as in other countries), if we needed a taxi into Havana Central, our tour guide finally appeared. He was a thin wisp of a man, swarthy-skinned, dapper, in casual light-coloured chinos and a white long-sleeved shirt buttoned up, except for the top button. His dark hair was oiled and brushed back. He introduced himself as Raoul, speaking perfect English. He picked up our bags, no luggage trolly, and silently led us to his parked car.

Winking at each other, we said simultaneously, 'Hope it's an old American car.' Sadly, it was not, more like the old Russian Lada.

However, our initial disappointment soon evaporated, and our luggage was carefully loaded into the boot. Opening the car doors, a bolt of hot air gushed out and we hopped in, settling quickly into anticipation. Raoul drove out of the airport perimeter and onto the dual carriageway which led to Central Havana.

'So, Ella, what do you think so far?'

'I'm so looking forward to this holiday. I'm going to have to pinch myself over and over to believe that we have made it here. I can't quite imagine what it will be like and hope our casa particular will be comfortable. It's probably going to be one of the best experiences of my life.'

Her excitement showed as her words tripped over one another.

I nodded in agreement, at this point unaware of how my own experiences would metamorphosise.

# 4

The car turned slowly into a darkened street on the edge of Havana Vieja, stopping outside a row of tall narrow buildings, or so they looked in the dark evening shadows.

Raoul turned off the engine and announced our arrival at our casa. Peering out of the car window, bending our necks like a tortoise, we looked up at one of the narrow houses, the only one in the street that seemed to have a light on somewhere in the building. He opened the kerbside car door and helped us out.

As we stood on the pavement, we noticed that the front door was set into a larger wooden frame (a feature we would see in many houses during our time in Havana). Raoul pulled a rope, hanging from the arched ceiling of the doorway. We heard a ring in the distance and then heard slow footsteps descending. The door opened revealing a lanky man with a slight stoop who stood outlined in the doorway. They spoke to each other in rapid Spanish, and then Raoul stepped aside as we entered the casa, squeezing past the owner and up the narrow steep cement stairs. Raoul followed, carrying our bags up three flights. We stepped onto a small landing with a half-glass door opening into an apartment, long neon wall lights nervously flickering their cold glaring light over us. The owner opened the door into a high-ceilinged room with white walls and woodwork, painted in what I call 1950's aqua green (the green of Nigella Lawson's cookware sold in John Lewis in London).

Standing in the dining area, Raoul informed us that another driver would collect us in five days, on 1st January, to take us on the next part of our journey. He gave a slight smile, bowed, turned on his heels and left.

The apartment was sparsely furnished and precisely neat. I looked around at the 1950's faded brown wooden furniture. A double-seater sofa with lace antimacassars, white and crisp, positioned in the centre of its back, a couple of matching armchairs to each side, but no antimacassars. In the middle, sat a small wooden coffee table with splayed legs, and a plain glass vase of plastic flowers on a white lace doily. The owner's wife, who was standing in the small kitchen situated off the living area, came out greeting us with a cheery smile and "Ola" and offered us a glass of cool fruit juice, which we gratefully accepted.

We were informed very formally, in perfect English, that breakfast would be served at 9 am and asked what we would like to eat. Equally formally, we requested coffee, toast, boiled eggs and fruit.

We were shown to our room and handed our room and front door key.

This introduction to a Cuban casa particular was less than friendly and I wondered if this would be the type of reception we could expect around Cuba.

Before going to our room, I stood a while and looked at the casa owner. I noticed his hunched shoulders and peered closely at his face, seeing a man with prominent features, deep creases along his nose, slightly sunken cheeks, with a "beaten-by-life look". He looked older than he probably was. Of course, that was an assumption trailing through my mind.

I cast a glance around the apartment, which reminded me of apartments I had stayed in previously in Warsaw, Poland, back in the early 1970s. The voice of communism and socialism still echoed around many parts of the world through its architecture and interior living and, like the casa owner with his hunched shoulders, a reminder of its long stranglehold on people's lives.

We entered our room and looked at each other.

'Oh well,' said Ella in her matter-of-fact way, 'it's neat, tidy, and clean. It's fine for our stay here but the beds look like army camp cots.' She sat down and jiggled around on her bottom, the springs squeaking. 'Where's the bathroom?'

Turning around, I walked towards a curtained-off corner of the room. Behind the thin cotton curtain was a chocolate-brown painted door, its paint slightly chipped and flaking. Opening the door inwards, lay a tiny bathroom which had a washbasin, a toilet, a mirror on the wall and a small shower head projecting from one wall. A low concrete wall about 20cm high had been built to create the shower area and a towel rail on the back of the door, from which hung two towels. Taking down one of the towels, I walked back into the bedroom saying, 'I hope you brought a towel with you because this is what we must use for five days. One half each of a small hand towel.'

'That is meagre.'

Ella smiled good-humouredly enjoying this new experience of Cuban frugality.

'Anyway, at the cost of £16 per night, we can't complain. This is Havana city living and reminiscent of the world over, but I have a feeling that the casas outside Havana will be different.'

We sat down on our low beds, falling backwards, and laughing. As we sat with our bags unopened at the foot of the beds, we surveyed the size of the room, the lack of cupboards, the high ceiling, and the twenty-watt lightbulbs.

'Let's get changed and find somewhere to eat and explore. We're here. It's warm, sultry and we must find somewhere to dance tonight. I'd imagined we would be staying in an old Spanish-style house, not an old utilitarian apartment. Uhm, I think the tour operator needs to be more honest as to the type of accommodation they have offered us.' My initial criticism would alter as we travelled further around Cuba.

El looked quizzically at me.

'Maybe they too have no clear idea as to the variety of accommodation available and go by the price of the casa.'

I felt a tinge of disappointment and thought to myself, "What's the matter with you? This is a new country, a new experience; you've stayed in worse places in other parts of the world." Thinking back to some of my garish hotel rooms in those early travels to China, echoes of recognisable bleak interiors, set off quiet laughter in my head. My first experience of travelling to China when I visited the Canton Fair in Canton, now known as Guangzhou, where I lodged in rooms with red brocade curtains at the window, verdant grass-green threadbare carpets, ten-watt bulbs and shrieking when I saw a pair of white slippers under the bed, thinking I was going to have to share with an unknown person. The room had resembled a bordello with its suggestive colours.

After having a quick chat with the owner of the casa particular (neither of us ever found out his name), we wrote down the address of our lodgings and asked him for directions to the centre of Havana Vieja, which he said would take about 20 minutes. We sprinted down the stairs and out the front door, following his directions down long, dimly lit, narrow cobbled streets and empty plazas flanked by white looming, stone-worked filigree lace spired churches. The streets were quiet at nine o'clock on a Sunday evening. As we walked, bruised, and flaking paintwork on most of the buildings arose before us and, nearing the end of one street, I noticed an elegant building called Hotel Beltran, its walls a soft buttery daffodil-yellow, brushed with a touch of terracotta, illuminated by large up-lighters, creating a "son et lumiere" up and across its walls.

I made a mental note to find out if there would be a room available there for our last nights in Havana. A surprise for Ella whose birthday was in the middle of January.

The hotel led us around the corner into Plaza Vieja. Our long journey and time zone change left us both disoriented by our new surroundings and unsure of what to do next. We were hungry and stood looking around at the size of the stone-paved plaza (which appeared larger than St. Mark's Square in Venice). Restaurants and bars were strung along two sides, while bar-b-q grills sent spirals of delicious-smelling smoke outside some cafés. Aromas of aromatic fish filled the air. All the tables were full of noisy and laughing tourists of all ages and colours. A flurry of white-shirted, black-trousered waiters ran around with smiles, trays held high and a wiggle of hips to the sound of live bands playing salsa music.

Music echoed and reverberated off the stone walls from all four corners of the plaza as though the very stones were singing, alive and in communion with their own historical memories, old and new.

Hunger and thirst gnawed at my belly, and we chose the Italian pizza restaurant right next to where we were standing. Eating outdoors on warm balmy evenings must be one of the most enduring holiday memories. Food, wine and smiles all seem to be tastier, richer, and more enlivening. We sat at a small square metal table, a perfect choice. A soft wind blew. The menu offered the same Italian choices of thin or thick stone-baked pizzas, pasta, and garlic bread; a typical pizza menu. We ordered one each and a glass of red wine, tart-tasting, that gently rubbed the insides of my throat as it warmly flowed down, and I inhaled a long slow breath of contentment. We paid 40 pesos, the equivalent of just under £40.

Ella said, 'Let's hope this is not going to be the price we pay for all our meals. I thought Cuba was inexpensive for eating out.'

'This is the middle of the tourist season and a dense tourist area. In all cities around the world, tourists pay high prices, getting skinned alive with a gracious smile, and we are sitting in an area which is now a World Heritage Site. Welcome to Havana, which I sense is going to throw some interesting surprises at us.'

Ella was not happy as she was on a limited budget and had to be careful with her money.

With the meal over and our initial hunger and thirst satiated, we wandered around and out of the plaza. We could have been in Seville or Granada. Beautiful slender-arched columns framed stone corridors, behind which housed restaurants, bars, art galleries, and private apartments and in the centre of the plaza stood an old bronze fountain, its spouting water silent of life. White cathedral domes peaked high above tall shadowy apartments from which streamed pinpoints of lights and narrow side streets ran off each corner of the plaza. Another deep breath and I inhaled all I imagined I saw through and around darkened corners.

A sense of peace settled all around, like the feel of a warm hand resting on our foreheads as we walked and talked, crossing over and through many small plazas until we found ourselves in Obispo Street, where the casa owner had told us we would find a few salsa bars.

People wandered up and down the street, music pouring out from many restaurants, the pores of their old brick walls oozing out ages of music.

Latin rhythms chuckled and laughed out over loudspeakers, our shoulders unconsciously wiggling to the rhumba, salsa, jazz and reggaeton. The middle of the road was cracked and broken, worn out as cars slowly rumbled along, but good humour and laughter filled the air.

As we continued down Obispo Street, with its many Art Nouveau bank buildings and old hotels, heavily carved marble edifices and inner-framed metal doors, we passed by Hotel Florida with a plaque dated 1885. We doubled back and stopped, as we had to go in. We let out a gasp of amazement when we entered the lobby. It was a palatial Spanish-styled hotel, a touch of a Moorish inner courtyard, worn and elegant with a black and white terrazzo floor, large terracotta pots filled with wide-spreading Royal Palm trees, decoratively standing by lofty bare stone columns, supporting the upper-terraced floors and the roof, with its mouth opened to the night sky. I love buildings with exposed roofs, allowing themselves to be one with the natural sky, and was transported back to my many visits to the palaces in Jaipur, India, which had the same feature.

Loud music and voices beckoned us from one of the corridors and we followed the sounds to a vaulted carpeted room where a group of young Europeans were dancing. We stood and watched the dancers from the side lines and had the feeling that this was not the place for us. We felt we were intruding on a private party and whispered that we would return after a couple of drinks, certain that the dancing would continue till late.

A further few hundred yards and Obispo Street intersected with Calle San Ignacio. Café Paris sat on the opposite side of the road, its neon lights flashing and a five-piece band playing softly under a large, canopied tree; so inviting. Our eyes met and we walked across to the bar, found an empty table and ordered ice-cold mojitos.

This was a new shared experience. Sitting there till past 1 am, sipping and savouring the taste of fresh mint which refreshed our tired travelled taste buds, with the lime and crushed ice and more than the usual two ounces of rum; we made plans for the next few days, our five days in Havana. We would need to find the best places to visit and let's not forget Ernest Hemingway's house and how to spend New Year's Eve, one of the reasons for coming. We mulled on whether we should have come with a salsa holiday group or, if travelling independently, we could find the best venues to dance. We were eager to explore this old and infamous city and savour new experiences.

Leaving Café Paris as the air became cooler, the bar emptying, and the surrounding streets becoming even quieter, we retraced our steps back down Obispo Street towards Hotel Florida and, at the entrance, peered into the lobby. All was quiet. We looked at each other, wondering why we had felt awkward. Were we too old to have stayed and danced there?

Our first night in Havana and the only salsa dancing we had done was still in Dreamtime, for tomorrow's dream was yet to be dreamed.

# 5

Our casa particular was not the place for a leisurely wake-up in the morning. There was no view of the Malecon (Havana's seafront) or the Straits of Florida, so we missed that feeling of throwing open our bedroom window and breathing in the fresh sea air. Its cement floors and austere furnishings, together with a sullen and dour-faced casa owner, did not invite us to easy chit-chat with him. We had a hurried breakfast and sprinted down the three flights of stairs and out into the 10 am December sun, relishing its warmth on our bodies. A sun already threatening to heat up considerably as the day progressed. Our joy at being in Havana was evident by our wide smiles and eyes as we strolled down the same streets from the previous night on the way to Plaza Vieja. This became our central starting point for most of our ramblings around the city, as we breathed in the sights, smells and sounds as Havana Vieja hummed within its own pulsating vibrations.

Walking along narrow cobbled streets, we passed antiqued mellow-yellowing apartment blocks, many with the same high, wide wooden-framed fronts with a smaller entrance door within its frame, as at our casa. One or two

32

of those small front doors were open, and I peered into cavernous courtyards with wide stone stairs curving up several flights into darkness. I had not seen inner courtyards of that magnitude and was reminded of the Tardis. We peeped through windows cut out in the old brickwork walls with iron grills, behind which were housed barber shops, bakeries, small butcheries; a humdrum of tiny shops where customers stood outside chatting to those inside. Side streets led into small plazas where cathedrals with intricate, finely chiselled stonework reached up into the blue morning sky. Old multicolour-painted buildings stood on opposing corners, some crumbled to the ground, rubble and iron posts standing guard over what was left of themselves. On the steps outside a cathedral, a man and woman sat with a basket filled with fresh bell-shaped white Jamaican flowers (endemic to Jamaica and Cuba) overhanging their sides; the sun, its golden shafts bathing both sellers as they waited for congregants to stop, buy and slip into those vaulted places of worship.

Those scenes were a photographer's delight.

Local churchgoers, some dressed in white, reverently carrying bunches of white ginger lilies and long creamy-coloured candles, entered and left the church singly or in small groups, their faces looking beatific and reverential. I do not think they were of the Santerían religion, although I had already seen a few small groups of men, women and children walking around Havana dressed in the more traditional Santerían style. The women and young girls with their slim-fitted dresses adorned with lace, and heads covered with lacy handkerchief-style scarves, their legs in thick white stockings and flat shoes. Their men were dressed in white from head to toe.

The sound of organ music, softly fluted warblings, sounding as though they were wrapped in muted cotton wool, and reedy pipe sounds drifted through the many porticoes and slit windows, high above in galleries, pointing their musical harmonies into the warming air. Ella was a devout Catholic and loved churches. She left me standing outside admiring the architecture while she went inside to light a candle or two. She had many family members to offer her blessings and prayers in churches for wherever she travelled, and I waited patiently knowing the length of time to light and pray for love and protection for her expansive family. Her smiling face appeared a while later, clutching a small bunch of Mariposa flowers, enthused by the decorative glories of the church. We both agreed that Spanish-style churches, whether in Spain or Cuba, were obscenely beautiful, their diverse architecture still intact after the revolution although some needed restoration after years of neglect due to Cuba's fading economy.

Havana, now listed as part of a UNESCO World Heritage Site, was in various stages of rebuilding, mainly the old city and forts, reminding us of their former magnificence. Its architectural influence of Colonial, Moorish, Spanish of course, Italian, Greek and Roman styles, as well as 1930's art deco. Their architectural ideologies and morals, skin deep in their philosophy and influence, was a living testament to a forgotten time, invading and inviting the myriad of brown skin colours from ancestral Africa to soft creamy tones of Europe and Asia, rushing and brushing past us. All this confluence of style, colour, discordance and vibrancy reminded me of an artist's palette of a little bit of this and a little bit of that, of clashing yet matching colours, which in one broad-brush stroke on his canvas, paints the enduring spell of this city.

Lunchtime was looming and Obispo Street seemed the obvious place to change some money and find somewhere to eat and plan our trip in detail. On our way, we repassed Hotel Beltran.

'I saw this hotel last night and want to go in and check something out. Can you wait here? I'll be about fifteen minutes.'

My cousin said nothing as she knew I was probably up to some mischief. I rushed in and, fifteen minutes later, came out having booked a twin room for our last two nights in Havana. A surprise, a birthday present for her.

As we crossed Plaza Vieja again, a solitary guitar player was strumming out "O Sole Mio".

We both collapsed with laughter, with El (I sometimes called her that) saying 'Are we in Venice now? Reminds me of that TV advert of "Just one cornetto" to the tune of "O Sole Mio" as couples were rowed in gondolas through the canals.'

We continued to giggle.

The sounds of building work could be heard all around from great booming bangs to small tap-taps of carpenters nailing door panels and sawing wood to repair worn out parts of the exterior and interior of so many of the surrounding buildings. We crisscrossed a warren of streets, stumbling into corner courtyards where solitary trees stood silent, caged, barely a sprig, barely a branch, behind an iron-railed enclosure.

'You know, Ella, for all the deterioration of these old buildings, peeling paintwork, broken balcony railings, the vendors we have seen on the street corners selling small quantities of avocadoes or potatoes, there is a real dignity here. Have you noticed how smartly dressed the men are in their white shirts and pants and styled haircuts? Do you remember the woman and man back at the first church we came to? We stopped and asked if we could take their photo. The young man could have been a GQ magazine model and the woman, I think he said, was his mother. Did you notice the pink curlers in her hair? Even with her curlers, she had a certain style that I love.'

She agreed. 'It's something about Caribbean people in general that I find I can't emulate. I think they have an inner "dignity" that you mentioned, which comes out in the way they put their clothes together, style their hair and in their distinctive walk. Did you not notice that about so many poor people in India too? No matter how poor they were, they would walk out of a shanty town in Mumbai, clothes freshly creased and crisp.'

We both fell quiet, lost in thought.

Entering Obispo Street, we headed to the Cambio. There was a queue thirty-deep and the temperature thirty degrees with higher humidity. I was now sweltering and red-faced, a most unattractive look. A sign said, "Lunch 1 - 3 pm". It was 12.45 pm. Thirst drove us to abandon the idea of the Cambio and we found a cool shaded bar-restaurant which had a shorter queue. We checked the prices on the menu before entering and were shown a table. Over lunch we found out the names of a few salsa dance bars from the very chatty waiters while they weaved through the tables of tourists, taking orders, shuffling to the rhythm of the small band playing by the entrance of the bar, or the odd male tourist with a large glass of beer in one hand, and a frothy smile dripping around his mouth, standing up and leaning forward, eager to share his tourist information.

We chatted while listening to the music being played by a young Cuban girl on a pennywhistle, while an older woman plucked on a double bass. An elderly man bowed deftly on a fiddle, tapping his feet as he played, alongside a big wiry curly-haired Afro-Cuban, twenty-something guy on a small acoustic guitar, and another with matted Rastafarian plaits on the bongo drums, a Bob Marley lookalike.

The overhead fans whirred and the gold tinsel, which hung in strings down the walls of the bar, gently stirred reminding us that we were in a season of celebration.

I had picked up a tourist brochure in the reception of Hotel Beltran and looked through the list of "Places to Visit in Havana". Architectural attractions, art galleries, museums, old hotels, forts, and churches abounded on every corner, just as in Granada and Seville. Vast cathedrals at one end of the wide cobbled enclosed courtyard and the familiar blue and white statue of the serene-looking plaster cast Virgin Mary. We had passed a few shops during the morning, and both decided we should spend our money wisely and, judging by the size of the local women, none of the clothes would have fitted us anyway.

Ella, who was a proud and independent woman, remarked, 'I'm lucky to have a small income. Not as much as you perhaps but, judging by our first day here, Havana seems an expensive place to eat and drink. I'm going to have to be careful about how much I spend on meals, clubs, and drinks, as well as on the museums or art galleries we visit.'

Even though I could afford more, I too hated paying the inflated tourist prices and, for me, the sooner we left Havana for the countryside the better. As Ella was talking, I had a quick look under "Entrance fees for museums and art galleries".

'I think we will be ok. Museums and art galleries are free here, so we could save our money for other activities.'

We knew we would not see it all so decided for the first two days to just wander around and choose a few places to visit which would capture a sense of this intriguing, contradictory, extraordinarily beautiful, and rhythmic city where, in my fanciful mind, the walls themselves sang of their history and their future. Ernest Hemingway's house was an essential visit which, according to the tourist book, was called Finca Vigia, meaning "the lookout", about 10 miles outside Havana. Along with a few salsa lessons, we also wanted to enjoy the outside café life, drinking in its savoury everyday life as it streamed past us.

Refreshed after lunch and returning to the Cambio, which had reopened, we changed our money, gasping at its low exchange rate, almost 1 peso to £1. The reality of money exchange and its buying power, seeing it printed on a board, is quite different to that of the reality of its physical buying power.

We would continue to be in a state of shock as the days passed and see our money flow through our fingers like a damaged New York fire hydrant.

The biggest decision we made over lunch was to go to Casa de la Musica, Havana, not too far from our casa, and the brochure mentioned the best time to go was 10 pm. Excited at the prospect of dancing later that evening, we hopped into a passing pedicab (rickshaw) which ambled along street after narrow street. The young Cuban kept turning around, grinning and shouting at other pedicab drivers, with reggaeton music blasting from enormous speakers at the back of the pedicab. His long sinewy legs lightly pressed down on pedals, as the wheels spun and passed through a passage of time, terraced buildings, colonial-styled overhanging arches, facades of coral orange, faded peeling aqua, strawberry pink and magnolia yellow, side by side, contrasting and blending into each other, a glorious convergence and melee of colour, all appearing as streaks of a night-traffic blur. The pedicab sped along, creating its own breeze. It twisted around sharp corners, further revealing buildings with watermelon-pink-coloured front doors which looked as though frenzied dogs had been scraping away the paintwork with their sharp claws, exposing layers of other aged and layered colours. Neither of us had ever been to a city such as Havana. To me, as we journeyed through the winding streets, every corner, peephole in a building, open door, even a large-bosomed woman hanging over a grapefruit-pink balcony and a sweating bare-chested bronzed body lounging against a half-open door, was like looking through a camera lens. Snapshots of an old city which had carved out its life through glorious architecture, now caught in a time warp, a living museum. Tall apartment blocks shut out the sun but somehow allowed pools of light to play along the surface of the streets as the pedicab rolled along. I remembered those images from old movies but where were the old American cars? We had briefly glimpsed a couple.

The pedicab finally burst out of the maze of streets, entering a wide busy road, and stopped in front of an old hotel called Hotel Inglaterra in Parque Central, opposite the Jose Marti Plaza. We slid out of the pedicab and paid the driver, stunned that we had been charged 10 pesos for travelling for what seemed only a couple of minutes. We had to shrug our shoulders, with realisation dawning on us that this was going to be an expensive holiday. In less than one day, we would have spent almost £100 between us.

The noise and happy clamour all around us was infectious and, turning to face Jose Marti Plaza, there on the right, parked along one side were long fin-tailed, rainbow-coloured, iconic, classic, 1950s American cars. They were parked in a row, shining, gleaming, the sun bouncing its rays off their sparkling paintwork of brilliant fuchsia pink, turquoise, lemony-yellow, royal purple, sexy fire red, their fenders exploding sunlight off their shiny chrome, their drivers mainly Spanish-looking, hustling, from what we could see, and the myriad of tourists milling around the cars, all grinning like happy kids. I found myself thinking in colours rather than in thoughts.

Finally, the image of Cuba was complete. Our holiday had begun.

We were compelled to walk across to the cars and have a look, barely able to contain the excitement of standing by those immortalised vehicles and asked a few of the drivers the price to have a ride around the city.

'$50 per hour, and that is cheap.'

We knew we had no choice. A longing to be a part of "Old Havana" was an important element of our time there.

Ella wisely whispered, 'Let's go over to that hotel. I think it's called Hotel Inglaterra. Have a cool drink and think about when we should take a ride in one of these, maybe tomorrow.'

Later that evening after having showered, dressed, and checked in the mirror at how we looked and not too sure what to wear to go out dancing at Casa de la Musica Habana, we agreed that so much of what we had seen and felt throughout the day was reminiscent of our early life in India and England. Dressing up to venture out to a late-night dance club was like being a teenager again.

We sat silently in the back of the taxi, each looking out into the dark streets, neon lights flashing over dingy dwellings and long American cars speeding by. We arrived outside Casa de la Musica Habana, its acidic-coloured blue and yellow sign hanging above the entrance like a beacon. We paid the driver, slid out and stood on the pavement. Reggaeton music, its pounding rhythms stirring our blood, a little wiggle and shake of our hips, we couldn't help it as we joined the queue at the entrance, aware of new feelings like soft breath on our skin. A man stopped by me shouting, '10 pesos, only 10 pesos for a night to remember.' I turned and looked up into the face of a tall black Cuban wearing a red baseball cap, his throat swathed in gold chains, a living portrait of Cuba.

# 6

The queue outside the club was of tourists, in couples or small groups of European men, dressed very indifferently compared to the local Cuban men, their faces flushed red, from overtan or with drink. Eyes wide and excited, corners of eyes deeply-creased, unable to hide their excitement of what they hoped was yet to come. The main street, Galliano, was busy with cars and trucks driving slowly past, heads poking out of open windows, some of the drivers shouting out greetings to the local Cubans who were hanging around by the queue of people waiting to go into the club. The long queue moved leisurely, and we imbibed its surroundings.

I waited, looking calm but, on the inside, feeling slightly nervous. I was unsure of the origins of this feeling and kept looking closely at the faces of the local Cubans who were milling around, touting tickets, chatting up the single women in the queue and being generally friendly and boisterous. Many of them held cans of Cristal, one of the local beers, flashing large gold jewelled rings on slender fingers, many wearing heavy gold-link chains around their necks. These did not look like costume jewellery. Their open-collared shirts exposed those glittering ornaments against their dark skins; much to my surprise as I was unaware that the local Cubans could afford such riches. So much for not reading up enough on the current state of Cuba. Having bought a lot of gold during my travels to India and Hong Kong, some of the chains looked like they weighed about 70 grams. There were a few Cuban girls, resembling glossy feathered storks, tight skirts hugging their bottoms, stork-like legs on even higher stork-like high heels, their close-fitting tops skimming their pouting breasts, their long ironed-straight hair or hair piled high on top of their heads, clutching tiny occasion bags, their knuckles white. They wore no jewellery as their makeup was dazzling enough.

Looking at each other, Ella winked as she often did, showing that twinkle in her eyes, her dimples deepening with mirth. Approaching a short flight of vermillion-red painted cement stairs, we passed through finger-printed smeared double-glass doors and into a dully lit lobby. Each of us handed over 10 pesos.

'Hey, do you think this is going to be a night to remember, as the tall Cuban with the red baseball cap said as we queued?'

El laughed, 'No idea, I just hope we get to dance with some great Cuban guys. Back home, I've danced with a couple of them, and dancing salsa is a whole different dance. What's wonderful about salsa is that it isn't as ageist as tango, from what you have told me about it in the past.'

'Absolutely agree. It was always such a relief to go to the clubs in the South of England and dance the whole evening. I always left feeling physically wrecked but joyful.'

As we walked through a short narrow dark corridor into the dance area, I thought about the many times I had attended milongas (tango dances) back home, eagerly looking forward to dancing the Tango. Instead, I often found myself sitting like a wallflower, almost wilting with frustration, watching as most of the men danced with the younger women, ignoring the older ones. It didn't matter how well we danced; the men needed to hold onto a piece of "arm candy". I mused on how I felt about myself. I was not ugly or fat and looked extremely young for my age, or so I was often told. Maybe I exuded an air of self-possession which most men found intimidating, as they need to feel unchallenged. Thank God the world of salsa dancing embraces women of all ages and if a woman can dance well, she will have the floor.

A large high-ceilinged room greeted us with tables and chairs on each side of a narrow gangway, which sloped down to a large wooden dance floor, and beyond lay an elevated stage with giant screens on either side. The stage flickered and flashed with illuminating coloured lights, set up for a 12-piece band. We had been told at the entrance that the band would be playing around midnight. The room itself was of cavernous proportions, walls of age-old paint of cordovan red and rich English clotted cream. Dark chocolate-brown doors deeply scuffed and pools of yellowing light hiding, or lighting up, moments of the intimacy of couples at tables nestled together, arms around shoulders, whispering, with foreheads touching.

I stood at the top of the central gangway for a short while, unsure of what to do. It had been a very long time since I had been clubbing, especially in dark rum-filled clubs. Ella appeared more relaxed, towering over many of the people around her.

There were a few dancers on the floor, mainly Europeans, their arms and legs gesticulating wildly to Puerto Rican reggaeton, not salsa. In the two days we had been in Havana, we had mainly heard reggaeton, a rhythm which sounded like a caffeinated heart on overdrive. We had come to dance salsa. Reggaeton was different and we both felt awkward dancing it, as it required a seductive body style which we felt too shy to exhibit. It was a sexually suggestive dance with knees bent and legs further apart. Leon, my salsa teacher back home had begun to teach me, but I usually giggled my way through the practice. That night, I would need a few mojitos to get rid of my inhibitions.

We found a table in a darkened and quieter space to perch ourselves and ordered long mojitos, at 3 CUC (local money) each, from a passing waiter. The atmosphere was heavily charged or was my heartbeat on overdrive? Young tourists walked up and down, young Cuban men in tight t-shirts and white jeans sauntered by. Then, out of the corner of my eye, I saw the "stork women". I tapped El on the arm and said, 'Look, do you remember seeing those young girls outside, by the front barrier? They look about sixteen. I don't think they are here for the dancing.'

The girls were all lined up on the right side of where we were sitting. A small older and stockier Cuban woman dressed in mourning black was fussing up and down their line directing them in a quiet way, where to sit or where to stand. A couple of the girls stood just behind me, one of whom had long bleached-blond hair wearing a tight feathered peacock-print top, her greenish eyes roving the room. For a moment I felt unsettled. I turned, looking over my shoulder to the back of the club where groups of men of all ages stood by the bar, drinks in hand, standing at least four-deep.

A saxophone hit its top note and, turning, I saw the whole band on stage. Wartime flashes of lights fled across the ceiling and surrounding walls and, as the band struck that first chord of a powerful Latin rhythm, with those baritone saxophones sounding like cannons firing, people jumped out of their seats and headed to the dance floor. Again, it was not salsa music, nor music that either of us wanted to dance to. So, we sat engrossed, watching the lovely "stork women" being approached or guided towards the men at the back of the club. There had been about twenty of them and, within minutes, had been partnered except for two.

'I wonder how much they get paid?'

'I hope a lot.'

While we had been captivated by the stories around us, our view of the stage was blocked by two men standing in front of us, both slender and of medium height, dressed in t-shirts and chinos with ankle-high canvas boots. They formed a dark outline against the bright stage lights in front of them. The one in front of me turned around and asked if he could put his drink on our table, an empty Fanta can. I shrugged my shoulders.

He looked in his early thirties, a mixed-race Cuban, with a boyish face and cropped hair. Smiling graciously, he thanked me. Immediately the other guy in front of El did the same and turned and asked if he could put his drink on our table. I looked at him. A light-skinned Spanish man with a cute face and shoulder-length curly dark hair. El looked at me and we both smiled. Leaning over, she whispered, 'Do you think we have been chosen?'

The club was overflowing with customers and noisy with the band in full crescendo, the crowd full of laughter, the dance floor writhing with young bodies, many holding each other intimately and one or two of the band's vocalists mingling amongst them. Waiters ran around in-between tables carrying trays full of beers and bottles of Havana Club rum and small shot glasses, sweat beading on their foreheads, white shirts wet, plastered to their backs. There was an electric party atmosphere, and I was restless, sitting and looking at dancers rather than dancing myself. I went to the back bar where all those men and "stork women" were standing, some of the men with big wolfish grins on their faces, some looking bleary-eyed, but all eyes were on the local Cuban girls. I made my way to the bar, pushing through those hot sweaty-bodied men and ordered ice-cold mojitos, telling the barman to make them extra tall and with extra rum. I downed one at the bar and ordered a further two. I skirted the throng of men and made my way back to my seat. As I approached, Ella was standing and chatting with one of the guys by our table. I thought, 'Good for you.' I loved that my cousin was so open and easy-going. Arriving at the table I handed her a mojito and was introduced to Jonnie, the taller of the two, and the other one introduced himself as Alejandro but quickly said he was called Alex by his friends.

The men asked if we were enjoying the music and Ella said we had come to dance salsa, but the only music here was reggaeton, which we found less appealing. Immediately

Jonnie told us that tonight was not salsa night, being a Sunday. Only on Friday and Saturday was salsa music played at this club, but if we wanted to dance salsa tonight, they knew a small bar not far from this one with salsa music and open till the early hours of the morning. He spoke perfect English and had a bright and easy way of chatting. The other guy seemed much quieter, maybe his English was less fluent.

We decided that we had had enough of spending two hours sitting and watching others enjoying themselves nor did we like the fact that this was a hooker and tourist bar, so agreed to leave with two total strangers to another unknown bar in search of what was now becoming the elusive salsa.

We left, walking out into the warm dry air. Poised on the edge of the pavement, waiting to cross the road, the three mojitos were having the desired effect upon my senses and as I stepped across the road, found Jonnie walking beside me chatting about his work and dancing at The Tropicana and did I know it, as well as teaching salsa during the day. El strode ahead with Alejandro.

I was unsurprised to find myself walking with strangers on the way to an unknown bar. On several occasions in the past and my various travels around the world, I found myself in situations sitting alone in a café or restaurant, striking up conversations that would last a few hours and end up going to a bar or walking along a beach, quietly confident that I knew exactly what I was doing. My instincts were my guide and, up to now, self-preservation was my guardian angel.

So tonight, meeting two strangers in a bar in Havana and walking with them, to find another to dance salsa, seemed normal and natural.

As we did during the day, we wove our way through small narrow streets and plazas and came to Bar Asturias in Prado near Paseo del Prado. An avenue of trees interspersed with tall 1920s-style lamp posts decorating each side. We entered through a high door into an impressive stone-carved building, its entrance lobby, a smallish dark bar backlit with acidic neon green lights, where finally salsa music was being played. El's face lit up with excitement, her dimples deepening around her mouth. We grabbed a small table and ordered drinks for ourselves, as well as our two new friends. For the next few hours, we danced blissfully with a variety of Cubans. Jonnie was a fluid dancer and El showed off her dancing skills. Alejandro seemed to sit, lost in his thoughts, and refused to dance. A tall dark Cuban wearing a suit of black indigo, a dazzlingly white shirt matching his teeth, and a narrow shiny black tie, asked me to dance and we spent the next twenty minutes dancing, perhaps a little too closely, with him whispering unintelligible words while we danced. Very eager to tell me his name, Michael asked if I would like to meet him the next day to go with him and his family to a beach.

While we danced, I was aware he was wearing a lightweight wool suit. I could feel the heat of his body soaking through it. I wondered at his choice of cloth for dancing in that heat. He looked impeccable, deeply darkly handsome, sweating inside his suit. I could imagine a rainforest of humidity dribbling inside his suit, like the tumble of the matrix codes. His outward appearance was more important than sweating in that wool suit. I thanked him as the last note of music drifted away and we came to a rhythmic end. His heat was too much for me.

The music played on for the next couple of hours and every time we got up to dance and put our drinks down, they disappeared upon our return, and we had to buy another. This happened at least five times.

I danced with Jonnie to a slow more-tempered salsa rhythm, having performed that piece many times before. We seemed to have a real connection and I loved the way dancing allowed me to express myself and be my true self. I never cared what others thought about my style or ability. When I danced, I was fully immersed in the connections I felt and, dancing with Jonnie, my true self shone. At the end, we both laughed and hugged, a secret shared between two dancers.

By now I was in Nirvana as it wrapped its arms around me, quite happy to go on dancing all night to the joyful beat of the music.

I felt a tap on my shoulder and saw El standing, suddenly looking tired and in need of leaving. We left the men in the club, Alejandro still sitting in the same chair, inert, as when we arrived.

Sitting in the front seat of the taxi, Ella told me she had arranged for us to have dancing lessons with both men and were meeting at 10 am at Hotel Inglaterra. I was sleepily happy and thought that a wonderful idea, saying I was looking forward to the next day.

An image flashed into my drunken consciousness of Alejandro sitting very still in that same chair while we danced. As I left, I remembered asking him if he was alright. He looked sullen and refused to answer.

In the distance, I heard her voice saying. 'Gina, that guy in the chair seems quite a moody person, not dancing, just staring at you. Do you think he is the jealous type?'

'What do you mean?'

'Not sure, seemed odd that he sat and did not dance at all.'

Maybe tomorrow there would be an explanation, but it was not that important.

# 7

Waking up in a rush in the morning so that we could catch breakfast at 9 am, after having had too many mojitos the night before, was detrimental to my skin and mood. I hated rising early during a holiday and preferred a civilised hour of breakfast around midday.

I decided I did not want to dance salsa at 10 am, feeling jaded and dehydrated, but El was in a perky mood, dressed and already seated at the breakfast table when I joined her, and to my surprise, the casa owner was smiling and chatting with her.

She did have a very good rapport with everyone she met. It must be those two little dimples in the corner of her mouth when she smiled. They seemed to enchant people.

Arriving at Hotel Inglaterra by pedicab, the two guys from the previous night were already seated on the front veranda, sipping espressos, with huge smiles on their faces. I felt a twinge of suspicion but put on a bright smile and greeted them both. On closer inspection of Jonnie, I saw that he was not Spanish-looking at all, but a light-skinned Afro-Cuban with shoulder-length afro-curly hair swept off his forehead with a black plastic Alice band. They were also wearing the same clothes as the previous night. Had they slept at all, I wondered. The quartet was already playing, the bongo drums just that little bit too loud for my slightly sore head. A balmy breeze blew through the length of the veranda, easing my mood. Again, I could not help but respond to the gentle sounds of the music and relax while sitting down at their table.

We chatted about dancing salsa in England and how popular it was. I mentioned that I had been dancing it for about six months but preferred Argentine Tango. El said she had been dancing salsa for over six years and was hoping to dance a lot in Cuba. The men told us that they had not left the club till about 4 am as a few of their friends had arrived at Bar Asturias and they carried on drinking and dancing.

Jonnie looked at his watch and suggested they all leave, paid for their espressos, and led the way across Jose Marti Plaza. I walked beside Jonnie, asking if he had a dance studio nearby. He smiled and said that was beyond his means. They were going to a friend's small café just off Obispo Street in O'Reilly Street and would hire the upstairs bar room for an hour's lesson. He told me they charged 12 pesos per hour each. I said nothing, already thinking, 'OK, this is the start of a new day, let's wait and see how much today will cost.'

Crossing the plaza, I noticed many older men sitting cross-legged on stone benches under the tall overhanging trees, some of them with crutches and walking sticks clutched in their bony hands, all very thin with gaunt faces. I glanced sideways at one man, wearing faded indigo blue pants and jacket, bare-chested, bare-footed. He wore a black

Che Guevara-style beret at an angle, his yellowing silver-grey hair poking out beneath his beret. I looked directly into his rheumy blue eyes as I passed by. The iconic Che was still alive in Havana - posters, books, t-shirts, metal badge pins; all still acknowledging him as the hero of Cuba, or was this tourist money for the locals? I imagined the wind softly whispering Che's name through the trees as we sauntered along in the direction of Obispo Street, which was quickly becoming our temporary new home.

I stopped, telling the others I was going to take a photo of the man by the lamp post. I crossed over quickly and went up to him, asking if I could take his photo. He quietly nodded and at the end said his name was Arturo. I gave him 10 pesos, not wanting to steal his soul. His dignity shone out and I held that moment in time, understanding its significance.

The streets all around us were thronging with tourists parading, shopping, and chatting; local men lounging or hovering in small groups, eyes darting, waiting, or like lizards basking and sitting on low walls in the sun.

The four of us turned into O'Reilly Street and entered a tiny bar called El Ojo Del Ciclon (Eye of the Cyclone). I puffed out my cheeks when I saw that sign and immediately felt a jolt at its insinuation. Entering the tiny bar and after hugs and kisses from a young woman, we ascended a dark narrow wooden flight of stairs, entering an upper wooden-floored bar area. The sun poured in through the smeared, unwashed wide glass window and on a high bar table stood a music deck. Jonnie turned on the music and I decided I wanted to partner with Alejandro as he was closer to my height. There was no awkwardness as the lesson started and Jonnie seemed to be at ease dancing with Ella.

Salsa is different in every way to Tango, it's all about those swaying hips, rapid feet and hand movements, more akin to Flamenco in its overt flamboyance. I was having difficulty keeping up and kept missing the beat of the music in its 1-4 rhythm. Was it the slight tingle passing through me as we danced, feeling his rough palms twining in and out of my hands as I was twirled over and under his arms? As the music changed from a fast to a slow salsa, I felt a shift in the way he began to hold me. I consciously pulled back from his embrace. I also experienced a slight feeling of annoyance, thinking, 'Is this his level of teaching salsa?' I was a relative beginner but a quick learner and had learned nothing in the first twenty minutes. Maybe I was being too harsh and should lower my expectations.

Again, El had no problem as she danced easily with Jonnie. She didn't need any lessons, being a natural salsa dancer. 'Oh well,' I thought and smiled.

Finally, the lesson was over and a light, lingering, tingling sensation remained. I did not consider my partner a particularly good teacher or dancer and later, chatting with El, we concurred that neither of them was that accomplished as a teacher, but it was fun to have been a part of the whole experience and connect with the locals in Havana.

The guys were reluctant to leave after the lesson and wanted to chat and have a drink, so we returned to the end of Obispo Street to Café Paris. We felt ourselves unwinding into a holiday mood and keen to find out as much as we could about local Havana life and discover where we could dance later that evening.

Sitting outside at the pavement café was a joyous way to watch the tourists milling around, local Habaneros, many of them dressed in white, the women's hair in long braids threaded through with small colourful beads. I could not but help feel clumsy and frumpy, although I was not. I continuously compared myself to other women. For all the confidence I exuded, I often wished I could feel it.

Lost in thought, I suddenly became aware of Alex (by now we were friends) telling El that he had been a salsa teacher in Zug in Switzerland (El's daughter lived and worked in Zug). It is one of the most expensive places to live in Switzerland and I wondered how much he had been paid as a salsa teacher. He pulled out his driving licence and showed it to us as proof. The date was embossed on the card, Zug 2012. Besides teaching salsa, he sometimes worked on building sites to earn extra money. I looked at him in disbelief, having just had an hour's lesson with him and comparing his teaching to that of my teacher back in the UK, who was divine to dance with. He pointed to the wristwatch on his left arm saying that one of his students had given it to him as a parting gift. El and I looked at each other. Jonnie, in turn, told us that he had taught at a bar called The Havana in Bristol when he had been living there, further saying that he was engaged to be married to an English girl from Bristol and was waiting for his emigration papers to come through. I took a deep breath at hearing all of this and dispelled thoughts brewing in my mind as to the truth of their stories.

Under the tree, the afternoon musicians were playing, and Jonnie grabbed my hand, pulling me towards the pavement at the side of where we sat. As we danced, many passersby stopped to watch and began to video us. The spontaneity of it was how I had hoped Havana would be, exuding that raw energy and undercurrent of so many hopes and possibilities that whispered in my mind. I was chimerical, creating stories and visions of how I would like my life to be and dancing on the pavement at that moment was one of them. I enjoyed Jonnie's easy manner and felt very comfortable with him, As I sat down, I glanced over to Alex and saw that same sullen look as the night before.

Jonnie turned to me and said, 'Do you know what it is like to live in Cuba?' I shook my head. 'It's like living on a beautiful paradise island, but I am caged and cannot fly away, and I am a prisoner here. I dance at the Hotel Tropicana every evening for so little money. I am young, what will become of my life here?'

I was taken aback by that statement and said to him, 'But I thought you said that you are engaged to be married.'

'I am, but I have no idea how long the papers will take to come through. I've been engaged now for four years.'

El very quickly changed the subject saying, 'Jonnie, we have a couple of nights here before New Year's Eve, can you recommend where we could go dancing?'

He immediately said, 'Yes, Casa de la Musica in Miramar. It's a beautiful place and there's a live band there tonight, playing around 11 pm. It's best if you get there around 10 pm so that you can get a seat. It will be very busy, full of tourists and locals. Miramar is in the more expensive part of

Havana. I can't go there tonight as I am dancing at the Hotel Tropicana but maybe Alex could meet you there.'

Alex shrugged his shoulders in a desultory way. However, when we said we were leaving as we wanted to take a taxi out to Ernest Hemingway's house around 2 pm, he immediately sat up and said, 'I have a friend who has a taxi and will take you out there for a very good price.'

El laughingly said, 'What? Are you going to come with us?'

He surprised us by saying he would like to go as he had never been. I looked at him and then saw Jonnie looking at him surprised but he remained quiet. Suddenly, Jonnie stood up and pushed back his chair, the bottom of the legs noisily scraping the gravelled ground. Light airy kisses were exchanged as he said goodbye, saying maybe we could meet another day. We never saw him again on that trip which was a pity. I liked his strong positive and playful energy.

Alejandro's mood changed like a chameleon as he led us down Obispo Street, over Jose Marti Plaza, and back to the Hotel Inglaterra. He walked over to a long-finned, green American Cadillac, parked to one side of the hotel. The driver was lolling in the back seat, eyes closed. He negotiated a price of US $24 to drive the ten miles out and back, waiting at Ernest Hemingway's former home.

The ride took us through Miramar, giving us a glimpse of another Havana, of plantation-style houses, white colonial gated homes, and tall-fronted art deco mansions. Another land, another time in Havana's history.

Such a contrast to so many parts of Havana and is reflected everywhere around the world. There is urban decay - the outskirts, with very little real estate investment, overcrowding, the local government's inability to restore homes and infrastructure with good quality parts and a chasm, distancing the beauty of inner Havana from its outer parts. Very much in the tone of the rich landowners of sugar, coffee, and tobacco; wealth separated them from the lives of the poorer local workforce.

The taxi travelled to a small area called San Francisco de Paula, a shabby suburb of Havana. It turned off the main road through a metal gate and then slowly made its way up a dusty drive to Hemingway's house. It stood nestled amongst tall trees. A large double-fronted, flat-roofed, single-storey house. Its walls were a pale cream stucco colour. Wide stone steps led up to the front door. It was my dream house. I adored American 19th-century colonial-style houses on which this house was modelled. I stood at the bottom of the stairs and absorbed the silence of the surrounding trees. The tourists were reverential as they entered, as we three were. I had no idea if he knew who Hemingway was, but I was impressed by his interest in everything he saw, occasionally commenting on the décor of the rooms.

For its age it looked surprisingly modern and elegant. The house looked homely as though Ernest Hemingway himself was still living there. We were told by a guide that, after Hemingway died, the Cuban government took it over and left the house and all its contents intact - the guns, the deer heads on the walls, the paintings of Hemingway hanging on the cream walls, and all his books. It was colonial elegance, not rustic. It was how I imagined the house of an American writer living in Cuba;

beautiful, comfortable, orderly, and of restrained wealth. I loved the high ceilings, the soft buff-colour floor tiles, and the walls of cream and faded pastels. We walked along a terrace at the back of the house where a metal stairway led up to Hemingway's hideaway, his office, which housed his original desk and a large brass telescope; the room where he was found dead.

As we strolled around outside the house, Alex said, 'Did you see those animal heads on the wall? They are white-tailed deer. I can take you to see them sometime if you like. They are in Cayo Saetia, not far from my home.'

I turned to him, 'So is Havana not your home?'

'No, I live in a small village called Santa Rita, near Mayari, on the Eastern side of Cuba. It's about one thousand kilometres from here.'

'What are you doing in Havana?'

'I've come to see my friend Jonnie and maybe look for some work, like teaching salsa.'

'Do you have family here?'

'Yes,' and lowered his head.

I mislaid El at some point as we wandered through the garden strolling down to the swimming pool, seeing Hemingway's famous and beloved wooden boat called "Pilar" dry-moored near the pool. It's a small two-berth boat and featured strongly in Hemingway's Nobel prize story, "The Old Man and the Sea". I've since heard that a man called Wes Wheeler has rebuilt a copy of "Pilar" based on the original, for a film he is making and that his grandfather, Wesley L Wheeler was the architect of Hemingway's beloved boat. However this is hearsay and an interesting story.

I finally caught up with El, walking down a path which led back towards the taxi. To one side of the path was a makeshift bar under a tall stand of trees, where lengths of sugarcane were being fed through a metal mangler, making fresh sugarcane juice, the same traditional way as in India (a special childhood memory). I walked over to the bar and bought three tall glasses half-filled with fresh sugarcane juice mixed with white rum and large cubes of ice, handing one to Ella and assuming Alex would maybe like one. He declined and I poured his drink into both our glasses.

At five o'clock in the evening, the sun was tired from its daylight work, casting dark swathes of plum coulis shadows across the ground. It was the perfect time to have a couple of drinks. We carried them over to one of the wide-trunked trees and leaned against its old worn warm bark. We stood side by side, savouring the moment, talking about Hemingway. Ella had not read any of his books. I had read a few and told her a little about him and his involvement with the Cuban Revolution, saying that he had often helped the rebels by smuggling guns for them on his boat.

I whispered about Alex's account of Switzerland, teaching salsa and the large silver wristwatch he was wearing. We both disbelieved parts of his story although the driving licence had to be authentic. We looked over to where he was sitting on a fallen log, waiting.

On the drive back into Havana, El sat in front and I was in the back with him while he dozed. My camera was in my hand, and I quietly lifted it to my face, taking several black and white photos of him. He looked like a pin-up boy, his light creamy-brown skin smooth, reminding me of a bar of

Galaxy chocolate, his black eyebrows a perfect arch and his hair cut in precise architectural planed lines around his forehead. I looked out of the window and, seeing his face reflected in the glass, my mind drifted away with a thought of how little I know about men and nothing at all about Cuban men, young or old. I was already fascinated by him. His mixed-race features, fine eyes, full lips, high cheekbones, and strong white teeth were all perfectly imperfect. He reminded me of my mixed heritage and the assorted features of my vast family and wondered if he too bore any of the stigmas which I had inherited from my people. Those thoughts and attitudes to our colour, accent, financial standing, being underprivileged, not being good enough, white enough, educated enough; from an old colonial regime where being white still held sway over the other.

Arriving back at Hotel Inglaterra, El invited our new guide to join us at the club later that night. He said he would try but he did not have enough money for the entrance fee. Later, we would discover that he had been given a cut from the fare we had paid the taxi driver.

On returning to our casa we passed through Plaza Vieja, stopping to buy an ice cream from a corner street vendor. As we queued, we heard a couple of tourists behind us talking angrily in English. They were saying that it seemed there were a lot of handshakes and exchanges of something between many young men everywhere, particularly among the pedicab and taxi drivers. We could not understand their anger.

That "something" unfolded a day or so later in a separate incident when I was taken by our new Cuban friend to buy cigars for my brother. I was beginning to become sensitive to the events gradually unfolding and slowly understanding how the Cubans see themselves and how we see them. I had not studied the social history of Cuba in depth, but I began to realise that it is not until Cuba is viewed differently from the outside that we will begin to appreciate the complexities of their lives.

As time would go by, and I became more involved in this Cuban liaison, I would glimpse those historical periods in Cuba, when people were moved towards violence, corruption and a whole raft of extreme experiences which coloured their aspirations and desperations and created the costumbrismo, those images which depicted the everyday life of Havana and Cuba, and which pulled me so deeply to the heart of Cuba. I saw and experienced them on my several journeys over the coming months.

# 8

The Tropics brought a whole new meaning to nightlife. Later that evening, lying on our beds in the casa, having eaten first in a small local café after our Hemingway visit, we showered, resting from the heat of the day before the late evening ahead. It was a familiar experience, a pre-life. El, who was the eldest granddaughter in our huge family, had many sisters with whom she had regularly danced during her teenage years. Those years had been spent dressing up for the local discos back in the 1970s and 1980s in Northern England, in the latest fashion, with hair and makeup done to perfection. I remembered the many photos I saw of my "girl cousins" as I used to call them, with their almond-shaped eyes highlighted with black kohl drawn and swept up to the sides of their eyebrows, curly hair caught up in a loose chignon, or waterfalling around their shoulders. I had been so envious of them and their social life.

I, on the other hand, was from the South of England, with no sisters, cousins, or girlfriends to go to discos with during my formative teenage years. No best friend to share secrets and dreams with. I had to wait till I was in my late teens and free of my strict family life, before emigrating to

London to join London Hospital to train as an SRN nurse. I called it emigrating because I was leaving my old life to build a new one. Only then did my disco nightlife start, and I made sure I spent a great deal of time making up for those forlorn years of teenage musical deprivation.

This night, we prepared ourselves, putting on our makeup meticulously and dressing to kill (unsure of who or what) in whatever we had brought that would be appropriate for the night. We remembered our high heels, those shoes that could make a woman feel and look sexier than she felt. Our heels clicked like castanets down those three flights of stairs and, stepping outside, we felt a frisson of excitement, as the evening air imperceptibly stroked our cheeks. I smiled as I felt a coil of anticipation rising inside me of the possibilities of the night ahead. What would they be?

Arriving at Casa de la Musica in Miramar, the first thing we noticed was a long line of "stork women" queuing quietly, the bright lights of the forecourt casting harsh shadows over their faces. At least twenty of those feathered birdlike women, wearing skirts which brushed over their bottoms, tops that kissed the smooth rounded flesh of their breasts, their bent white knuckles clutching small purses. That constant soft tropical breeze rustling their long black or blond hair like soft feathers. Their eyes were darting, staring downward or boldly forward. Their faces, marbleised in those moments, spoke of hope. That night they would meet someone who would momentarily, or perhaps permanently, change their lives. This was Cuba.

Being tourists, we were allowed into the club ahead of the locals at the cost of 10 pesos each. We entered, weaving through numerous crowded tables, and found one, halfway down on the edge. We ordered two daiquiris from a passing waiter, hips a-swaying and sashaying. This place certainly had the hallmarks of an entertainment venue, with its large semi-circular cavernous stage set for a twelve-piece orchestra and show dancers. I suspect it had been a private residence in a long ago time. An excited buzzing crowd of tourists had filled the club, single men scattered around, couples at tables. Having settled down with our drinks, I turned around in my usual way, to survey everything around me and saw the "stork girls" filing in and walking down both sides of the club room taking long strides in those high-heeled shoes which purposely made their legs move in that slow sensually inviting way of "you may or may not". Again, I noticed an older, short woman in black, her full breasts protruding forward, shortening her waist, directing them where to sit and stand. By now the orchestra was syncopating as they warmed up and I headed out to the Ladies, where another group of the "stork girls" was chattering excitedly. Some had glazed eyes and a sweet-smelling aroma of smoke trailing out of their delicate nostrils, cigarettes hanging from red lips.

I wondered what it was like to sell one's body for sex. If this was their only income or an extra job, they would earn more in one night than in six months. It was a thought which held no judgement, just a ruefulness at the state of the world in which we lived. I realised how lucky I had been throughout my life to have had opportunities and many choices to allow me to live the way I chose. Although I also knew I had made far too many mistakes and would continue to make them, so I did wonder, for all my choices and independence, if in comparison I was that lucky.

Returning, I saw El chatting with one of the girls who was perched on the edge of her chair next to her. I joined them for a while and asked in halting Spanish how much she would earn tonight. The girl smiled and quietly said '$100'. I reached over and took her hand and squeezed it. It was an unexpected gesture, leaving me to ponder over my action. I suddenly had to leave, whispering that I was going outside for some fresh air.

Passing through the interior of the lobby it exuded an old-fashioned faded glamour with deep Chinese lacquer-red painted walls, large mirrors encased in distressed ornately gilded frames, mirrors like silver pools, catching reflections of eager and expectant faces. I caught my reflection but didn't recognise myself. Chandeliers hung low with dazzling iridescent crystals, their twinkling lights creating small pools of silvered light on the stone floors. It had a sense of a permissive playground for hedonistic socialites of a forgotten past.

I walked out and sat at the top of the stairs in front of the club, watching the taxis arriving, disgorging eager tourists and locals - what would they each get tonight?

Something about the night made me think of Jack. Feeling a dull ache, a tightening in my chest, unbidden tears suddenly rolled down my cheeks. I wiped them away and took a deep breath. Two years had passed. It seemed like one minute of my life. I had stood by the front door of our apartment, watching him finally leave our home of twenty-three years, with a smile on my face (that stupid vacuous smile) but sobbing inside, anxious, having held him tight around the neck, finally letting go of him. That memory was frozen. I stood for a long time, listening to the last of the dying engine of his car, recalling one of his earlier comments that "I was too old for him".

Raising my head, I saw our young Cuban standing opposite, staring at me. A light, almost indistinct, tremor went through me. He looked so vulnerable and hapless standing by the taxi stand. I arose and walked over to him, stork-like. We greeted each other with a light kiss, like old friends.

Another 10 pesos passed through my fingertips for his ticket, and we entered the vibrant atmosphere of the club. The "stork girl" had disappeared and El stood and gave him a big hug. He seemed delighted to see her. In her usual direct way, she softly said, 'There are a lot of prostitutes here. Is this a regular place for them? I thought this was not permitted in Cuba.'

A wide smile broadened his lips. 'Didn't you know that the Casa de la Musica is always full of tourists and prostitutes? The girls here earn good money, much more than a doctor or a teacher. They can afford to help their families and make their lives better. They earn more than I will ever earn teaching salsa unless I can become a professional salsa dancer like Michael Fong.'

That night Los Van Van, a popular Cuban Band was playing. I hadn't heard of them, but it seemed everyone else in the club had. When they started to play there was an explosion of music. It was throbbing, luscious and vibrant as only the big band sounds of Cuban musicians could produce. It had so many layers of Salsa, Mambo, Rhumba, and Jazz all fused, creating energy and fire which does not allow any lover of Latin music to sit and idly tap a foot. The music pulls one's inner carnality, freeing all inhibitions and self-doubt. It's in those moments, when the cage of our inner self is released and free to fly, to dance, to express, a cadenza to wrap around and around in another type of hedonism.

Reggaeton music was not played that evening.

The "stork girls" were quickly paired off, many of them leaving the club on the arm of an estraño embrujado (bewitched stranger). I would love to have heard the men's stories later, to find out if any had a similar experience to what I was about to have, as it is not only foreign women who become ensnared by the charms and deliciousness of the Cuban magic.

By then, the dance floor was a swarm of freneticism. Local Cuban men of all ages came up to us and grabbed us, pulling us out of our seats and close to their sinewy bodies. A powerhouse of energy carried us through the rest of the evening. I danced briefly with Alex who was more like a professional stage dancer, and I responded to the fluidity and grace of his movements. El was caught up in the arms, or under the arms, of fedora-hatted, slim-bodied men, with her dimpled smile even deeper.

Later that night, on the way back to our casa particular, Alex mentioned again that someday he would like to be a famous salsa dancer like Michael Fong. Neither of us had heard of him and remained quiet. I began to muse on Alex, remembering how he looked as he dozed in the car a few hours earlier. His sullen expression then smiles, his remoteness when Jonnie was around, then his engaging energy when on his own with us. He sat next to me but chatted with El. I glanced sideways at him, enraptured by his mixed-race features. A straight Spanish nose, a soft wide African mouth, almond-shaped eyes, plucked arched eyebrows, and curly hair cropped close to his head.

We left him on the corner of our street.

Before drifting off to sleep, I asked El if she had enjoyed the evening. She turned over in her bed, 'I could not have imagined that Havana would be so thrilling. Tonight's dancing will be with me all my life. I have never danced with such amazing dancers as those men at the club. Their bodies were like swaying serpents, and they wrapped their arms around me as though I was a part of them. I felt smitten while dancing. How was it, dancing with our friend?'

'It was as if we were on top of a mountain and a musical wind wrapped itself around us.'

Laughing gently, she said, 'I had no idea you were such a hopeless romantic. I hope this island magic does not cast its witch-like spell over you.'

I laughed as sleep overcame me.

# 9

For the next couple of days, we toured Havana Vieja, enjoying being tourists in this contradictory city of grandeur and decay, a city from another century. We finally took a ride in a fuchsia pink and cream long-finned American car, with cream leather seats, picking up one outside our second home, Hotel Inglaterra. We sat in the back with the roof down, the wind in our hair, while the slim, sandy-haired Cuban drove us all over the city and out towards Havana Forest on the edge of Havana City and back to Plaza de la Revolution, where a large metal outline of Che Guevera hung with the words "Hasta la Victoria Siempre" (Ever onward to victory). He drove us to Lennon Square; John Lennon of course, a bronze statue seated on a bench with the famous Lennon glasses atop its nose. We later found out that there is a woman who looks after JL's glasses, cleans them, and then puts them back on the face of the statue.

Anton our driver was patient and full of smiles, keeping up an endless stream of chatter, telling us how much he had paid for his taxi (over $35,000). At the end of the tour, we gave him $60 instead of the $50. We received his biggest gap-toothed smile as we walked away.

Our afternoon explorations led us through many cathedrals, dotted down the side streets, passing the Bueno Vista Social Club restaurant on the way to Plaza de San Francisco de Asis, next to Havana Harbour. At the side of the Convento de San Francisco de Asis stood a modern dark bronze statue called El Caballero de Paris, a well-known street person who roamed Havana during the 1950s. The statue reminded us of Darth Vader from Star Wars. At the opposite end of the plaza was La Conversacion, a suspended highly polished sculpture of two bodyless people conversing. Huge art pieces stood boldly in plazas everywhere we walked. One of our favourite places was the Museo Nacional de Bellas Artes De Cuba, near Parque Central, which is full of glorious paintings and avant-garde structures in a variety of materials. A particular installation, of an oversized beetle with a human head, crawled up a wall. I stood for a long time staring at it, seeing in it the symbolism of Cuba. The hard outer shell reminded me of its diverse and rich history, its resilience, its political alliances crushing the people, yet its uniqueness which continually allows them to transform themselves. Our eyes feasted on Cuban art; modern, eclectic, and traditional, all enriching and enlightening our curious minds.

This is a once-upon-a-time place, a louche world of Mafia-run casinos and legendary stories of Hemingway downing 16 daiquiri shots in one run; stories one could only imagine. My imagination overflowed and I could feel and see all of this, walking down street after street, sidewalks of four-storey-high stuccoed buildings, greens and pinks saturated with luminosity shrieking at each other for their rightful place in streets full of arched colonnade portales. A city of Spanish colonial and classical columns, statuesque and proud, gouged and crumbling. A myriad of coloured 1950s American cars drifted by in slow motion. I was falling in love with a mythical city, breathing in the sights of metal-laced balconies resting on crumbling brickwork, looking up at care-worn women leaning over them. Aqua blue patterned Spanish-Moorish chipped tiles covered distressed walls, barred glassless windows, children playing in open courtyards or sitting in doorways with Cristal beer cans on sticks, a child's makeshift gun, and old men, half-asleep on steps, loosely hunched over their bodies.

Young men swaggered past, their muscled bodies pushing through their white t-shirts, casting quick fluttering eyes in our direction. A vision of Alex walking in front of me. The city of Havana seemed petrified in time. I too felt trapped in the time loop.

30th December was hot; one more day till the end of 2014. As we walked down Teniente Rey near Plaza del Cristo, we saw him walking towards us wearing the same clothes from our first encounter, a parrot green t-shirt and beige chinos. We greeted each other with smiles and asked him if he knew where we could find an inexpensive restaurant. He pointed to El Chanchullero, opposite where we were standing, saying the food was excellent and about 12 pesos each. That was better news than the 40 pesos we had paid on our first night. He nodded and continued walking.

As we entered, there was a sign on the outside saying "Hemingway did not come here", maybe a marketing ploy as so many other places had large signs up stating Hemingway's association or maybe many habaneros felt the need to distance themselves from him. However, it turned out to be a superb cosy brunch bar with excellent food.

The day drifted, gradually shifting into early evening as we meandered down Paseo de Marti towards Castillo de San Salvador de la Punta, a large grey fort at one end of the Malecon. A small open-air café sat opposite, and it was time for another delicious ice cream. As we chattered, we again saw Alex, approaching with a friend.

'What's going on? We seem to be bumping into him a great deal today. I get the feeling we are being followed.'

'Yes, it's quite odd,' I mumbled and fell silent, feeling pleased I had seen him again.

The two men walked over and sat at our table. That was a fortuitous meeting as we chatted about how we would spend New Year's Eve, with Alex suggesting we meet the following evening and he and his friend would hire a car and take us over to the fort opposite where we were seated, for a fireworks display.

At 8 pm the following evening, we left the casa and waited outside till 8.30 pm.

We had half-expected them to not arrive and after waiting thirty minutes, hailed a passing pedicab who dropped us off at Plaza Vieja, our central spot, a compass point. We looked around the semi-darkened streets, conscious of the lack of human activity and returned to Obispo Street, choosing one of the restaurants we had seen during our earlier walkabouts. A few diners, mainly tourists, were scattered around.

Looking at me quizzically, my cousin said in a low voice, 'What do you think happened to the two guys? Do you think we should have waited a bit longer or waited outside the casa instead of on the street? What if he had turned up and found us gone? She fell quiet for a moment. 'It's odd that they didn't turn up, especially since Alex told us that he would have to pay 10 pesos for a taxi to take us to the Fort. I wonder if he had to pay for the taxi and maybe we are supposed to repay him if we ever see him again. once we return to Havana. It would have been fantastic to see how the local Cubans spend New Year's Eve.'

A glass of red wine was brought to the table. 'On the house,' said the waiter.

'God knows. I feel that my hands are forever opening and closing my wallet. How much do you think we have spent in just a few days here? I'm not going to think about that tonight. Let's order a bottle of champagne, this will probably be the one and only time we will visit Cuba.'

'Don't you think it's quiet for New Year's Eve? Maybe local Cubans eat at home first with their families and party in the streets later.'

'Maybe. I guess that is what we would do at home, so why not here as well? Or maybe this happens to be a particularly quiet year, or this area is quiet.'

While we waited, pre-recorded music began to play and the women in the restaurant were invited to dance with the manager of the restaurant. We all lined up and began copying him. He had started to dance to a song that I absolutely hated, "The Birdie Dance". I stood there and refused to flap my hands like a chicken and shuffle from side to side. 'Enough,' I thought and sat down quickly, downing the whole glass of red wine. I loved dancing but not to that type of song, which I recognised as popular around Europe, but it was not my musical enjoyment. I looked at the manager who was smiling broadly and wickedly and could not help laughing back at him. The level of ambience in the restaurant remained non-festive and, after a couple of hours of eating and drinking our champagne, as the hand of midnight drew nearer, we left, grabbing the remains of the champagne, in search of a more rumbustious end to 2014.

As the hand of time reached out to midnight, the church bells clanged and gonged twelve times in unison all over the city. We found ourselves caught up within small groups of young Cubans who pulled us into their circles of fun and spontaneous singing and dancing. We were carried along in a rush of laughter and excitement through the many small, and by now familiar, streets with a gathering momentum of revellers. Some men had guitars and drums hanging around their necks and wafts of hashish drifted through the air. I knew it was forbidden and punishable but tonight it hung in the air with indulgence, spreading itself over all of us pleasure-seekers and pleasure-lovers. Groups of people, so many in white, huddled together around makeshift fires in disused yards, or linked arms, spontaneously dancing and kicking up little dust clouds around their feet. Film clips of Havana magic. Brown arms circled our waists, inviting us to become Cuban for that night and enjoy the start of 2015. We arrived back at our casa at 5 am, elated and tired; happy we had chosen Havana to spend our exit from 2014.

As we were leaving our casa towards midday, for the second part of our trip, the owner handed us a piece of paper with a phone number on it, saying that a man had turned up at 8.30 pm the night before, asking for us. I immediately called the number, the answer a long low ring.

We left Havana for a few days to travel around Cuba. I was glad, as I had been thinking about him just a little too much and, for a few days, needed to spend time with El in and around other parts of the island.

On our return, the driver dropped us off at Hotel Beltran. As we entered the lobby, El's eyes widened. She could not believe we would be spending our last two nights there. She dropped her bag and gave me a huge hug, her lovely dimples even deeper than usual. Our bodies relaxed in the wonderful Spanish colonial hotel, happy and content, in a place that felt like "home". Its large inner courtyard opened to the sun-drenched blue sky, with palm trees in large pots against tall pillars, walls of fading daffodil-yellow and doors the shade of multi-hued blues and greens of the Ionian Sea.

'Oh, my goodness, I'm in Spain, Greece. This is amazing. I cannot believe we are going to be staying here, what a wonderful surprise.' Her voice was filled with unsuppressed delight.

'Happy birthday surprise.'

Carrying our bags up to the first floor, we walked quickly along a brown stone-flagged corridor and entered our cool darkened room, with wooden slatted shutters closed to block out the midday sun. The bathroom was luxurious. Half its walls were of mellow cream tiles, almost cream-cracker cream. An old-fashioned bulbous white bathtub, on stumpy metal clawfoot legs, rested on a stone floor. Instead of two half-pieces of towels, two soft white towels hung from dark brown wooden towel rails. Large twin beds were covered with white cotton jacquard bedspreads, instead of the low camping-style beds we had first slept in.

Putting my bags down, I took out the creased slip of paper given to me by the previous casa particular owner and called the number.

A voice answered at the other end. It was Jonnie's, sounding slightly cagey. I asked to speak to Alejandro and was told he was out but would call me back. El looked at me quizzically and said, 'Gina, I hope you are not falling in love with him.'

For a moment, I was unsure who she was referring to and then taken aback by her comment. I wondered if I had been acting differently or talking about him too much, both of which I could not remember during our time out of Havana. Of course, I ignored the remark but did wonder why I had phoned him.

A couple of hours later, while out walking, my phone rang, and it was him asking if I would like to meet up and have a salsa lesson.

We three met at the veranda café of the Hotel Inglaterra. Again, he was wearing the same green t-shirt and beige chinos as on our first meeting, but they looked fresh. I wondered if those were the only clothes he owned.

He asked why we had not met up on New Year's Eve. He had to pay the taxi 10 pesos. El and I were unsurprised to hear that, and we reassured him that we had been waiting outside the casa. We did not see him arrive and, thinking that maybe he had forgotten, we then left at 8.30 pm and went over to Obispo Street. He shrugged his shoulders and seemed to forget the incident.

Our conversation turned to cigars, and he asked if either of us wanted to buy any. We were very close to the Cohiba cigar shop, and he could take us there. El decided she would like to go off on her own and explore, so we agreed to meet back at our hotel in a couple of hours.

The two of us walked down some unfamiliar streets chatting softly while he asked what work I did in England. He was in a quiet mood, full of smiles, and I noticed that his eyebrows seemed to have been plucked into an even finer arch and his hair closer-shaven. I remarked about his new haircut, and he grinned, saying it was the latest fashion out of Puerto Rico. He said many trends from there were followed by the younger Cubans. He remarked on my clothes, saying I looked very fashionable. Blushing, I brushed the comment aside.

Instead of going to the Cohiba shop, he hailed a pedicab and said he was taking me to a friend's house where he could get a box of 25 for $100 instead of $200 from the shop. I knew they were expensive so agreed to go along, as my brother had requested this small gift from Cuba. Ten minutes later, the pedicab quietly pulled up outside a grey concrete utilitarian-style block of apartments. We entered a dark and dingy lobby and walked along its corridor, stopping outside a barely visible small brown door which was ajar. Entering, a petite Spanish Cuban woman greeted him with a big hug and handed him a box of cigars. He turned to me and asked if I could give him $100, which I did, in $10 notes. Taking the box of cigars from him, I watched him hand over the money. As I turned aside for a moment, out of the corner of my eye I saw him split the money, putting some inside his chino pocket with one hand

and, with the other, handing over the balance. I suddenly remembered the "handshakes and exchanges of something between many young men and pedicab taxi drivers" spoken by the English tourists, while we had been queuing for our ice creams, the previous week. OK, I understood. If you want something in Havana, ask a pretty boy to take you just around the corner, where you will get what you want cheaper, and he always gets a good reward. I guess that is how life works in Havana.

On our way back, we passed a small bar and went in to have a coffee. Sitting opposite him, he started to talk about himself and what he wanted to do with his life. His English was not fluent, and I asked how much English lessons cost in Havana. He replied, saying about £60, and his eyes were downcast. My immediate thought was, 'maybe I should help him out with English lessons, he would then have more opportunities to get a job', forgetting that he lived in Switzerland. I remarked on his work in Switzerland and asked if he spoke English while teaching dance classes. He said he spoke German more than English there, so his English never improved. I casually suggested that maybe I could send him some money, once back in the UK, for English lessons and, at that, he seemed very pleased. As we left, he suggested that we meet later that evening around 10.30 pm at a local hotel which had a show and was playing salsa music.

He met us outside, dressed in a suit the colour of burgundy wine with a contrasting black velvet collar, and a black open-neck shirt which suited his handsome face. We paid for his ticket to go in. He was charming and gracious, ensuring that he danced alternatively with us. It was a fun-filled evening. The music was the best salsa we had ever heard and many of the pieces we had danced to, back in England. It was an evening where our feet barely touched the dance floor. We danced with Cuban men and tourists, to every possible version of sol and salsa. Now and then, I glanced over at him. I caught his eye and smiled.

On our last day in Havana, El wanted to take one of the open-top buses and see the city. It was a blistering hot and moisture-drenched day. We decided that we each needed a little time to ourselves to enjoy the last moments of Havana. I phoned Alex for a final salsa lesson while she went off on her own, agreeing to meet up at Hotel Beltran around 4 pm. We lunched together and went our separate ways.

I met him at Jose Marti Plaza by the statue. Again, I saw Arturo, the bare-footed elderly man dressed in blue with the Che Guevara beret, sitting on a stone bench under the same trees. Walking over to him, I asked if I could take his photo again. He spoke softly in English and agreed. I gave him about 15 pesos, knowing that these photos of him would adorn my home with memories of my last afternoon in Havana.

We walked across the plaza, with my camera in hand. I was in street-photography mode, shooting photos mainly of him while sauntering over to the café in O'Reilly Street, El Ciclo, to discover that the owner was absent, and we could not practise there. We hopped in a pedicab and rode out to the apartment block where I had bought the Cohiba cigars the previous day.

The entrance to the block was full of dark spaces as we mounted a couple of flights of concrete stairs, the little light coming in from tiny windows high up in the wall. As I followed him, I thought of how I rarely allowed myself to take risks that would put me in jeopardy, but I felt completely safe in this city. At the end of a couple of flights of stairs, we stood outside the door to an apartment in deep shadow. A gentle tap and it was opened by a black Cuban woman with blue curlers in her hair. Her shadowy figure let us in, and we were led to a small room with a double bed and an improvised shower area. He closed the door and turned on some music. I was taken aback, not sure how to interpret this. Had the woman thought I was here for sex? There was a knock on the door and the woman handed something to him. He threw a small towel on the bed. I looked quizzically at him, now feeling a little bit nervous, but he only smiled and said, 'Let's dance.' We danced for forty minutes, having a better salsa lesson than the first and chatting all the while.

I kept chatting to hide my desire for him. I paid him 20 pesos for the lesson. Would that have been the price for sex too?

Our departure from Cuba was imminent as we rode back in another pedicab to Hotel Beltran. Sitting in the cab, I was relieved that nothing more than dancing had transpired in that room, in that cement box of an apartment, although there were obvious signs of other activities available. The towel on the bed was such an overt hint.

I was attracted to him but, leaving Cuba in a few hours, I felt no inclination to be physically involved with him in that room, or any other place, and liked him more for being a gentleman. My camera, my sub-ego, was at the bottom of my bag and I wanted to capture what I saw as I looked closely at him. It was an expression I wanted to replicate on film, but unsure how. On impulse, I leaned towards him and kissed him on the cheek, then leaned back and took his photo. He looked at me and laughed, 'Now you kiss me. We were in that room for forty minutes and you did not kiss me. Why?'

I just smiled and shrugged my shoulders.

He laughed out loud and said, 'Thank you for the kiss' and kept on smiling for the remainder of the ride.

What I had done was for an effect, to capture his face on camera knowing that the kiss would change his expression, but I didn't fully know the effect it had on him.

Arriving back at the hotel, instead of leaving, he asked if he could wait in the lobby until I left. Ella was finishing her packing and asked if everything was OK. I finished mine and went downstairs to settle the bill. He was sitting at a metal table in the inner courtyard chatting to one of the hotel staff. I went up to him and told him that we were leaving. Looking at him, I took off a thick silver ring and handed it to him, saying that it was a friendship ring. I wished him well and said that maybe I would return to Cuba one day.

He stood up and looked at me and, with a wide smile, waved goodbye and walked out of the lobby into the bright sunlight.

# 10

We left the sunshine and warm nights of Cuba and landed in the grey cold heart of the English winter, with its damp bone-chilling air and wet misty evenings. The sun disappeared by 3 pm into its dark fathomless horizon, awaiting the dawn of a new day and I too joined that horizon each winter's afternoon.

Our arms tightened around each other's necks before we parted company at Gatwick Airport.

'I had such a great holiday with you. I hope we can travel together again. Maybe even revisit Cuba. Let me know. I wasn't sure how well our holiday would work out but thank you for my wonderful birthday gift. Staying in the Hotel Beltran was a perfect ending to our holiday. So really, any plans to return to Cuba sometime soon?' asked El, with that twinkle in her eye.

'Uhm, not yet. I think I would like to, simply because ten days was not enough. I think we only touched the surface of that fascinating island. We missed seeing all the beautiful beaches and chilling out under the palm trees. I think it's back to work for now and maybe return towards the end of the year. I'll let you know.'

Giving me another huge hug, she whispered in my ear, 'Be careful with that guy. He is very sweet and nice, but you know nothing about him except that you are attracted to him.'

'Am I so transparent? I liked him in the moment of some holiday fun but nothing romantic passed between us. Did you think something had? We spent very little time together and you know, with all the travelling I've done, I've never become involved with local men and don't intend to start now.'

'Remember, I've been to that same place of hurt and longing, and your eyes give away your feelings.'

Once again, I was taken aback by her keen, but subtle, observation of me without passing any comments.

Back home, the flat had a solitariness to it that also lay within me. My home was usually my refuge with its art collected from my travels. Chinese, African, and Indian paintings hung on walls throughout. Corner up lights played softly on my favourite oil painting of a serene-faced African Zulu woman, with a sunset-red halo of a hat surrounding her beautiful finely carved face, the painted oils shining out in chocolate browns, burnt caramelised oranges and classic blue. I would gaze at her serene face for hours, her smile warm and enigmatic. Now, that lovely Zulu woman reminded me of the many Cuban faces I had just left behind. So many happy memories of travels around the world, admiring grand edifices and works of art, and so often a lone traveller; often wishing there had been a lover's arm around my shoulder, gazing at the same sights and dreaming the same dreams.

Forty-eight hours had passed since returning from Cuba and I had not been thinking of him particularly, more of the whole experience of that lovely island. Sitting on my voluminous sofa, with my fingers wrapped around a cup of hot coffee, I was already regretting that El and I had not seen more of it. I knew we had missed burying our toes deep in soft sand, sunbathing and swimming languidly in warm waters, sipping ice-cold cocktails on plump white cushioned cane beach chairs, as the sun dazzlingly slipped below that line of infinity where the sea meets the sky. We had not danced our fill of salsa or sol or seen enough of the many other cities and towns throughout Cuba. It was a tourist trip for me but not the type I truly enjoyed. I loved to get to the grassroots of a country, to explore the heart and soul of the cities and villages, peeking and poking my curiosity into their lives, hoping the locals would indulge a romantic foreigner.

One week, then two weeks passed, snuggling back into the hibernation of winter. I continued with my business, working relentlessly but finding the business climate was changing or was it me?

My passion was ebbing for it. I'd sit in the office every day, phoning clients to secure business. Anxious that I was not confirming orders for the next season, three months in advance, knowing the consequences of a lack of sales and profit. During the evenings, I'd look at the photos of Cuba, selecting and cataloguing them, as was my usual way after travelling. I had taken so many, not realising just how many I had taken of him. I looked at one, taken of him sitting on the veranda of Hotel Inglaterra on the second day of our meeting, tracing the outline of his high cheekbones with my fingertip, his arched eyebrows. I looked at his elongated eyes and wondered what it was about him that I found attractive and yet had a feeling of unease. There was a cunningness in his eyes with a hint of sweetness and innocence which felt like a snake sliding across the back of my shoulders, warm and dangerous. He was a head taller than me and lightly muscled, accentuated by the tight t-shirts he wore. He walked lightly on the fronts of his feet like a gazelle ready for flight. Despite that nascent nagging of a feeling, I began to find myself thinking of him more frequently; picking up the phone at night and then putting it down again, about to send a text and then cancelling it.

Towards the end of January, on a drizzly Sunday afternoon, my phone rang. I'd guessed by the code that it was a Cuban number and a young woman's voice started to chatter excitedly, saying her name was Rosario and she was a friend of Alex, who was next to her and wanted to speak to me, but his English was poor. I heard him laughing in the background shouting out, 'Ola Gina, como estas? te queiro.'

I laughed too, not knowing yet what 'te quiero' meant.

Rosario said, 'Is it OK for me to call you Gina? Alex has been talking about you, saying how nice you are and that you met in Havana, and you gave him a silver ring. He wants to know if you will come back to Cuba again.'

'Oh, I don't know, I have no plans to return yet. I would like to. I loved visiting your country.'

He shouted, 'Come back soon.'

The connection broke.

I pressed the off button, laughing, and then it began. His beguiling eyes and smile drenched my thoughts and the seed of a plan to return to Cuba began to flourish.

When would be the best time to return? How could I justify it? Who do I have to justify it to? What will the family think? What is there for me here that I could not find in a new country? Why did I need to continue to live my present life, repeated day after day, without the two people who had been with me for so long?

Thoughts, thoughts, thoughts!

A few moments later, the phone rang again, and it was my brother from France, with a big cheery 'Hullo' and eager to hear about my holiday.

'So, Gina, tell me everything about Cuba. You didn't send me any photos, as you promised. How was our cousin?'

'We had a great time, lots of mojitos, not enough salsa, lots of culture, lots of travelling. We both loved Havana and its eclectic mix of architecture. I'll send you photos by email shortly. It looked like the whole country is locked in time, a living museum. Less touristic compared to so many other places.'

'Yes, but that can't be good for the Cuban people surely? I have read a great deal about Cuba and watched its politics unfold over the years. How did you find the people? Did they seem happy, have fun, and drink a lot of rum? They have great food there.'

Our conversation continued for an hour and then he said, 'Your voice sounds a little sad, did you meet a handsome Cuban man and now want to return.'

'I don't remember saying anything about meeting anybody.'

'You are such a romantic but please, be careful. You have been through so much grief in the past couple of years, and

I don't think you are strong enough to take any more heartache. A holiday romance is not the answer.'

I felt slightly irritated by that remark.

'Why do you and Ella think I've fallen for a guy I've just met? I'm not a schoolgirl.'

'Sister, you know I love you, but you have not yet come to terms with Jack leaving you. You are still grieving for him and, on top of that, Mum's death has left you painfully raw. I know she is always with you in your heart. You are still so vulnerable. You are such a strong woman but hide your sorrows too deeply. All I am asking is that you be a little careful but, if you get a crazy idea to return to Cuba, please take me with you.'

I heard the chortle in his voice. I laughed too as I hung up.

Sighing deeply, I realised I was beginning to become entrapped in an affair I had not even started, and the words of my cousin and brother began to bother me. Maybe in a new country, without all the difficult reminders of my current world, I could find a new beginning, a new peace.

# 11

Oh, those cold stormy winter days were making the idea of revisiting the sunshine of Cuba more tempting and the murmurings of tiny plans began to form, but I decided that I would keep them to myself. Looking in the mirror one morning, I felt I needed to regain a more youthful figure and lose at least five kilos.

'Where does this weight come from?' I ruminated, puffing out my cheeks. I wasn't vain, as such, but had always been self-conscious of my physical self, which was probably one of the reasons I had never allowed myself to be with many men, overexposing my vulnerability.

I had to feel confident and trust myself with him or trust him. Over February, I embarked upon a strict routine of running five kilometres a day, five days a week, along the beachfront, no matter what the weather.

Today's weather though was a maelstrom. The storm blew deep down into the yellowy-grey waves of the English Channel, churning and roiling in frantic swirls, scooping up pebbles as the ice-cold sea washed over the iron rails of the esplanade. I was thoroughly soaked by the ferocity of the salty spray despite hugging the sides of the beach huts. I stopped to catch my breath, feeling the same tumultuous energy of the waves rushing through me, as I thought about whether to return to Cuba and what was driving my need. Every step I ran, I argued with myself as to the genuine reasons for wanting to return.

'Why do I find it impossible to be honest with myself sometimes?' I thought as I shivered, with my cold wet clothes sticking to my body, my beanie hat pulled down low over my eyes to keep off the rain.

It seemed this was not the day to continue my run. Instead, I headed back home, my feet squelching in my trainers, the wind howling and following me down the road like an urgent messenger from Hell.

'Messenger from Hell? Do I always have to have such dramatic ideas about everything?'

Giggling at the thought, I felt lighthearted and invigorated by my morning jog, beginning to feel and see the benefit of them.

I arrived home, dripping wet by the front door, and unlocked it. I took off all my sodden clothes and trainers in the small lobby of my flat, not wanting to leave a trail of slushy water down the carpeted stairs. I looked up and caught sight of myself in the hallway mirror and let out a huge laugh at my reflection. I looked like the proverbial "drowned cat" and thought, 'I doubt he'd fancy me much, looking the way I do.' I then caught an imaginary glimpse of him, also laughing at me in the mirror.

Standing in the shower, the steaming water like a gentle tirade warming my body, I decided that I needed, more than anything else right now, to change the future of my current life. To find a way to expunge the sadness of the recent past, of my broken marriage and the death of my mother. I knew that, at the heart of me, I was a happy and optimistic woman, full of life and determination, resilient and strong. I had risen like a phoenix on several occasions and visiting Cuba only a short while ago had awakened in me the beginning of a new rise of that fiery-red mythical bird. I smiled as the steamy waters caressed my body, enjoying the silkiness of my skin, thinking of him. Closing my eyes, I remembered dancing with him in that small room in the heart of Havana, full of apprehension and doubt as to his intentions which were, on the surface, no more than dancing salsa. I giggled at that memory and at the same time knew that although I would not call myself a prude or sexually unadventurous, I had had no desire to have a physical relationship within the staged parameters of that gloomy room, bordering on the seedy, where money had been exchanged for the activity between us.

The memory of leaning over towards him in the pedicab and kissing him on the cheek, as he accompanied me back to my hotel, sent a slight shock through me, as my shyness, even in the privacy of my mind, awakened in me a tingle of wanting. I heard the phone ring in the distance through the soft thrumming of the water on the shower floor and made my decision.

The first two months of winter passed quickly and, on a bright early spring morning on 7th March, I booked my return flight to Holguin. There had been many late-night and early-morning phone calls between England and Cuba, lasting about one or two minutes of 'hola', 'como estas?', 'how are you?', 'what are you doing?', 'when are you coming back?', 'te quiero' or 'te amo'.

I asked my Cuban salsa teacher, after one of our private lessons, what it meant when a Cuban man said 'te quiero' or 'te amo' and he grinned broadly and winked (he winked often).

'Well, "te quiero" could simply be a friendly term as within friends or family, or it could mean "I want you" in a more sexually desirous way. "Te amo" means he could be in love with you.'

I was amused at these endearments and felt a silly thrill when I heard them and thought it had been quite some time since any man had said, 'te quiero' or 'te amo' to me. I then let it slip away to a corner of myself, knowing it really meant nothing.

Flattery is deceiving and, as the days passed, those four small words soon had me excited and curious.

Soon after my return from Cuba, I sent him £60 to pay for English lessons, as I said I would. Once I say something, I have to carry through with it. It had taken the bank four weeks to transfer the money to one of his friend's bank accounts in Matanzas. I had been so happy, knowing I was helping him in some way. During one of our brief phone conversations, I'd asked him if he had found an English teacher and started lessons. His reply was vague, with a light laugh, and at that time I did not pursue the conversation again, although thought I ought to learn a few more Spanish words.

The business had been my passion for years, having many successes, but along with those were constant concerns which consumed and left me despondent. My fashion business was fast-moving and demanded continual creativity and aggressiveness; testing my abilities to improve year after year. I felt stretched, like a worn-out threadbare piece of elastic. The beginning of that year had signs of a new recession, and orders were non-existent, but February was seeing a flurry of substantial orders flowing in, indicating that 2015 would be a profitable year. Once I had secured orders for the next season, being early autumn, I could step back for a month before preparing for Christmas orders. So, I could revisit Cuba at the end of March for ten days. Getting business, even after 30 years was continuously tough without respite; planning a year ahead for each season, foreseeing and creating new trends to be ahead of the competition.

That evening, I texted him to say that I would like to return to Cuba at the end of March to visit him. I did not think too deeply about my reasons or motives. I decided I was going to return to see more of that beautiful island, travel deeper into the Cuban countryside, and delve into its heart and soul. I loved the idea of having a local companion who spoke some English, a native who knew Cuba well, to hire a car and drive its length and breadth, to dance and … I let my thoughts slip away.

Later, as I was falling asleep the phone rang, his voice very excited, his Spanish and English tripping over each other, asking me when I would arrive.

'I'll be at Holguin Airport on 25th March, the plane lands at about 2.45 pm. Will you be able to hire a car for me? I have already checked out some car hire places, they are all expensive, but I know there is one at the airport that's a little cheaper.'

I took a breath.

'I've emailed them but haven't had a reply. I'll send you my details so you can reserve a car for me, and I'll google translate these in Spanish and send them to you tomorrow.'

I slowed down.

'Is that OK?'

'OK, no problema. It's easy for me to contact them. I'll get a nice car for you. Buenos noches, Carina.'

The next morning before the day took over our working life, I called my son to ask if he would like to have a coffee.

As we sat amidst the early morning gaiety and classical music in Café Nero, I told him I had decided to return to Cuba for ten days and would be leaving on 25th March. He looked up at me quite shocked, 'What's going on here? Did something happen to you while you were out there with El?'

'I know this may seem like a sudden decision, having just returned from Cuba. But, in honesty, I feel so restless and truly don't know what to do with my life. You know that the past few years have been tough in all sorts of ways.'

He looked at me and nodded.

'I can't seem to get over the past and I feel I am just hanging around with no real purpose.'

'What does that mean?'

'I'm not sure, maybe on my return I will have a clearer answer for myself and you. Going to Cuba with El and both of us chatting about our lives, marriages, husbands, loves and losses, it was a realisation of how quickly we have gone from 15 to 55 and feel left behind in our lives.'

I stopped for a moment, sipping my coffee, and looked at him.

'We've both found it difficult to meet anyone in these past years. I think we had a similar ending to our relationships which left us both in a void.'

He narrowed his blue eyes and asked, 'Did you meet someone?'

He smiled impishly.

'Oh, is that why you've been out jogging every day?'

I gave a short laugh.

'I did and I didn't. You remember we've both chatted about wanting to move from here and find a new way of living. I want to return and see if there are any possibilities to find a new way to live my life. I'm not saying I will find it there, but I might find something to stop my restlessness.'

'You have always been restless, Mum. It's your nature. You're like the storm we had yesterday. It's those nomadic ancestors of ours who continuously chase both of us.'

He reached across to me and took my hands in his. This surprised me as he was not often affectionate towards me.

'Just be careful out there and don't take too many risks. You don't know the Cuban people or their culture. I know you have always been a cautious traveller and kept yourself safe but, this time, please be even more vigilante.'

His brow was furrowed, and his eyes suddenly looked troubled.

I gently squeezed his hand and said, 'I'll be OK.'

As we both walked back to the office, I knew I was not being truthful with him.

While I busied myself, in preparation for this trip, I remained calm on the exterior chatting with friends. I was still jogging and visiting trade shows to ensure I was always in touch with the latest business news and gossip, but my innermost thoughts were like that of a woodpecker. Peck, peck, pecking away at my rational mind, asking myself if I was really attracted to a man so much younger than me. Was I being truthful or fanciful, imagining that a country like Cuba could be the answer to my constant restless yearnings?

I was becoming irritated with those thoughts, so took off on a quick shopping spree, buying some pretty underwear and Chanel Chance perfume, and replenishing my supply of white t-shirts, and favourite staples of white espadrilles and flip-flops. I knew it would be hot there and bought a couple of cotton dresses from Vivien of Holloway, 1950s-style halter neck printed dresses, perfect for the retro look I loved.

Three weeks later, on a warm spring morning, I boarded the Thomas Cook flight at Gatwick Airport to Holguin, Cuba, with my small pull-along packed, visa to be issued at the airport, a car already hired and one very excited woman and Cuban man waiting to see each other in 9 hours and 45 minutes.

# 12

Flying always gives me a sense of discombobulation as though time itself is the traveller. It seems we are barely in the air when the descent begins, gliding from crystalline sunshine in clear blue space through layer upon layer of fluffy clouds, and dropping down into another level of space, hanging on outspread wings, revealing yellowing ground below, dotted with spreading green. The ground rushes up to meet us, scattered crops and Lego-size buildings, larger and larger they become, until a strip of grey-black tarmac meets the plane's wheels.

I was like a teenager, barely able to contain my excitement, strapped into my seat, belt loosely clipped across my blue jeans. I had been very careful to dress simply and casually, so wore my favourite semi-fitted faded blue jeans with a sleeveless button-through denim blouse, Indian embroidery with tiny mirrors on the yoke, glinting as the sunlight poured through the small round windows of the plane. Hair in a loose ponytail, I wore little makeup and would freshen up once I had landed.

The image of him waiting for me, well I could not quite imagine it, half-afraid of myself and for myself, not truly believing that I had decided to return after such a short time. Surely the message to him would be obvious? Would he be pleased I had returned and, if so, what was he hoping for? All these thoughts, already accumulating like autumn leaves, are being brushed together in one big pile.

I could not believe I was once again walking through immigration, passport stamped for the second time entering Cuba, the arrival hall washed in glaring sunlight, dust particles drifting up and down the myriad shafts of light. I stood impatiently in the queue, stamping my espadrilled feet. I just wanted to get through all the formalities. I smiled as I watched my bag slowly lumbering along towards me on the conveyor belt. It seemed to take an inordinate amount of time as this was the only flight in with a plane half-filled with passengers.

Bending to pick up my bag, I looked across the conveyor belt out towards the large front door of the arrival hall and, through the glass doors, saw him standing outside dressed completely in red, including his trainers. I remembered seeing the men in Havana dressed completely in a mono colour. Approaching the final exit, two further customs officers were checking the luggage tickets against the counterfoil on each passenger's passport. I flashed mine and slowly walked forwards, a few yards towards the exit. Suddenly I stopped, unsure of my next move. An acute attack of nerves overcame me, a slight tremor in my stomach, as I caught sight of him again, his handsome face shadowed by his hand over his forehead, peering from the sunlight into the cavernous arrival hall.

Why were there no locals inside the arrival's hall, as in most other airports around the world? A moment later, I realised that most of the passengers on the plane were package-holiday tourists who would be met by tour guides and taken directly to their holiday resort hotels.

Once again, I was the only independent traveller on that plane.

Needing a few moments to gather myself together, I headed to the Ladies where I quickly freshened up; brushing my teeth, putting on glossy pale pink lipstick and reapplying my smudged eyeliner. All those hours on the plane had left my skin dehydrated. I glanced to the left. A female attendant stood with her back against the wall, a slightly rotund woman, with black hair scraped back tightly in a ponytail, and long black eyelashes covering her deep dark eyes. I suddenly remembered an old song about "dark Spanish eyes" and I grinned. She rested one hand on a long-handled wet mop, streaks of wet floor around her feet, studying me with a shadow of a smile, but not her eyes, and then I saw her shake her head, almost imperceptibly, from side to side. 'Demasiado, Senora' and in English quietly said, 'Go slowly here, vale.'

I frowned, interpreting that as "take it easy" but not sure what she was referring to. It sounded like a warning. That was the fourth in three months. The first two were from Ella, then my brother and son, three weeks before I left. Running a brush through my hair and retying my ponytail, I looked at the attendant and thanked her but not sure for what. Turning, I walked out towards the Cambio, a money exchange, on the opposite side of the Ladies, unsure how much money to change. Shocked once again at the poor exchange rate, almost 1 peso to £1, as I remembered the low exchange rate the first time in Havana.

Shrugging my shoulders with irritation and tossing my ponytail, I pulled my luggage behind me, lengthening my stride and resolve and walked out into the sunshine. He came towards me and gave me a huge hug.

'Ah, Gina, you have returned. So nice to see you, but you look different.'

Stepping back, he looked me all over with a tiny frown between his eyebrows and then grinned. A shyness crept over me leaving me feeling a little self-conscious. Stretching out his right hand, he took the pull-along from me. He walked lightly ahead towards a small white squat building, Rex, the car hire firm. I'd left the booking of the car to him. By the side of the office stood a bright red Peugeot, its new highly polished body flaming brightly in the afternoon sun, glints of sunlight bouncing off the chrome front fender. I gasped. He heard and turned back to me, 'Do you like it? It's new and the last car the company had.'

I walked into the slightly dark interior of the office, made darker by the blazing sun outside, and sat down on the low metal chair in front of a sprawling desk. Before completing and signing the paperwork, I asked the man across the desk from me the cost of the hire car for 10 days. When he told me, I held my breath then let out a whisper of a gasp saying that the cost was too high and asked if he had a cheaper car.

He looked at me, shaking his head from side to side. Alex, standing next to me, whispered, 'What's the problem, Gina? You not like car?'

'The car is beautiful, but it's so expensive. £1350 for ten days is more than I had expected to pay.'

'That's the usual price for foreign cars in Cuba and this is new, a convertible, a luxury car. I don't have any others for at least three to four days. Do you not want it?' the hire man asked in perfect English.

I did a quick mental check remembering that I had asked for a standard car, not a luxury car. Seems he made his own decision to hire this one, without telling me about the cost before my arrival.

I signed the car hire agreement, paid for it by credit card and stood up with a bright smile.

'OK, let's go.'

Outside, with the key in my hand, I turned around and asked him where his luggage was, thinking he would have come prepared to spend the holiday with me. He mumbled, saying he would get it later. I tugged at my ponytail with a little worry but pushed the thought aside.

Sitting behind the wheel of this left-hand drive, I whispered to him, 'I'm a little nervous about driving here as I'm not used to driving on the left-hand side of the road.'

The car hire guy was standing at the side of the car, so Alex whispered back, 'It's OK, you drive and later I drive. The man he says my name not on paper so I cannot drive.'

He touched my arm and told me not to worry.

As I lowered the roof of the convertible, I felt a discomfort in my stomach as though something was out of order, but my pride kept me quiet.

Taking a deep breath, I smiled and drove away as the sun's heat mellowed a bit, and a lighter breeze stirred. We swopped over, a mile down the road, safely away from the airport. As we drove, I asked him what type of casa he had rented, and he replied saying it was a very nice villa which belonged to a friend of his outside one of Holguin's beach resorts, Emerald Bay.

Speeding down a long black ribbon of tarmac, we left the urban towns behind, rushing past green fields of sugar cane, with unfamiliar salsa music playing. I turned to look at him and saw small dimples in his cheeks as he smiled broadly, dimples I had not noticed the first time. I let my head fall back against the backrest and let the sun and the breeze kiss my face, cheeks, and lips. I loosened my hair and sunk lower into the seat. The now quiet of my mind embraced me fully. 'Is this meant to be?' I thought. I did not know him but had already entrusted him with hiring the car and our accommodation. What would that be like?

I felt his hand reach over and take mine, drawing it onto his thigh.

# 13

The door closed softly behind us.

The room was still and silent except for the light beating of my heart. That time had arrived. That moment I had envisioned so frequently, wondering how to make that first move, alone together after these last few weeks of hurried phone calls and urgent texts.

Putting the luggage somewhere or other, I turned to him in the intimacy of the room and put my hand out to him which he took with a gentle smile on his face as if to reassure me.

Would this be a moment as played out in the movies of erotic urgency, with hands tearing away ties, buttons ripped, lips locked while layers of clothes fell to the ground, bare backs against a wall, naked legs hooked?

I could feel the slight awkwardness of two relative strangers moving towards each other quietly, tentatively, allowing each granule of time to unfold. I circled my arms around his neck and felt his lips on mine even before they touched, a soft breath on my face. As we kissed, his full warm lips enveloped mine, drowning out my senses. I sank into their softness, remembering how often I had imagined the touch of his lips on mine, in the quiet of the night, in my darkened bedroom.

My lips tingled as he pulled our bodies closer. Every muscle was taut with excitement and suppressed longing, and I felt slightly shaky. That kiss seemed to float in eternity. I felt his fingers slowly unbuttoning my blouse as I pulled and unbuckled the thin leather belt around his waist. I was aware that it had been quite some time since I had been with a man. I pushed that thought away and hoped my body would be desirable to him.

The back of my legs felt the hard wood of the bed frame, and we both suddenly started laughing, his eyes sparkling and, as I sought again his soft lips, we fell onto the bed. With one hand, he undressed me and with the other circled my neck. The gold chain around my neck pressed against his arm as I lay long and naked under the single bare neon strip hanging from the middle of the ceiling.

Self-consciousness kept invading my need for him, while our now-naked bodies wound together as he caressed the smooth velvet of my skin, sweeping his fingers through my hair, slowly melting away my shyness and fears.

I hated the constant taunt of the "older woman" which played through my mind. I could not let go of it, not even now.

He lay lightly on top, sensing my anxiety. Looking at me with smiling eyes, he whispered, "Te quiero."

I stroked his strong muscular back, his skin almost transparent to my touch and sensed his arousal becoming stronger.

This first time was not a physically pleasurable experience as I realised that going without sex for some time had caused a problem for me that I had not known until now. He seemed unaware of how I felt and neither of us was physically satisfied. He rolled off onto his back and, as we lay side by side, took my hand in his. I smiled to myself at this gesture which I took to be his understanding of the situation.

Turning on my side, propped on one elbow, my eyes travelled the length of his bronzed body. It was a marble statue of gently rippling muscles, defined and smooth, lithe as a dancer, graceful in its perfection. His body was naked of hair and his eyebrows now a perfect thin arch which accentuated the slight upward sweep of his eyes. A quick flashback to our first meeting reminded me how his eyebrows had been thick and dark.

For a while, no word passed between us. He lay on his stomach and, looking at me, asked, 'Gina, you come to Cuba for sex?'

For a moment I heard a loud silence in my head, followed by a tremor of shock reverberating within me.

'What did you say?'

'I ask, you come to Cuba for sex?' as he buried his face in the crumpled sheet.

'So, you think there is no sex for me in Anglaterra?'

'Si, but your body it seems like nervous and anxious. Are you, ok?'

'Si. I'm fine but I came to see you and, yes, I want to have sex with you, but that is not the most important reason for coming to Cuba.'

I did not quite know what he meant but maybe the terrible pain I felt while we had sex had physically affected him too.

He reached his hand up to the gold link chain hanging around my neck and held it lightly between his fingers, stroking it gently for a few minutes. I waited, not realising I was holding my breath.

'Gold is expensive in Cuba, not many people have such things. I like it, maybe you buy one for me.'

'Why?'

'You come to Cuba and maybe you give me a present.'

He buried his face in the crumpled sheet again. Closing my eyes, I smiled. The older woman, the beautiful young man. Knowing how much I had paid for my chain and for what had transpired in the last hour I was not prepared to exchange it for gold or pesos.

'My God,' I thought, 'he is fast,' and I realised that this was probably not an uncommon practice for him, or was it just a supposition on my part? I remembered his story about being given a heavy silver watch by his student in Switzerland. Shifting my body slightly and removing his hand from the hanging chain, I again smiled, quietly saying, 'Maybe but not yet, possibly later when we know each other better.'

With that, he looked up at me with a smile and rolled off the bed saying he was hungry.

# 14

Darkness had replaced the day's sunlight and the air was that wonderful tropical warm. The warm I loved, the warm of my childhood sitting with my family on wooden-string beds as the shadows of evening deepened, sucking on juicy warm mangoes, and drinking sweet lassi. The chattering of stillness reminded me of my passion for sub-tropical heat and life. That life, an old memory, a slow bubbling, as I walked down the short flight of red brick stairs with Alex in front, to the car parked along the side of the casa.

Driving to the beach at Guadalajara was in comfortable silence, stopping and parking behind a double-storey 1970s hotel building, defused yellow lights glowing behind small windows. Walking down the side of the building, a small door opened into a sparsely furnished bar filled mainly with local men in string vests and shorts, bare dark-skinned feet resting on top of flip-flops and a few young women serving behind the bar, with music in the background.

Following him, he led us out through another door directly onto a sandy yard where there was a makeshift bar with the usual-coloured lights suspended from the edge of a thatched roof.

Buying some beers and white wine in cheap plastic tumblers, we walked further down to the beach edge, which was in luminescent darkness; the sand glistening under a sky full of twinkling speckles of stars and a peace broken by the soft tumbling of waves, its salt-enriched waters tickling the edges of the sand and my feet lost themselves in this metaphor, allowing them to be wrapped in its watery sensuality.

Sinking down, sitting cross-legged by the water's edge, we seemed to be enveloped in easy silence, listening to the murmur of a breeze, feeling the tiny grits of sand, hundreds of years of crushing and grating, as I dug my toes deep into its warmth, remembering my comment to Ella that I had wished we had been able to do this.

Now I was.

A while later, he quietly asked, 'Gina, you like here?'

'I love the beach at night, in its quiet and stillness with only the rippling sound of the waves.'

'Ripple, what is that?'

'Well, it sounds like each wave is tripping over the other with a little "boom". Something like when two people are tangled up and roll down a hill giggling and gasping. Can you hear it?'

'Oh yes, I know what you mean, sorry I am not so good at English,' he said, laughing at the image of a ripple being like two entangled people.

'Did you use the money I sent earlier, to find an English teacher and start English lessons?'

'I am not well off, so I use the money to help my family.'

Somehow, even in this second meeting, I did not believe him but let it go, believing that in gifting him the money it was no longer my concern what he did with it. It was a gift.

In the darkness, I shrugged my shoulder and, turning to him, kissed him lightly on the cheek. He pulled me up, laughing, and ran with me towards a fallen tree trunk, pulling me down onto the powdery sand, and gently kissing me.

Later, I stripped off, the darkness covering my shy body and swam in its warm luminescence diving into its darkness, as deep as I dare.

# 15

A thin slice of light fell through a chink in the black curtains, nudging me awake. He was sitting on the edge of the bed. My eyes flickered open.

'What time is it?'

'5 am. Gina, I cannot sleep. I go to my home and bring back some clothes. I take the car and come back soon.'

'OK, what time will you return?'

'About 10 am, vale?'

'Oh,' I said slowly.

Through my sleep haze, another discomfort welled up.

'Is your home far?'

'About 80 km to Levisa.'

He had told me before.

He bent over my foetal-curled body and lightly kissed me.

The door clicked shut behind him.

Oppressive heat enveloped the room as I opened my eyes and turning to the bedside table, checked the time on the mobile, 10 am. I sleepily remembered he mentioned something about returning at 10 am and jumped out of bed to shower.

No hot water, tepid, trickling out of a small shower head. Water drip-dripping in a long single niggly stream out of the shower. Oh, I needed powerful jets of hot water on my body, to revive the constant ache from an accident I'd had over twenty years earlier in Qingdao, China. The morning shower was my separation from sleep to aching wakefulness. Third-world countries and less tourist-developed countries regarded bathrooms and showers way down the list of luxuries for us sophisticated travellers. For me, that morning shower was tantamount to a good or bad start to my day.

Opening the bedroom door, the garden patio was bathed in shadows and light, the heat already crushingly hot. Peering out, much like a curious cat, there was a deep quiet and a slight buzz in the air, a familiar tropical languidness, unseen buzzing insects somewhere. No one was around and, putting on flip-flops, I walked across the red-bricked patio to look for the casa owner, hungry and in need of breakfast.

Suddenly, my host appeared through an arched doorway along the side of the casa and asked if I wanted some breakfast. He laid a table for me under a pink Bougainvillea bush, bringing coffee with condensed milk and fruit, enquiring if I wanted anything else to eat. Declining, I did however ask how far the beach was. I could not hear the sea.

He mumbled something about it "being across the road", waving his hand in several directions and "over that roundabout" which was invisible. He stopped for a while.

With a slight sigh, he said that Alex had called him to say he would return at 2 pm.

Why had he not called me instead?

Sitting alone in the mid-morning heat, I mused about the strangeness of the past few minutes. My thoughts had already begun to spin like a merry-go-round, and I hated merry-go-rounds.

I called him. His phone rang for over a minute.

'I am feeling a little bit out of my depth here,' I thought, as I sat in the shade of the Bougainvillea. 'I seem to be doing it again. My expectations and dreams are high on a pedestal and now here they are again, crashed into an empty wasteland such as this.'

It looked as though this casa had been dropped into an arid landscape of loose red soil, with unfinished walls covered in red dust and sunset-orange Bougainvillea. Peering over the low surrounding wall, the ground on the other side was littered with large broken stones and bottles. Builders' debris lay scattered. Other houses stood partly built, spiked concrete pillars on rooftops waiting for a roof.

I felt hot, tired, irritated, angry, and dumped in this "dream villa" that he had chosen through his contacts and, in his mind, stylish and suitable for a foreigner. I hated the place. I had so wanted to stay in a small beach house along the coastline and had spent hours back home trawling the internet for such an idyll, eventually giving up and asking him to arrange accommodation, and so he did. I had decided that maybe beach huts were not available for tourists, not yet anyway, and when I asked him to hire one for our stay, maybe he did not understand what a beach hut was.

The phone rang.

'Hi, Gina. Sorry. I go home to get some clothes and fell asleep. You OK? I come back soon. Sorry again, I have no much money on my phone.'

I sighed again, not knowing quite what to do in this place. It was now mid-day, even hotter, and I was without a car in an unfamiliar landscape, in a stranger's home and, beyond the wall somewhere out beyond the main road, was the beach that I so wanted to walk over to. It seemed that all human life had disappeared as I walked out through the gate in the patio wall, out into a barren and deserted compound, down a dusty footpath and out towards the main road. My feet were already covered with red soil. I felt as though I had just been part of a story, walking from one land to another. I had no idea in which direction the beach lay, as last night we had driven there, but where? No beach signs, no indication, and no direction.

My skin began to prickle with sweat, not perspiration but sweat, which started to form on my forehead and down the sides of my face, tasting its saltiness as my tongue passed over my dry lips. Suddenly, I caught sight of a building in front of me that looked like the bar from last night and crossing the road realised it was the same one. I hurried, going down the side of the same building, seeing the white sands and the picture-blue sea in front of me. I was on my own again in familiar territory with my aloneness in a foreign place. Buying a Sprite from the thatched-roof bar, I walked, my feet sinking into the soft sand, burning them gently with its hidden heat. I found a white plastic lounger under a large low-hanging Seagrape tree, its leaves a rich dark green, the colour of wet seaweed. The beach was crowded with local families quietly sitting around. Many were swimming far out to sea, the waves gently rising and falling. The late-morning sun made the sand sparkle like a thousand tiny jewels.

I must have fallen asleep for a while. Voices next to me woke me and a group of teenage girls lay in the sand in tiny bikinis. My watch said 2 pm and the phone had been silent for hours.

I called him again.

Maybe he has no credit on his phone.

Retracing my steps back to the casa, I saw that the car was not parked outside. Walking back through the gate in the wall and crossing the inner compound, the owner appeared and asked if I'd like some lunch. My hunger overrode my irritation, and I followed him inside the cool shelter of a tiny building which served as the guests' dining space. I was brought a plate of rice and chicken stew, with a large bowl of fried banana chips. Eating but without tasting, my mind now niggled by contrasting feelings and thoughts of the past twenty-four hours. Was it only twenty-four hours?

A dark shadow appeared in front of me, looking up from the white tablecloth I saw the casa owner again. By now, I had learned that his name was Ernesto. He told me that Alejandro would be here in thirty minutes. Again, I wondered at the strangeness of not being phoned directly.

My meal finished, I scooped up the bottle of cold water and went up to the patio and sat at the same table by the Bougainvillea bush.

Time passed slowly but, eventually, the sound of loud music broke through my reverie, and I saw him – with the roof down, large sunglasses atop his head, wide smile, eyes sparkling like brown crystals, his hand raised in a wave. A large, burgundy-coloured suitcase, like an American Tourister, lay mannequin-like on the back seat. I continued sitting while he turned off the engine and dragged his case up the narrow flight of stairs of the patio and walked over to me. Looking at my watch which now showed 3 pm, I decided to smile, though inside was a fury. He walked over to me lightly, bent over, and brushed my cheek with a hurried kiss, then sank into the metal chair opposite.

Neither of us spoke for a while. I had no idea what to say to him as my thoughts swirled the edge of a whirlpool.

'What is this?' I asked, in the quiet of my mind, 'Did he maybe not believe that I would arrive at the airport and so did not bring clothes with him, or had he just arrived in Holguin himself from somewhere, or does he not have a suitcase?'

On and on. No answer was clear to me.


Later that evening, we dressed and drove back towards Holguin City as I had asked if there were any salsa bars around. Casa de la Musica was opening at around 10 pm. Lowering the roof, we drove through the warm dark evening, the CD player on, its volume thunderous. He sang along in a very tuneless voice, the dimples in his cheeks deepening, his neck stretched forward. He danced in his seat as we drove, alternate hands coming off the steering wheel, foot down at 100 kph wherever possible. I couldn't help but laugh and forgot about the afternoon as the night sky twinkled along our Milky Way.

Entering Holguin city, the red Peugeot, even in the late evening, made an impression and he made sure he was noticed. He drove slowly, approaching Parque Calixto

García, the central Plaza, near Terraza Bucanero, a white marble plaza edged with palm trees. I saw the lights of Casa de la Musica above the top of the windscreen, its name blaring out in neon blue, flashing and blinking. The sound of music could be heard above the blast of music from my car. Horns hooted and Alex turned his attention, waving at various people along the way, all shouting back greetings to him.

We parked in front of the club. I watched him as he put his index finger on the controls of the car roof, looking out the window, watching some of the Cuban men looking at him. The Peugeot was a sexy red convertible, and he was using it for arousal. A crowd of young Cubans and tourists strolled languidly outside the entrance to the club, the night air picking up their perfumes and smiles as they all plied their wares, one way or another. We both opened the car doors at the same time, slowly emerging to the covetous eyes of all around. Paying a small amount of money at the entrance to the club, we strolled in, its floor already wet and stained with drink. There certainly was a buzz, which embraced and swept away the many uncomfortable memories of my earlier day.

Thinking of that night I would have very little memory of that first evening at the club, except for a few too many margaritas and Alex, who seemed to make one beer last the evening. Salsa music curled and coiled its way from the band playing up on a stage, bathed in stark-coloured lights. He took me by the hand and steered me towards the dance floor and the hours drifted into the early morning when eventually we left with the night sky lightening as a new dawn was born.

# 16

The morning awoke in the afternoon, with no specific thought as to what to do. I had decided after the previous day's events, to let each day unfold as I was in Cuban time, in a new Latin culture. My whole adult life had been spent in the Far East and the Indian sub-continent, and experiences there, had not prepared me for what I sensed would emerge. Casual holiday, or business, relationships had not been a part of my travelling and yet here I was in Cuba, in a country still steeped in the past, where deep deprivation had prevailed on the psyche and economy of over 11 million people, and I was considering allowing myself to be drawn into a maze where I could lose myself in pandemonium.

As the languid afternoon drifted, we drove to the beach, which I now knew as Emerald Beach.

Finding the same sun lounger as the previous day, under the spreading Seagrape tree, he curled his body in a ball, ensuring he had a large umbrella over him and fell asleep. Standing there looking at him, I stepped out of my shorts, grabbed my swim goggles from my bag and walked down to the water's edge. As the sun-kissed waves washed over my semi-submerged body, I immersed myself in the shimmering diaphanous sea. Diving deeper into its sunlit depth, I felt the rippling undercurrent stroke my skin, feeling its flow leave a trail of softness as I swam underwater. I had never been a confident swimmer, but these waters seemed to be a guardian angel, and, in those moments, I became a mermaid.

Happiness was an inadequate word to describe how I felt.

Walking out of the sea back up to the sun lounger, I found him still asleep. I ordered some food and cool drinks from a passing beach waiter who brought the food over within 20 minutes.

I nudged him with my foot, and he sat up, happy to see some food and drink.

'Alex, do you not like to sunbathe or swim?'

'No, I don't want to burn my skin dark brown. I am already brown. It's not good for me. I no like to swim much.'

And that set the pattern for the rest of my time with him. There were only a couple of other occasions when we went down to a beach in Corinthia, near Mayari, where I swam and he sat on the white sand, always colourfully dressed in primary colours, drawing hearts with a stick.

Later, sitting on the patio of the casa, he said, 'Gina, I was thinking that maybe we go to my family home to Levisa. There is not so much here, and we have more fun with my family. I no like the beach or sunbathe.'

'Oh, I have paid the casa owner £270 to stay for three nights and I don't think he will give me a refund.'

'Yes, but it is not much money, you think?'

He looked me straight in the eye, unblinking, and then dropped his gaze to the ground.

It seemed like a huge amount for three nights to me, but I left it at that.

As I pushed the metal-legged chair along the bricked ground and stood up, Ernesto arrived and was unsurprised when I told him we would be leaving. He stood in front of me expressionless.

Closing the door to our room, I was only too glad to leave as I had not enjoyed the barren atmosphere or the red dusty soil that was constantly blowing around in the air. This place had a vacuous feeling that left my soul as arid as the earth under my feet.

Sitting in the car, roof down, I turned around to look back at the Bougainvillea-draped walls of the villa and saw a place filled with the hope of a new beginning but still unfinished. I felt a surge of sadness flow through me. An empathy arose for this place and for myself despite my feelings.

'Hey, Alex.'

I had to raise my voice above the roaring engine and wind as the Peugeot cut through the small towns and countryside, heading out towards Levisa.

'Was there a reason for you calling Ernesto, instead of letting me know what was going on once you left early this morning?'

We were now approaching agricultural countryside. Tobacco and cornfields flashed by, and long stretches of startlingly brilliant-green fields were saturated in the afternoon's rays of sun-kissed gold.

He did not reply but leant over to turn off the radio.

'We go stay in a very nice casa in Mayari. I like Mayari. I have many friends and family live nearby. It's a small town. You will like it, Gina, and not so expensive.'

No reply to my question.

American Jeep taxis flashed by on the opposite side of the road, horns tooting and lots of waving of hands. He smiled and laughed.

'My friends, they pay big money for those Jeep taxis. I like, but no much money to buy, maybe one day, but not now. They earn lots of money. Few people have cars, so up and down the road from Holguin to Mayari they make much money. Sometimes they drive taxi from Mayari to Havana.'

He shrugged his shoulders. I watched his face closely as he spoke. Ideas started to form in my mind.

'The scenery along this road is not what I expected. I had no idea Cuba was so beautiful. I know when I came with my cousin to Havana and we went to Trinidad and Vinales, most of the time we held our breath.'

He did not know what I meant by that, so I explained it to him. He gave a big laugh saying, 'Oh, then I think you will hold your breath here too much.'

Slowly I unwound as the kilometres slipped beneath us, crossing railway tracks, roundabouts with statues of long-legged men standing tall, symbols of heroism held aloft in arms pointing towards the sky. Small roadways led to dual carriageways as we cut through dusty old 1970s Russian cemented towns, stylised statues at the side of roads or at the entrance to smaller towns. Shouting out the glory of the past, a constant reminder to its inhabitants. All familiar to me, yet unfamiliar. I eyed all around as though through a camera lens. I enjoyed that sense of viewing as it created short stories in my head as we travelled.

At one point, we stopped for fuel at a small garage, turning off into a side road. He jumped out of the car and went through a semi-broken doorway, returning with a large plastic water container filled with petrol and put it into the boot of the car. He got back in, looking around, checking to see if he had been seen. Returning to the main road, we drove for a few minutes until he turned off to the right, following a worn track through a cornfield, then he pulled out when far enough away from the road, and parked up at the side of the field, hidden by the tall corn crop. While he filled the fuel tank, I remained silent, just watching and wondering what had just happened.

Before he jumped back into the car, he asked me for 20 pesos for the petrol.

'How much is it per litre?'

'About 1 peso per litre.'

Quick calculation.

'That works out to about £1 per litre, seems expensive.'

'You will see here in Cuba much is expensive for you. I buy this petrol cheap, but we must be quiet. I know those guys, and this is the way of Cuba.'

He glanced at me quickly before starting the car.

I thought it best not to ask too many questions as we turned around at the side of the field, bumping along the rutted track, hearing the rasping, scratching sounds of dry corn on the car's paintwork, then finally driving out onto the main road, and picking up speed to get to Mayari before the sun set fully.

'We stay in Mayari tonight.'

Along the route, I spotted a group of people at the side of the road, a broad track cutting off to the right. He swung the car hard off the road, stopping just in front of them. A woman with two children looked up with delight and came rushing over to the car, shouting out with broad smiles, calling out his name. A look of delight was on his face, barely pulling up the handbrake as he jumped out of the car and went over to hug the woman and children. A light-skinned woman with burnished-gold hair and brown eyes, about thirty-five and her two children of contrasting skin colours, around ten to twelve years old. Down the grassy slope, a dark-skinned man slid down the bank, with a white-toothed grin, greying peppered-black hair cropped tightly. He rushed up to Alex, both hugging each other till it looked like they would have no breath left.

'Gina,' he called back to me, 'this is my Uncle Roberto, my papa's brother. He fights in Angola, just like my papa.'

Roberto came over to the car, leaned over the door frame and took one of my hands in his calloused hands. His skin was warm and worn. He looked directly into my eyes with friendliness.

His wife, Eugenia, came over and shook my hand lightly. The two children looked on from the verge side.

A rapid exchange in Cubano ensued, with laughter and references to the gleaming red Peugeot. I saw the look of pleasure on his face as he returned to open the car door and slide in, gently easing the car into automatic as we waved and sped off.

The sun had begun to set, the sky the colour of fiery nectarine, slashes of deepening shades of purple indigo and aubergine blue, as we arrived at the outskirts of Mayari. The sunsets constantly reminded me of an artist's palette of late-evening colours.

It was a grand entrance into a small Cuban town with music turned up, blasting out like a Mardi Gras, and I felt just that little bit too conspicuous as he tooted his horn at the cars in front. I found myself slipping down the seat. Many young men, lounging against walls or walking, and some sitting atop the bices, (cycle rickshaws) waved and hollered to him. I watched their faces, as I had done the previous night at the Casa de la Musica in Holguin. Their eyes were bright, surprised as though caught in a car's headlight, smiling and shouting out in Cubano. He drove the car very slowly through the town's only high street. The day's work was over, and many were out shopping along the roadside stalls of vegetables and fruit. In one cerulean blue wall, a small cut-out window appeared, some legs of blood-red meat hanging from hooks outside the edges of the hole in the wall, and a few women, slightly overweight with bleached blond hair, rested against its wall chatting.

There was a cinematic feel to the drive through this town. It was a show, a parade and he was the star in this beautiful Milan-red, shining, brand-new Peugeot. I could tell that, somehow, this had all been planned. This grand entrance, as though a victory entrance. I sat still as the hot torrid air of the day slid down a cooler curve, the dusk quietly descending, enveloping us as we twisted down dusty side streets for about five minutes, coming to a halt outside a tiny green-fronted, white-gated entrance. He jumped out and beckoned me to follow. Slowly, I uncurled myself and swung my legs out of the open door, feeling the warmth of the red dusty road beneath my feet. Walking up a couple of stairs to a small casa, we were greeted again with big smiles by a white-skinned Spanish Cuban couple. I was greeted warmly by Marita and her husband, Carlos, and shown a room which led off the downstairs corridor. I immediately turned away and walked out telling him I did not like this place.

He appeared embarrassed and looked at me.

'Is there anywhere else?' I gently asked him.

Without a word, he jumped back into the car, drove us down a few more streets and stopped outside Casa Carolina. This would be the place we would stay for a few days.

Inside, Maria and Tonio greeted us as though we were long-returning friends. Casa Carolina was a small house, painted yellow on the outside, with a white-gated entrance to the front room. Its furnishings consisted of overstuffed brown leatherette armchairs and a sofa, family pictures on the wall, a youth of about fifteen, lounging on a sofa, watching TV, looking up with a small 'hola'.

Amidst the chatter, Alex returned to the car and pulled out the suitcases, dragging them behind him. We made our way through a narrow corridor, with small bedrooms off it, and then into a kitchen which led to an outside covered restaurant. I was surprised to see this taverna-style restaurant, with its thatched roof, Italian style or Greek style, and plastic grapes hanging from inside the roof, wooden tables covered with blue and white checked tablecloths and chairs, uniformly spaced, and the sound of the beating heart of salsa music. More coloured lights hung from the inside of the covered thatched roof.

As we stood outside for a few minutes, a young girl brought a couple of glasses of cold juice, its coolness quenching my parched throat.

We walked up a narrow iron spiral staircase, with Tonio carrying both suitcases on his head. Upon reaching the top rung, Maria led us down an open airy corridor which further opened out onto a large balcony, overlooking the surrounding rooftops. Our room was the only one on this level. A double glass-fronted door, lined on the inside with faded pink curtains, opened into a cool cement-floored room with an overhead fan, and a wooden frame bed with a matching pink canopy sat in the middle. The room looked like a bridal suite. I felt uneasy as to its suggestion. Checking the bathroom, its walls were painted in the same soft daffodil yellow as Hotel Beltran, with a matching vanity unit and wall tiles. I thanked Maria in stilted Spanish, and she smiled broadly.

Alex asked if I liked it and gave a visible sigh of relief when I said I did.

That room with that open balcony would become a haunting place as the days unfolded and I returned there to stay on several occasions.

A few hours later after showering, we ate in the downstairs restaurant. A large plate of Enchilado de Camarones (Cuban shrimp), which turned out to be his favourite dish. In fact, throughout the whole trip, he ate this, one of the most expensive dishes in every restaurant, accompanied by cold Bucanero beer.

Finishing, we drove to a small town called Nicarao, about 10 km from Mayari, winding off the narrow main road down a steep loose-earthed track. Around a dairy plant, the track opened out and led up to a one-storey squat-shape building which glowed a faint white in the night light. Further along, other lights suddenly blazed as we drove up to a collonaded building fronted with swaying palm trees, long Cadillacs, black army-shaped Jeeps, and young men dressed immaculately in white, with assorted shapes of young, coiffured women. There was an exciting buzz, with booming beating music pouring out of the building, noisy laughter and chatter, and the sound of cars taking off and motorbikes roaring out into the night. I loved this newly charged energy. The club looked like it had been recently built in what I perceived to be a Miami-style nightclub.

We looked at each other, parked the car, jumped out and strolled into the entrance amidst the gaiety and youthful energy of what I called "the beautiful Cuban - los jóvenes".

We sauntered through one of the arched entrances into an open white-washed space, with a meagrely-stocked wooden bar along one side of the room.

It was empty of people. An exit door led out into a garden amid more palm trees and red Poinsettia bushes all around. These were not the small potted version we buy as gifts in English supermarkets at Christmas but some were small trees with huge luscious flowers. Beyond, lay a further green-lawned area, dotted with stubby trees with diamanté lights entwined amidst their fronds and further ahead a glint of silver water of Levisa Bay along the Atlantic Ocean.

Two marbled outdoor dance areas lay at the back of the club, one covered and another open to the night sky, surrounded by flashing lights, illuminating the faces of the young dancers. A gentle waft of evening flowers drifted off the skin of the young girls as we passed.

I loved the way music changes one's mood when played in an outside space, the evening air seductively sultry, whispering promises of a new life, bringing an unrestrained smile to my lips.

I was suddenly aware of standing alone. Turning full circle, I saw him amid a group of men. He turned and looked over his shoulder in my direction. Leaving the group with one of the men, he introduced him as Norrie, his cousin, the son of his papa's sister, Silvana.

I immediately liked Norrie. He walked up to me and gave me a huge embrace, smelling strongly of metallic aftershave, with a hint of musk.

He introduced himself in perfect English. He had those large soft, deep dark-liquid eyes of childhood, a straight nose, slim face and body, straight hair closely cropped with the front raised in a coif, dressed in the uniform white, as so many of the men I saw around me. I loved that the men here paid minute detail to the way they dressed. Many of them looked as though the gym was maybe their first home.

Whether Spanish Cuban or Afro-Cuban, the white social uniform they wore spoke to me of personal and national pride. Vanity, well somewhere there is always vanity, which in itself creates the need to feel secure and proud and, of course, it's the usual hunt and chase. In white, they are not the white peacock but the effervescently magnificent coloured male peacock.

The three of us made our way to the bar for a mix of beer, cola and a mojito for me. I pulled out some pesos, paying for the drinks. I let that irritating thought slip through the cracks of my fingers as I took out the pesos, smiling that ever-gracious smile of mine.

As the evening wore on, Norrie stayed with us, dancing with me for the remainder of the evening while Alex continually slipped away, returning an hour or so later, staying for a few minutes, and then slipping away again.

This continued until we left around 2 am, with Norrie saying that he was off to see his girlfriend and hoped he would see me again soon, circling his arms around me in a warm embrace.

Later on in this story, Nicaro became a centrefold of stories yet unlived but already a part etched in tears.

*Within the beauty of the green lies the viper*
*Its tongue flickering as though smelling the air*

# 17

The air was still and anticipatory, a virgin air, young in the day and future memories still unspoilt.

We woke a little late as the previous night had been one of partying and dancing in Nicarao and the after-party was a gathering in the forecourt of the local garage - hanging out. Old Buicks, American classics, taxi jeeps and my shiny red convertible, parked against an old worn wall in a shadowy space. Prickles of humidity hung loosely in the air. I could reach up to the dark sky and wrap its moisture around my hand. Alex wound his arm around my waist, smiling and happy. He was in his element, with a European woman, a shiny new car to ride around in, and money in his pocket. A popular guy, having bought everyone ice creams, beers and white rum for his father, Papa Luis, with my money (I find myself already saying this too many times), lounging against bumpers and bonnets in this patch of dimmed darkness. This late-night air, with its accumulated daytime warmth, encircled us all. We stood, waiting for something to happen.

That was a pervading sense I always had on my many visits to Cuba.

I stretched out as I lay in bed, sheer pink drapes hanging on four sides of the bridal bed. He was already up and dressed in white. I found myself saying 'already' as though I had lived this life for a long time. I showered and asked him what I should wear today. Not something I would usually ask of anyone, but I felt it was appropriate to ask.

'Something elegant. We are going to meet my family and have lunch with them in Levisa.'

Cuba had intrigued me for years and, coming here on my second visit, I felt I had slipped back to the 1950s with tales of old Havana, where Hemingway supposedly drank mojitos at the famous Bodeguita del Medio. I had a real affinity to 1950's fashion and, being in the fashion world, the elegance of the 50s played a great part in the clothes I wore. I had brought with me a Vivien of Holloway fitted blue and white abstract floral-print halter neck dress, with a boned bodice; meant for a fuller bust but I slipped it on, pulled my hair back into a ponytail and felt I looked like a film version of an American teenage sweetheart, not really wanting to but this style had echoes of that era.

We had a quick breakfast of honey-sweet mangoes, tortilla de papas and black coffee, and then headed out through the iron-grilled security gate of the front door of Casa Carolina and jumped into the Peugeot which, by 11 am, was suffocating inside, its seats burning hot.

He leaned over and gave me a quick kiss, and then opened the roof of the car. The relief, as the heat escaped out the top, was like an explosive vacuum of air. The car moved away, and a thin layer of red road dust drifted upwards off the unmade streets, swirling around and settling over and into the car, covering the interior seats.

We travelled quickly with Marc Anthony singing "Y Hugo Alguien", the volume up to its maximum cacophony, ensuring that everyone and everything from Mayari, where we were staying, to Levisa, his village, knew he had something no one else in his sphere had.

I closed my eyes and rested my head on the backrest.

We turned off the black tarmac road, through a metal gate, down broken-pebbled pathways, past rusting wire fencing, small wooden homes half-hidden behind screens of Papaya trees, glimpses of tiny gardens within which sat women, of all colours, on tree stumps, bright plastic chairs, or on wooden-fronted doorsteps. We had to drive more slowly along narrower lanes until I feared my car would get deeply scratched by broken wooden posts or pieces of wire jutting out from torn fences.

We pulled up outside a dwelling set in its own wilderness.

At the sound of the dying motor, white chickens scuttled out from both sides of our pathway. A neighbour popped up from the house on our left, and his Uncle Roberto suddenly appeared from nowhere, with another big hug amidst huge grins of delight at seeing each other. He turned to me and introduced me to his uncle again. Roberto came over, leaned over the door and shook my hand, scratching the inside of my palms.

I got out of the car, but he was already through the gate and walking up along the side of the house from which a ponytailed teenage girl emerged and threw her arms around his neck.

I stood at the gate and looked at the squat one-storey house in front of me, with mildew-streaked white walls and some unpainted wooden shutters on broken hinges. I looked up at the roof - broken slates. The sun shone high in a fondant blue sky. Thick green vegetation grew along the sides of the fence of the house, tendrils like snakes twining in and out of the holes of wire meshing and creeping in zigzags along the rough grassy garden. As I walked across the yard my feet kept twisting. I was wearing cream high-heeled rope espadrilles, elegant be damned. I felt ridiculous, turning up here dressed the way I was. I could already see the impoverished condition of the dwelling and thought it was his family home. I followed him along the side of the house, almost tripping over a small white pig as it scooted alongside me.

Walking to the back of the house, I entered a small, grey-walled kitchen area where the same young girl, his cousin, an elderly man and a woman sat at a wooden table covered by an indistinct patterned plastic tablecloth, with the biggest and warmest smiles, greeting me. He hugged them and walked out the back door.

I followed him through a small backyard littered with domestic debris, broken chairs, rubbish piles, uneven vegetable patches, and an empty clothesline with broken plastic clothes pegs, dangling perilously. I ducked under this and walked just a few yards further and had to slide between two narrow posts to cross through to another backyard. This was his home.

Already my head was like a camera, moving at the fastest shutter speed possible to take in all that I could see in front of me. I had to stop and catch my breath, and smile but not show on my face what was spinning around in my head.

I had entered rural Cuba. I had been brought to the very heart of Cuban life in its verdant splendid vegetation, a private paradise but also the true nature of how poor Cubans live. I walked forward slowly, steadying myself on my espadrille heels, conscious of my incongruent fitted dress. In front of me stood a grey concrete shack with a blue corrugated tin roof. A large brown water tank on one side, a straw haystack in another corner, and vegetables growing in neat rows. Brown chickens clucked and skittered nervously.

A narrow stone path led to the back of the house where his father stood by an open door. A tall thin man, with a big, white-toothed smile and skin as dark as ebony, a bony face, brown eyes, the whites bloodshot. He stood erect, with a knife in his right hand and a potato in the other. He hugged his son, his son hugged his mother, and his father came down the path and hugged me, then took my hand and led me up to the house.

Moments later I heard a pig squeal in the distance.

I walked from the sunlight into a small dark den of a kitchen, peeling electric wires exposed their copper innards, hanging down along damp walls. Immediately, small glasses were produced and thumped onto a concrete slab that made up the kitchen counter. A large bottle of white rum appeared in Papa's raw rough hand, quickly pouring out a thick clear dripping liquid, the famous Cuban rum. I looked at my wristwatch – 2.30 pm.

No one spoke English. I spoke the barest of Spanish, but smiles lit up on faces as, one by one, new neighbours and cousins came into the small kitchen. The air was filled with laughter and chatter.

I heard the sound of a pig squeal.

I walked back out into the yard, into the sun, down the path, and through to a coconut grove. Alex followed me and, proudly spreading his hands, said, 'Welcome to my garden, to my paradise. For you, I am going to climb that tree and get a coconut.'

He pointed up the trunk of a tall curving palm tree.

I looked around.

'So, this is paradise.'

In bare feet, he shimmied up at speed, with a machete in one hand. He knocked a coconut out of the top of the palm with one heft of his machete and shimmied down again. I heard a thump as the coconut hit the ground. Picking it up, he cut off the top and handed it to me, its white liquid in a womb of soft coconut flesh. He winked and said, 'Do you want some rum in it?'

As I stood among the coconut palms, I sipped the cool milk, closing my eyes, feeling the effect as it trickled down my parched throat, relishing the first sip of mid-afternoon and as I opened them, glints of sunlight, glints of the unreality of what was going to unfold in a few minutes, visceral experiences that would alter my perception, a cultural world that would unfold like one of Gauguin's Tahitian paintings.

I heard that screeching squeal again.

As we slowly turned around and walked back into the small yard, a man entered carrying a white plastic bag, with air holes at the top, slung casually over his left shoulder with something wiggling inside.

Papa, now bare-chested, and Norrie, brought out an old green metal table. They set it down by the water tank and wiped its surface with a dirty wet cloth, grinning and chattering. I saw that same potato knife in Papa's hand, as he wiped the blade with another dirty piece of cloth. The man with the white bag came over to the table and carefully laid it down, while the "something" in the bag kept jerking but now less vigorously. I had guessed what it was. The mouth of the bag was untied and slowly pulled down over a pig's body. Freedom for just a few seconds.

I moved closer to the table, and it was the same pig I had passed not more than one hour ago. His four legs were tied together, his breathing shallow and strained. I wondered what was going to happen. The sun grew hotter, the laughter louder, the music increasing, shouting from three large speakers inside the house.

He lay there on that scratched table, squealing in fear; angry and trapped. I looked at his soft pinkish-white skin, almost like that of a baby, his little black eyes surrounded by long white eyelashes, his small ears covered in bristly hairs, soft pink on the inside, his trotters transparent and delicate, reminding me that I was somewhat of a pig today as I walked on my high espadrilles. Was I too being brought to a slaughter, for I uncomfortably knew that it was imminent?

Alex walked up to me.

'Gina, this is in your honour. My family's way of welcoming you to our home. We do not have money, but we still honour our special guests.'

I looked into his eyes which were dark and hard.

The little pig lay still. Two men turned him on his back, cut the string, and spread his legs. Papa walked up to the table, smiling, and continuously chatting with all around. He ran one long brown dirty-nailed finger down the centre of the pig, marking the place of the heart.

I grabbed my camera from my bag and as I lifted it to my eye. I saw, through the tiny narrow square lens, Papa raising his knife above the pig's heart, his forehead covered in tiny pricks of sweat, and swiftly and accurately bringing the blade down in one movement. The knife sank smoothly through that soft white skin, tissue, veins, and artery, deep into his small beating heart, as blood exploded out.

As I clicked, I caught my breath and as I lowered my camera, the little pig squealed in agony and intense pain. I felt my body jerk. His legs held fast, the bloody knife removed, and Papa's finger again poked into the hole in his chest to stop the blood flow. His finger was quickly withdrawn and replaced by a slender baby corncob. His heart had been plugged. His legs jerked but he stopped squealing. My heart rate was on speed. The corncob was still in place until no more blood flowed and the pig lay silent. He now laid on his side amidst streaks of his blood, red on the green-topped table, an altar. The inside of his little ears was still pink, his skin baby white. I felt the tears well up and run through my veins as the life left that little creature.

I looked for Alex and saw him standing near his father, a spot of blood on his cheek, his face impassive.

Again, I lifted my camera to capture the faces of the family and neighbours watching the matanza, the killing of the pig. I now felt like a hunter. The jungle that I was standing in was a cultural jungle, brought over from centuries-old Spain, an old agricultural custom.

I shot through my lens and witnessed each breath of this animal's life escaping, in sacrifice. I'd captured this whole event on camera. What was I?

I had stood in awe of the knife as it was plunged into an innocent creature to honour another creature. Two different cultures unified for a common purpose, the honouring of giving life to welcome another.

Papa stood, his knife hanging in his bloodied hand, its point dripping with blood.

# 18

Paradise is a word that conjures up for many people a holiday destination of white sands, iridescent aqua blue still seas, golden bodies, warm breezes, romance, long ice-cool spirited fruity drinks sipped while languidly lying in white swaying hammocks, hung between wind bent leafy green palm trees.

It's paradise longing for a romantic idyll.

It's also the modern version of the Aztec sun worship, offering one's white body on an altar of sand in exchange for that golden skin, changing from an insipid to an exotic sensual body, leaving behind the abode of one's virtuous old dead self and arising as a new version of the paradise of self.

The paradise that I saw while driving around Cuba had a sense of all of this, but I never quite found it. The paradise in its broadest tourist sense is what I saw as I drove down ribbons of broken-tarred roads, dense and vivid dark green forests of coconut and palm trees, with cows or horses tied to their trunks; skinny-boned horses pulling large wooden carts, their drivers, burnished brown-skinned men of Spanish or African origin, sinewy muscles from long labour in fields of broad succulent tobacco leaves, catching my imagination back to a time of fury and a flourish of hedonism. I drove through miles of snaking red soil tracks meandering through lush verdant mountains in the distance and trails of white smoke spiralling upwards into blue skies swirling with shaped clouds, telling stories of the ground below.

And on that hot afternoon, I stood in that tropical backyard, surrounded by those tall broad-leafed banana trees, hearing the rustle of wind all around, as chickens scratched their horny claws through the dry fallen leaves, as the pig lay dead on that green table. I was in a paradise of my own imaginings and that little pig represented to me a part of his virtuous old self. The matanza - the killing of the pig - had all the religious marks of a sacrificial ceremony.

Its arrival in a plastic bag, tied and trapped, brought in by a silent man, laying him down on the table, the music in the background like the church organ playing its plaintiff refrain of repetitive salsa beats, the rum being held between cupped hands like the chalice of blood held high above a purple-gowned priest. The pomp and ceremony of the ritual were enacted in front of another similar type of congregation. A congregation of friends and neighbours, a community of people come to celebrate a new sacrifice of an innocent pig in honour of the extranjera, dressed in blue and white, a new sacrifice. How much was I aware of my part in this sacrifice?

Time would reveal its true intent.

The warm urgent breathless air shook the leaves of the plants and trees which edged the garden, sunlight catching their tremulous movement and casting their shadowed patterns on the ground.

I stood and watched those flickering patterns as the chickens pecked amongst those dried fallen leaves under the table. The pig had breathed his last breath. I bent down and caught a drop of blood as it dripped off the side of the table down to the fallen leaves.

As I stood up, I looked at the blood on my fingers and searched for a piece of cloth to wipe it off. I picked up some dry leaves instead.

Laughter caught my attention. The energy was renewed and lifted high. I was offered another glass of rum, which I eagerly took and drank in one gulp.

A large drum of water had been boiled, brought over, and put down on the ground by the table, ready for the next step of softening the tiny bristles on the pig's body. Papa Luis was by now the head priest, with his altar servers by his side, knives at the ready. He presided over the table, dark-skinned bony-ribbed bare chest glistening, sweat continuing to bead his brow, white teeth flashing with smiles, and his blue jeans bloodied down the front. As he dipped a bristle brush into the hot water and rubbed the pig's skin, others joined in and several brushes ran up and down its body, loosening the bristles. Papa took a knife and started to scrape the bristles off the skin; they fell easily away. Norrie too, with his knife, and then I was pulled forward and a knife roughly shoved into my right hand, amidst easy laughter and patter. I felt slightly dazed by now and found myself passing the knife over the bristly skin with awkward moves.

Shivers went through me, and I could not believe what I was doing. Alex stood by my side with a knife in his hand also scraping the pig's skin. I had to stop, I had to step back. I understood the culture but, for now, could not be a part of this. Alex stopped too. I saw a grimace on his face, a smile a little hard to discern, an action he had obligatorily joined just at that moment but did not enjoy.

I continued to take photos of everything around me. I was intrigued by the number of people now involved in preparing the pig for the roasting and fascinated by the theatre playing out in front of me.

Being brought up a Catholic, I was well-used to the ritual of Mass, the offering of holy communion, the chalice holding the body and blood of Christ, turning water into wine, the benediction, the smell of warm incense held in a small ornate gold thurible, swung back and forward on a chain; the preamble of the mass before the communion, joining God and man in one moment. So, the cleansing of the pig, ritualistically being performed, now pulled me in and I became a part of its ongoing process, its sacrifice, its changing from life to death and reincarnation. We too would eat of its flesh and drink of its blood in its new altered state.

I turned away and Papa had disappeared, but I noticed an eight-foot-long pole propped against the rusty water tank.

With the pig, finally cleaned of all its blood, skin pasty-coloured and smooth, its eyes closed, mouth closed, ears still wide open and pink on the inside, its interior now had to be emptied and cleared, ready for the fire.

First, a hole was cut around the curly tail and the tail was removed. Bits of faeces oozed out and the flesh around the hole was bound lightly with plastic string.

The soft fat fleshy stomach was slowly cut. Up, up, up from its bottom end towards the neck in a long straight line.

Deft hands opened the stomach, revealing sausage-like entrails which jetted out in a rush. All the organs were removed, and blood from around the heart was poured into a small metal mug. Warm water was poured inside the emptied body to clean it. That eight-foot-long pole was carried over to the table and inserted into the anal hole, slowly and carefully working its way up towards its open mouth, and out.

A mixture of garlic, chillies, and onions were all chopped together and rubbed along the inside of the pig and used as stuffing. I'd seen a couple of the women, when I'd first arrived, sitting on low wooden stools, peeling garlic and chopping onions. That had been for the stuffing.

A needle and black thread appeared and the rip in the pig's body was surgically stitched with precision and its tail-end securely reattached. A pig needs to have his tail for dignity. It lay softly stiff, that black-stitched line vivid, its legs straight in the air, alert in death. The pig on the pole was carefully resurrected off the table and propped against the water tank. I looked at it, martyred, the imagery too apparent for words. Its shiny baby skin glowed softly in the setting sun, long white lashes over closed eyes. I had never seen that sight before nor felt the emotions. I looked at a life which I had seen just a few hours earlier, almost tripping me up as I trotted by. I had witnessed its brutal, yet ritualistic, killing and death, prepared for a feast in my honour.

I was numbed, sad, intrigued, and accepting of what I had witnessed and yet I'd had the strangest thought as I scraped the pig's skin. One of my adventurous delights, that I was truly a part of this Cuban culture but acknowledged that it was too primal, and maybe too early, for me to fully appreciate life out here in rural Cuba.

Papa Luis had cleared an area in the yard and laid down four stout banana trunks in a rectangle, coconut husks gathered by several neighbours and friends were thrown in the middle of the rectangle and petrol was poured over the husks. At each end of the fire pit were two metal tripods, one with a handle. The petrol was lit, and the dry husks caught alight in a fury of heat which gathered speed and rushed heavenwards, the sounds of the burning husks crackling in demonic laughter.

The poled pig was carried over to the fire pit, each end of the pole lifted and slotted onto the two tripods. It now waited above leaping flames from the fire beneath it, its ears still erect as if listening for a final chance to escape. Gradually the flames died down, the husks turned to red embers and the elderly next-door neighbour sat on a low stool by the fire turning the handle of the spit. I stood in my white espadrilles, in my figure-hugging dress, with the heat from the fire blasting over me, and watched as that once-delicate skin gradually charred, its reincarnation into feast food.

Music screeched out and the yard was crowded with people, beers, rum held out or clutched to chests, rapid Cubano (Cuban Spanish) spoken amidst a chorus of laughter, the killing of the pig forgotten - the party continued.

As the hours passed and the sun sank low, mellow darkness descended and the house lights were turned on, bathing the interior yellow. I was asked to take my turn at the spit. I sat down on the low stool, in communion with the little pig, its ears crisping brown, watching the ceremony of life as it passed all around me. I saw joy and fun, spontaneous dancing, and glimpses of life through the shutter of my eyes. As the pig turned on the spit, my stomach turned too.

I never eat pork.

Sitting by this roasting pig was a real incongruence for me but I carried on by absorbing myself in my surroundings as more lights began to flicker from the tiny houses on either side of me. As more friends arrived, Roberto stood behind me talking to Norrie, who drew me into the conversation, telling me that Roberto had recently returned from being in Angola.

I'd finally had enough of pretending to enjoy turning the spit and rose from my low seat, feeling my cramped body uncrunch as I slowly stood up. I looked down at my feet and saw black flip-flops instead of my cream espadrilles. When had I changed my shoes?

Having been there quite a few hours, I began to feel unsure of what to do next. Alex had again disappeared somewhere, from when I had last seen him sitting on a low stool next to a neighbour, with a small knife in his hand cutting out the white flesh of a coconut and nibbling on it. He had disappeared in the Peugeot.

The smell of cooking and happy noise was floating across the dusky evening sky, the smoke from the firepit slowly spiralling upward in thin streaks, laying a soft mist to hang in the evening air, its hot glowing embers gradually beginning to die down, the pig's roasting was coming to an end.

At the edge of the back veranda, a small wooden table had been set up with an assortment of plates with Papa taking charge. It seemed he took charge of quite a lot of things around this place.

I walked up the short path and entered the kitchen. As usual, lots of women were there. A very large lady, with the biggest grin imaginable, was stirring what looked like a stew of some sort in a large pan, too big for the electric ring it was sitting on. She stopped and turned to give me a hug. Later, I found out that her name was Silvana, the garlic peeler, Papa's sister.

A rice cooker sat next to the electric ring, with chopped tomatoes, cucumbers and various other vegetables lying on the concrete surface of the kitchen counter. I was pulled into their circle.

This was basic beyond basic, and I loved it. Of course, I had to go to the toilet but the thought of just a thin red faded curtain separating me from the kitchen and the people outside was embarrassing, but I shrugged my shoulders and plunged in, letting the red curtain flutter behind me.

I came out and, immediately, a glass of rum was put into my right hand. Another shrug off my shoulders. No washing my hands after the toilet here, I'd look for fresh water some time or other.

Off to the side of the kitchen was a tiny room, with an uneven concrete floor. It looked like it may have been an animal pen at some time, but now a small table rested on the uneven floor, one leg with a wad of paper under it. Upon the table stood another one of the electric rings with a shallow wok-like pan of oil, bubbling furiously with thin banana slices happily crisping away, jumping and then falling back into the hot oil.

Everywhere I turned and looked, smiling faces greeted me; they seemed such genuine friendly faces. I walked into the family living room, bare except for three dark brown wooden chairs with hard seats, a small dining table and two dining chairs and three enormous black speakers, blaring out a mixture of salsa and reggaeton. Suddenly the heavy pulse of the music coursed through my body or was that the rum?

Norrie walked up to me, took my hand and spun me around and my feet began to dance the Salsa. This is what I had hoped Cuba would be like; vibrant, sensual, and deeply connected and I found myself dropping down into my dancing body. In this tiny, tiny house, in a tiny part of a garden at the end of which lay a coconut grove of paradise, I felt my body automatically responding.

'Gina,' I heard Alex call.

Oh, he had reappeared.

'My papa wants you.'

I left the dancing behind and walked outside, adjusting my eyes to the semi-dark. There on the outside table, was the full-roasted pig, crisp and brown, with its little ears still erect. A sweet aromatic aroma came off its skin and Papa beckoned me over. As the honoured guest, I was the first to be served.

With that self-same knife, he cut a thick slice of meat off the side of the pig (I still saw him as 'the pig') and put it on a plate atop a bed of rice.

Looking down at that piece of fatty flesh, pale yellowy oily juices oozing from the cut meat, my body shuddered slightly, in memory of the matanza. As I brought the meat to my mouth and bit into it, I felt its heat burn my tongue and seer my teeth. I felt eyes watching me from all sides. I chewed into its bland flesh, saltless and tasteless to me. The communion I'd felt earlier with the pig now felt like an ex-communication. I smiled and I lied, I said how nice the meat was but had to go and get another glass of rum, a spirit which I needed to commune with, and which was having a heavy effect on me, one that by now I badly needed.

The scenes of the day, the effect of the killing of the pig, the cleansing, the blood, and the pole through the pig's rear end, really did have a religious impact on me, leaving me feeling small and bewildered. Thank God for the rum and returning inside I carried on dancing and smiling. The man I had come with drifted in and out of the moments of my time in his family home; sometimes he would come over, put his arm around my shoulders, pull me back and forward in a salsa move, and then disappear again.

Amidst the continuous chatter and laughter, now intoxicated, I slipped out again into the night air and saw the dissected carcass of the pig, lying in lumps of white meat scattered on a metal platter. The elderly next-door neighbour called out to me as I slipped through the gap in the fence, the way I had come in, and crept my way past the morning house before walking to my car, now sitting in darkness.

I leaned against the warm metal, its paintwork shining darkly in the half-moonlight. Images appeared in front of me of the squealing pig bound in the bag, its pink body tied and laid out on the green table. Papa's face with his toothy-white grin, knife held aloft slowly plunging through layers of its soft unwilling, screeching flesh. The bloody knife dripping blood drop by drop onto the sandy ground. I watched myself standing in my white high-heeled espadrilles, gazing, dazed as the pig rotated on the spit, its white trotters slowly charred by the fire. I closed my eyes at that moment, shrouding myself in the darkness, alone again.

The light sound of softly padding feet through the dry grass brought me back as he approached. The night light shone on his lightly sweating face as he looked questioningly at me.

'Gina, you ok? Why you are here and not inside? My Aunt Silvana told me you had gone.'

'I'm quite a lot drunk on rum and I don't like pork meat. Seeing the pig killed, and then eating it, is too much.' (I had to keep my English simple.) 'I know this is normal here in Cuba, where you all live with animals, look after them and then kill them for food. I understand.'

He put his arms around me and drew me to him, holding me lightly. I was beginning to find his behaviour strange or maybe knowing him so little and being in his family home with the barest knowledge of Spanish, made me shy and uncomfortable alone without him around.

His disappearances would become a habit throughout my time with him.

'We go in now as my mother, she is cooking more food, rice and chicken and I am hungry. I no like pork.'

# 19

The next few days moved slowly through the March heat, with blinding sunshine by midday, and hot breezes swirling the red dust like mini whirlwinds into the air, covering everything in its path.

We woke mid-morning to the sounds of brain-bashing music from the music shop across from the casa, accompanied by the blaring of other varieties of Latin beats from the bicycle rickshaws, amidst the chatter of passersby and tooting horns of gliding cars and trot-trotting pony and traps which acted as small buses.

The sun filtered through the curtained windows and four-poster bed, bathing the room in a red grapefruit-pink glow.

I showered and dressed, then walked to the edge of the balcony wall, looking out across the small flat-roofed town and the sand-dusty road below. All life seemed to move at the pace of a millisecond, and I began to slip into that stream space, languidly having breakfast, then following his suggestions for the day ahead, which seemed to centre on driving extremely fast to see his Aunt Silvana or his papa and staying hours at either one or the other's house.

The day after the pig kill, we drove to visit his Aunt Silvana who lived at the edge of Santa Rita which bordered Levisa, with a small banana plantation separating the two.

Once off the main road, we twisted down a winding track edged with a tumble of small bushes and broken inhabited houses, past a power plant along a track where straw-hatted horse riders rode skinny-ribbed ponies, burdened with large white bags of unknown contents. At the end of the ribbed concrete track stood a small square whitewashed house, surrounded by a high wire fence. Off to the right of this small artisan-style house, another track disappeared into an overgrown banana plantation. A place I sometimes walked through with Silvana when I got to know her a little better.

Parking up along the front of the fence, I opened the heavy door, swung my legs over onto the burning ground, and waited a moment as I drew in my breath, surveying all around. Pushing open the low blue metal gate in the fence I walked up a small path, with a covered patio ahead. Sunburnt and bleached dry grass lay on each side of the path (is it ever green?) and a few white large-headed wilting chrysanthemums in flowerpots languished on their tall stalks. Under the covered patio, Norrie was standing, barbering a young man's hair. A large white cloth covered the front of his body. He stopped cutting and came over to me, extending a big hug and "Hola".

His Aunt Silvana came out to greet me and I recognised her as the large lady who had been cooking in the kitchen the night before. The previous night, she had long hair and this afternoon short, cropped afro hair. She was a large-bosomed robust lady with ebony-dark skin, like her brother

Papa Luis. Her black eyes twinkled in their darkness. She too gave me a huge welcome hug and pulled me inside the house, repeating, 'Vamos, vamos.'

A cool wind blew through from the open back door. The small lounge was immaculately tidy, with two huge four-foot-high black speakers at the front of the room, and black leatherette sofas with white lace-edged antimacassars across their backs. My eyes were drawn to a small glass table upon which stood a two-foot-tall blonde-haired doll with large round China blue eyes, dressed in a long white lace-embroidered dress, almost like a christening robe, reminding me of a similar doll I had seen in Havana on my first trip, in the house of the tarot card reader. That doll had a black face and body, sitting in the corner of a tiny curtained-off back room, upright on a pile of plastic flowers, an altar to a Haitian deity.

The remainder of the room had a four-seater dining table with wooden chairs and a few framed pictures; some from magazines, others of family members, hanging on bare concrete walls. A shaky ceiling fan whizzed slowly around, barely stirring the air.

On one side of the room were a couple of curtained openings. A young pregnant woman pushed the curtain apart and shyly smiled at me. She was Norrie's fiancée, Mariana, and they were expecting their first baby. She was olive-complexioned, her straight black hair pulled tight off her face, bare of makeup, and wearing a loose t-shirt and shorts. Flip-flopping, she walked through to the back room, which was the kitchen.

Next to her room was another curtained-off room, which I presumed was Silvana's and her husband's, whom I had not yet met.

I was invited into the kitchen, a small dark room, like the one at Papa's house, with the same concrete work surface, a two-ring cooker and a rice cooker. At the other end was a sunken basin with a single tap. There was a pot of something bubbling on the cooker and a large pile of banana slices, ready for frying. I already knew that fried banana slices were a popular dish in Cuba.

I needed the toilet and noticed a semi-transparent red curtained-off cubicle at the side of the kitchen. I decided I would wait.

A bottle of rum appeared, and I quickly declined as, judging by the heat of the day, I knew the rum would knock me out, but I was sorely tempted. It was Dutch courage I needed and an ability to speak passable Spanish but, somehow, I managed with a translation book at the ready and Silvana's paper and pencil at hand.

She was effervescent, chattering away with Norrie's fiancée and Alex. I caught bits and pieces of words which I understood. Their Spanish was a colloquial dialect and later, when I got to know Silvana better, she would sit at her dining table and laboriously write down what she was saying so that I could slowly read and hopefully understand. At first, I had difficulty understanding as my knowledge of Spanish grammar was limited, having begun to learn Andalucian Spanish. Her grammar was what I deemed to be colloquial, but I read and understood the gist of it, which was often very amusing. As I listened more to Cubano (Spanish Cuban), I realised it had its own style based on a variety of cultures through time. Sometimes out in the countryside, it was unrecognisable as European Spanish.

As we stood in the kitchen, a slim swarthy-skinned man entered wearing a large straw hat pulled low over his forehead. He smiled a gap-tooth smile, just nodding his head, and holding a machete in his hand. He was handed a glass of water, murmured something, turned on his heel and went back out to the yard.

This was her husband, Carlos. I was led out to the back courtyard, overhung with large mango trees, which grew on the other side of a low wall. A row of small green mangoes sat ripening on top of the wall, their yellow-green skins glistening with oozing juices and insects. Beyond the wall was an open untended space with a few more leafy, widespread mango trees. The heat in this small backyard was shimmering above the wall, the smell of the small mangoes pungent and I noticed thin curving lines of brown sticky liquid oozing from the broken stems. 'Mango pickle,' I thought, and remembered my family making pan-loads back home in India.

I heard the squeal of pigs and tentatively walked over to a smallish wooden shack and, entering a low-lit space, saw about six large white females; some standing, others lying sideways on the ground, with newly born piglets snuffling and snorting, suckling on their mothers. A gentle whiff of roasting filled my senses.

Carlos was in there, with his straw hat slightly pushed up above his forehead, sweat gathering in tiny droplets on his face, standing gumboot-deep in mud and straw, cleaning out one of the pigpens, humming a tune to himself. He made no sign of being aware of me and, turning, I walked back out into the blinding sunlight.

Sounds of laughter poured out of the kitchen and Silvana appeared at the doorway, with a small knife in one hand and a large yam in the other. Behind her stood Mariana, looking at me with curiosity. I smiled. They smiled. Neither spoke English.

I liked Silvana. She must have been about 50 years old. Standing there wearing tight shorts, and a too-tight top that showed off her large bosoms. Her size was matched by her spontaneous laughter and twinkling eyes. At that moment, I think we both wished we could speak one or the other's language well.

They both came out, Mariana carrying a tin bowl with a mound of yams. They dropped down to low stools and began peeling them; their chatter was the sound of chirruping birds. I was invited to sit next to them.

'Gina, coffee con leche?'

'Si, pero sin leche.'

A small chipped white mug of hot black coffee appeared, along with a small glass of white rum. I was feeling nervous. Being here, not knowing any of the family, but sensing welcome and goodwill, I was thrilled to be in what I perceived as the heart of Cuba, visiting a local family, invited into their home, with music playing, heat and a warm breeze filling the now somnolent afternoon. I caught another sharp metallic taint of oozing mangoes. Looking up at the trees in front, they hung like sensual, semi-ripe little bosoms. I knew this perfume well, having grown up surrounded by mango trees, plucking them off the low-lying branches with their stickiness seeping from their torn stems.

Through the open doorway, Alex was chatting with Norrie. I pulled myself up off the stool and walked back through to the front patio. There he was, sitting on a high metal stool, a large white sheet covering his front and tied around behind his neck, and Norrie was cutting, shaping, and shaving his hair even closer than it already was. I caught both of their reflections in the small mirror in front of them. This familiar scene made me smile. How many times in third-world countries had I walked past the local barbers? Down dusty alleyways, around corners of courtyards, and along narrow streets. That clean white sheet covering a body, with their head showing, children and men of all ages. A scene that spoke so much of the society of that place. In bright sunlight or the darkness of the evening, with a low 10-watt light or kerosene lamp, stood those barbers cutting hair for a meagre sum of money. Standing behind their customers, with feet flattened in old dusty leather-thonged backless slippers, their heels worn-down, both human and leather, from years of standing.

Norrie looked up and smiled and introduced me to a very young boy around 12 years old, sitting off to one side, whom I had not seen.

'This is Raul, my cousin, he is my Uncle Luis's son.'

I looked again at him and remembered that he had been turning the spit at the pig kill the previous day. I was unaware of the relationship as on that night I had pretty much wandered around on my own, absorbing all the sights and sounds that had intrigued me. He was swarthy skinned, his light brown hair curling around the nape of his neck and forehead, and he looked like Papa's wife, Laura; nothing like Papa. Norrie smiled when he saw the curiosity on my face.

'Gina, I'll explain. So here in Cuba, we have very big families through marriage. Lots of mamas and papas, uncles and aunts.'

Alex looked ahead, silent, smiling.

'Uncle Luis is not Raul's papa but only married to his mother for many years. Raul's mama has many other grown-up sons living in Cienfuegos. His papa is now married to another young woman.'

Because of Alex's light skin I presumed that Raul was his natural brother. Months later, another story would unfold.

Meeting Carlos, I knew he was not Norrie's father but decided not to ask. I did wonder about the attraction between Silvana and Carlos. On first seeing them together, they seemed unmatched. In all the many times I visited their home, not once did Carlos come out dancing or to family functions with us. He was always looking after the pigs and chickens or sitting in their backyard whittling on a piece of wood. His face was always in repose.

As we were chatting, a stream of young men approached the house from two different paths; the path we had travelled on and another through the small banana plantation, off to the left of the house. Some were walking with arms around their shoulders, others on cycles, but all coming in through the small gate. Some hung outside the fence admiring the Peugeot. Alex got off the high stool and wandered down to chat with them and Raul jumped up to take his place.

All the young men had come to have their hair cut, there must have been about eight of them, or else they had heard about the red beauty parked outside the fence. Of the young men visiting, one was introduced to me by Alex, as one of his many best friends, Tajo, who had decided to hang from the roof of the patio by his fingers, with his legs dangling loosely in the air, just above the patio floor.

By now, there was a palpable excitement in the air. I'm glad the pigs had just given birth, so no pig kill tonight.

Suddenly I heard the car start up and Alex raced away without saying where he was going or goodbye. I looked at Norrie who said he had gone to get cigarettes for his mother and rum for his papa and would be back soon.

Almost four hours passed, and early evening had set in. The barbering was over, and the family sat eating their dinner, offering me some of the rice and chicken but I munched on the fried banana chips and sipped more white rum and black coffee.

The sun had now set, the air still, no sound from the pigs or chickens, a few crickets chirruping, and loudspeakers blared through the silence of the house. Norrie and his girlfriend had gone off to their bedroom, and Raul had returned to his own home in Levisa. Silvana and I sat outside at the back of the house, with Carlos sitting on a low stool opposite, a can of Bucanero beer on the ground, with a long wooden-handled knife, whittling a long stick. They spoke softly to each other.

I remembered wondering what they were thinking of this foreign woman, a friend of their nephew, sitting with them, not speaking, even though Silvana tried to make conversation, with me catching a word of understanding here and there.

The roar of the car was heard as it sped down the path at the front of the house. I rose and walked through the house to the front porch and out to the gated fence. He raised his hand, waving, stopped the car and jumped over its closed door, greeting me effusively with a big hug.

'Ola, Gina, como estas? Sorry, I took time. I went to see my sister, Valeria, and then buy food and cigarettes for my aunt, and rum for Papa for later this evening.'

'Oh, what's happening this evening?'

'We all, the whole family, are going to the Club in Nicaro. But first, we go back to Casa Carolina, eat and dress. Is that ok?'

'Sure,' I replied, holding back my irritation at having been left with his family for so many hours.

He looked at me and smiled that disarming smile and hugged me again then, leaning over into the back of the car, pulled out a large white plastic bag, with the feet of several chickens sticking out from the top. A second bag clinked with the sound of glass bottles.

Around 10 pm, we left Mayari and drove back to Levisa to pick up Papa and Laura, then back to Santa Rita to pick up Silvana, Norrie, and Mariana. They were all freshly dressed. Silvana with long hair pulled off her face, and hair with beaded braids. I think a wig. Oversized gold-colour hoop earrings, a tight top of a stretchy blue material spreading across her ample bust and extremely close-fitting white pants. Norrie was dressed in white too, which glowed against his chocolate-brown skin, enhancing the liquidity of his eyes. Mariana wore a hot pink off-the-shoulder top and white jeans. Her hair was loose, lying far below her shoulders. A waft of night perfume drifted off her skin as she brushed past me to climb into the back of the car.

Even skinny Papa was dressed in white, with an open shirt at his throat, loose-fitting white pants, and trainers, with his wife, Laura, echoing him.

I have no idea how five people got into the back of the car and couldn't resist laughing with delight, seeing them sitting in the back hugging each other and giggling. I did love the fact that these new strangers had this closeness, this family-ness. They must have been uncomfortable, with many a wide and skinny bottom pressed together.

We drove off through the warm night air, the sky by now an inky black, a few pinpoints of sparkling stars above. The car stereo reverberated, the air around echoing. A buzz of loud and happy chatter from the back.

We arrived at the club and being Saturday, it was filled with large groups of families. Young men, some I now recognised from earlier in the day, who saw us and waved, smaller groups of luscious young women, their dark eyes, from where I was standing, smouldering as they glanced around. But these were not the "stork women" of Havana. They all looked local, out for the night, and it was a memorable party night. Whatever I felt during the day vanished in this night air.

Papa insisted on dancing with me, and he was astonishingly good, but I should have known that as he was Cuban, and music coursed through his body and blood.

It was an intoxicating night where I began to be drawn into a life which I had not been a part of since my childhood. That close family bonding and caring, where life was truly about being out together and moving to the ebb and flow of the sounds and rhythms surrounding us.

The three men in our group and a few other male friends, as well as Silvana and Mariana, ensured that I danced until the arches of my feet in my high espadrilles ached happily.

As the late-night drew towards early morning, there was a crashing sound and screams. The outside area of the club quickly emptied, with young girls running across the lawn and people scattering all around us.

Alex took my hand and drew me towards the car telling me to get in and lock it. The rest of the family seemed to have momentarily frozen in place.

I sat in the car and looked out of the passenger window towards a lit area of the lawn at the rear of the club. I saw a young stockily built man crossing the brightly lit green lawn, clutching the back of his neck with the front of his white shirt blood-soaked, and approaching with a knife in his hand. He then half-ran to the driver's side of my car and I saw a bloodied knife in his hand. He banged on the driver's window and, looking at him, I shook my head.

Alex came running up to the car behind him, at which the bloodied man turned around, sidestepped, and ran off. Approaching the car, I saw that the front of Alex's shirt was covered in blood, and I leaned over to open the driver's door and let him in.

I looked queryingly at him at which he said, 'It's ok, I'm not hurt. We have fights here in Levisa and Nicarao all the time. It's the drink, the fire in their blood and boredom. Many young men get badly hurt here all the time. I go get my papa and family and we go home.'

On the ride back, the music played softly, the chatter was animated and loud, and I caught the odd word. 'Cuchillos', 'malos', 'siempre peleas', 'policía', 'no es seguro' and 'lo siento, Gina'.

There was no explanation as to the origin of the knife fight and Alex's bloodied shirt. I didn't ask. The family would have gladly filled me in, but not him.

The early hours of the night ended back in Papa's house, drinking through two bottles of white rum and carrying on dancing.

Another stepping stone in their daily lives and, observing this, nothing seemed out of place. It was just life.

# 20

By now, it was almost the end of the first week of my second trip and I was eager to visit Santiago de Cuba and Havana and get down to the local beaches. But so far, the first week had centred around visits to his aunt's house around 11 am and then his disappearance for a few hours in the car, so I had no choice but to remain with the family.

Silvana tried hard to entertain me. We would go walking down through the banana plantations, meandering along narrow alleyways in between little houses, the ground hard and dry, emerging into a large, gravelled clearing with a few low buildings, their peeling painted doors and windows closed. On one corner of the clearing stood a small corner shop, old and tattered posters flapping off the wall, a line of people waiting in the sun for the shop to open, or older men sitting on low stone walls, with legs crossed, thin cigarettes between fingers or lips and younger men crouching or sitting on fallen logs under green spreading mango trees, heads bent or swinging from hands loosely holding on to low tree branches. There was this "waiting" in the air, which I had already noticed in Havana, a type of patience because that is what was needed to live here locally.

'Alejandro, I like your family, but we have been with them a lot and it's difficult for me as I do not speak Spanish. I would love to go to Santiago de Cuba as I have heard so much about it.'

'OK, we go there for lunch, but it is far and it's not such a nice place.'

I had not been, so I had no idea if this information was correct.

'But we go tomorrow, as today we go get my sister, Valeria, and visit the waterfall in Salto de Guayabo, not far, but the road up there is broken.'

Valeria lived about fifteen minutes from Mayari, down a series of twisting alleyways and houses, which became smaller and smaller until we arrived at one lane, amidst a clearing of what was a random banana plantation.

Parking the car, he jumped out and quickly walked down into an even narrower alley about one arm span wide. I slowly followed, unsure if I should, but he turned and beckoned me. I walked down to a small English-looking garden shed of a wooden dwelling up three small steps, where a verdigris green door was ajar. Stepping up to the front door, I walked into a room with its walls painted the same colour. An old well-washed net curtain at the small front window, a matching green metal collapsible chair snuggled close to a round table and a few framed fading photos on the wall, made up their sitting room. A narrow vertical opening with another long net curtain led to a backroom.

I stood and waited, hearing light-hearted voices and laughter in the back. I felt humbled, standing there in someone's private house, a total intruder. I felt privileged to be there.

The net curtain moved, and I saw slender dark brown fingers curl around its edge. A tall narrow-hipped woman entered the front lounge. Her hair was neatly cropped to almost a number one crew cut. A wide-mouthed smile of delight and she quietly said, 'Ola, Gina, nice to meet you. I am Valeria, Alejandro's sister.'

She came up to me and gave me a warm embrace, putting me at my ease. She looked me straight in the eyes and said, 'I live with my mother here, in the back bedroom. Sorry, our home is so small.'

She took my hand and led me out, followed by her brother.

She sat in the back of the car, speaking little, while we drove up to the waterfall, along a steep hill with large fallen rocks along the road. It looked like there had been a landslide during the rainy season at some time or other. He negotiated this road very well and I had to tell him that, which brought a broad smile to his face.

After a while, she started to speak to me in English. I asked her what she did and, in halting English, she said she taught in a primary school in the local village. Brother and sister chatted away, softly laughing, with CD music playing quietly. Another hot day, with the roof down. Along the rutted road were small white villas with decorative metal fencing, cemented into low walls. One of the walls had a full-length dried crocodile lying, basking in the sun; an image, a flash, and we drove past, slowly crawling up the hill where giant mahogany trees grew on both sides of the broken path.

Stopping outside a low wooden fence, we walked through and along a planked walkway to the waterfall, white and frothing, in full flow and beyond, folding interlocking hills spread out far into the distance, as though on a painted canvas. Their surface was covered in thick hazy blue-green vegetation, a thin silver-mirrored ribbon of a river deep in a gully. I thought it would be quite a trek to walk down there.

With both of us dressed in white, we looked like a couple although I felt self-conscious about this scene from a movie, as that is how it felt. We stopped at scenic spots, taking photos of each other, with him standing at the edge of a waterfall, on a large rock, posing with both hands making a heart shape. This did not feel natural to me but, in my usual way, I waved and laughed.

Like so many of the past days, we ended up at Silvana's house again.

Later in the afternoon, Alex asked, 'Gina, you like Cuba?'

'Yes, of course, you know I do. Well, what I have seen so far. Are houses expensive to buy here?'

'Oh yes, in the countryside, like this house. Come, I show you my neighbour's house.'

We slipped through the back gate to the adjoining house, which was open but empty of occupants. It was in better condition than next door, with a bathroom still in progress of being built and a more fitted kitchen with a refrigerator. His face was bathed in smiles, as he said that his neighbour wanted to sell the house and leave Cuba to live in America with his son. I had a faint recollection during one of our conversations saying that it would be fun to buy a small house here in Cuba.

I looked around at it again and thought, 'This could be an idea, living next door to Silvana.'

It had a couple of bedrooms. The fact that it had a power station next to the two houses did not matter to me, as this was only an idea that it could become a holiday home and be let out as a casa particular.

Immediately, he became enthused, outlining all the modifications that could be done if I wanted to buy it and come back and have somewhere to stay in Cuba instead of in casa particulars.

'Where is the owner? Could you ask him how much he wants for his house?

At that, I wandered back through the little gate into Silvana's chicken yard where the birds were peck-pecking the hard ground scattered with corn seeds and the white pigs again snorting and snuffling in their wooden shed.

By now, I was getting truly bored of spending almost one week being taken to Silvana's house and then left for hours while he disappeared on a pretext of getting more rum for his papa who, it turned out, was away working at a steel mill in Moy. A place I would visit later that evening.

We took Valeria home.

I suggested that we go to Santiago de Cuba, as it was still early in the day, although a good two-hour journey away. Without a word, he turned the car around, driving off onto the motorway, stopping along a wayside booth and returning with two tiny Union Jack and Cuban flags on a stick, which he promptly stuck on the dashboard with a large smile of triumph. The flags fluttered side by side but not in unison.

We drove but never did get to Santiago de Cuba itself. Instead, we stopped at a large tourist restaurant, which looked like a whitewashed Greek taverna, covered with reddish-brown roof tiles, almost terracotta in colour, with outside undercover seating, its wooden floors a shiny tobacco brown. All the tables were covered in fluttering, pristine white tablecloths, held down by large water glasses and small bowls of flowers.

Smiling staff led us to a table by the edge of the patio, where the view stretched far out to a sun-drenched marine blue sea, white flecks skimming the surface of the waves and a low drystone wall girthing the sides of a precipice which fell steeply into dark deep waters below. An old fort lay at the far end of a walkway, large-mouthed guns protruding over battlements. The walkways thronged with tiny wooden sheltered booths, with a few people walking or browsing.

I quickly took this all in as we sat at the table, aware the diners were mainly tourist groups and I began to feel self-conscious sitting with him, beautiful and muscled, his white shirt opened halfway down his chest. Thank God, no gold medallion hung around his neck. I did openly stare at him, as did others, and I mused on this with a myriad of thoughts. Looking back at the photos of that afternoon, I did smile, partly through embarrassment at both of us in white. What would my mother have said? (No idea where that thought came from!)

Our food arrived. A set menu, an array of El Camarones, shrimps in tomato sauce, served on a pile of rice, salad, a bowl of banana chips and cold beer. I never drank beer. This was Cuban food at its best and I had a TripAdvisor moment thinking about what star rating I would give this place.

A frisky breeze picked up and we relaxed, almost for the first time since my arrival, and chatted about his life in Switzerland and returning now to Cuba. A flicker of quivering emotion fell across his face for a moment. He talked softly about returning without any clothes or money and wondering what he would do, in a place where jobs were few and salaries low. He said he loved his family and country but would have preferred to continue his previous Swiss life. I asked the reason for returning, but he turned his face away and remained silent. I'd already noticed this response on several occasions.

Looking around at the fort, I asked if he knew anything about the history as our silence lingered too long. He gave it a cursory look and said he knew little, except that once upon a time it had something to do with pirates. He'd learned about it from his history classes a long time ago, but he wasn't that interested in history. I gave up on this and decided to find out about the place myself, later.

A waiter came over bringing some more cold beers and I asked him the name of the fort. He gave a very big smile and said El Morro, like the restaurant name, but way back it was called Castillo de San Pedro de la Roca. Alex gave him a very sour look. The waiter turned away, smiling, and winked at me. Of course, I returned his smile and winked.

Sitting there, sipping beer, with the sun beginning to soften, the breeze continuing to blow, the tourists gradually leaving and the space around sinking into a languid silence, I mused the history of the Caribbean, pirates, gunrunning, the Cuban revolution and, of course, Ernest Hemingway popped into my thoughts. I remembered reading about his involvement in the Cuban revolution and helping the revolutionaries by transporting guns in his boat, Pilar, in times of need. He seemed disinterested in most things about the current state of Cuba but was interested in fashion, fast cars, money, and his mobile phone.

We drove back to Mayari, at over 100 mph, with the fuel gauge hitting on almost empty. Alex may have seen the film "Fast and Furious", and I decided that I must be Letty Ortiz, as I liked her. Although I loved the fast driving as the roads were long and straight in this part of southeast Cuba, fuel was expensive and fuel stations were few and far between, the cost of fuel seemed constantly uppermost in my mind. I often had to ask him to drive more slowly as I was spending a small fortune on fuel. He would laugh and say, 'No problema, Gina. You have money,' and accelerate, pushing the car beyond 100 mph. There were times when we got caught out by the traffic police in built-up areas and a conversation would ensue with a note passed between the two.

His mobile buzzed and I heard the scratchy voice of Papa speaking quite urgently.

'Gina, we must go to my papa and collect my mother. She is not well and have to take her to hospital near Moa. Sorry, I know we were going to the club, but the hospital is far and no transport for them.'

I had no idea that a club visit had been planned.

We raced through the early evening, quickly darkening as it does in the tropics, along ridged cemented roads, rarely a streetlamp but I guess these were familiar roads, and our journey lasted for what seemed over an hour. The hand brake was pulled up sharply, as we stopped abruptly in front of an edifice of a white building, though its walls glowed yellow under arcs of lamplight, Hospital General Guillermo Luis. In fact, my memory does not serve me well as, years later, I looked up this hospital and it was an aqua-green colour, but maybe it had been repainted over time.

Laura had spoken little on the journey, but she looked pale with dark circles under her eyes and Papa, who sat next to her, held her hand, talking softly all the while.

He got out of the car and helped her up the short flight of stairs, where a petite nurse stood waiting. Her starched, white uniform cap sat squarely atop her head, her crisp white apron covered her small but ample frame and a nurse's stopwatch was pinned on the left side of her apron.

I had a flashback to when I was eighteen and had enrolled as an SRN nurse in King's College Hospital, London, wearing the same uniform. So that's what I looked like. Flashbacks can be excruciating, as I remember thinking that I had looked like a little dumpy pigeon, with a small head, a wide A-line skirt, thin legs, and flat shoes.

At the top of the stairs, the nurse helped Laura through the hospital door, walking and supporting her under her left arm, with Papa by her right side, nervously touching her elbow.

We waited for more than an hour in the car, which was parked to one side under a lamppost.

'You know Gina, life here is so hard for all of us. The government helps us with food coupons, cheap travel, housing, education, medicines, and good bus transport, but most of us have so little money to buy a car or anything else. We are all helping each other out. So, getting around quickly is muchos difficile. Tonight, my mother would have to take a bus which would take about two hours to come here, and we do not know what the matter with her is, so that's a problem.'

Looking at his face, I saw genuine concern, worry and tension etched deeply into his sad eyes. I took his hand and he gently squeezed mine. A moment for me of sharing and affection for these people whom I had recently met. Thinking about how much easier it is back home, in most areas of our lives. Thinking too, that these people were swept up in an old man's dream and vision for his country decades ago. A dream of hope and revolution to change the quality of all their lives but, in fact, one that plunged his country into deep economic despair, those trails of dreams still linger around in the everyday lives of most of these people.

The hospital door opened and, seeing them, we reparked at the bottom of the stairs. Laura and Papa walked slowly and gingerly down the stairs. She looked less pale and Papa less fraught. I never did find out what was the reason for her hospital visit.

Papa worked nights at the local nickel factory in Moa and was driven there for his night shift. We dropped him off outside high imposing fencing, floodlit, dazzling rays of light, spreading across the entrance, resembling more of a high-security prison. With a toothy grin, he put his head through my open window, kissing me on the cheek, then waved to us as he walked away with small, measured steps; a diminutive figure as he passed through the high entrance gates. Earlier I'd asked him how he would reach his home in the morning and Alex replied, saying he would take the 7 am bus to Mayari and would get another local bus to Levisa village, then walk back, cutting through the tangle of small paths to his house.

We drove Laura back to Levisa.

The late evening passed and, on returning to Casa Carolina, we sat in the back garden drinking cold beers and fresh mango juice, listening to the sharp sounds of the crickets and spiky background noise of reggaeton, emanating from the music shop across the road. Did it ever close?

I heard myself say softly, 'I've only five days left of my holiday here and would love to drive to Havana. I know it's almost 1000 km, but we could stay overnight in Cienfuegos, which I hear is another lovely city and would also love to spend a day on one of the many beaches.'

'OK, but first, tomorrow is Sunday and there is a birthday party for Jonathan. He is going to be one year old and that is very important in Cuba. Many cousins, families and friends will be going, and we will kill a pig for the baby. After, on Monday, we will leave early and go to Havana. I must meet a friend of mine there, so that is good.'

*He has taken control of my car*
*and I seem to have lost control of myself.*

# 21

Seven of us were packed into the car, roof down, as we drove once again through winding dusty roads to a place I cannot remember. I do remember that it had a raised air of prosperity. The houses were detached, sitting opposite each other on either side of the red-soiled street, front fences covered with Bougainvillea and tall red Canna lilies creating a guard of honour along the fencing. Large saccharin pink, bell-shaped flower heads, with their petals punctuated with darker shades of sugar pink and orange, were growing tall and elegant, like so many of the Cuban people. There were also red Poinsettia-flowering trees; not like the little pots of gift flowers we get here in England at Christmas, but explosive fulsome flower heads, the heat feeding their lushness. Looking out the window at them, I recalled the many times on this trip, while driving through small towns, when I'd seen them first before seeing the squat concrete-walled apartments. Their blaze of colour distracted the eye from the ugliness of former Russian architecture.

We rolled up and rolled out of the car amid raucous laughter and many colloquial swear words I'd become familiar with. Children played in the sandy street, little girls dressed in frilly ice cream-pink dresses, or little shorts and frilly tops, and the boys in sports shorts and tops, white trainers, and artfully cut hair, just like many of the teenagers and grown men. Maybe they had been to Norrie to have their hair barbered.

I was immediately introduced to Florencia, Papa's older sister, who stood outside by the fence. She was a slender, tall willowy woman of my age, of similar colouring to Papa with brown feral eyes. I looked deeply into her eyes and saw uncertainty, with a point of recognition of two women measuring each other up. She held Jonathan in her arms, a light-skinned little boy with large doe-like eyes. The birthday boy.

Alex walked with me into the garden and Valeria was sitting quietly on a green bench, under a dust-covered blossoming royal Poinsettia tree, dressed in snake-green shorts, an off-the-shoulder gypsy-style top, with her long bare legs crossed, and her close-cropped hair looking worn and faded brown. We smiled and waved, and I went over and hugged her

Off to one side of the house towards the back, the ritual of the pig kill had begun, this tiime it appeared less ceremonious. The setting was different, and my mood and emotions were no longer curious but, already, disinterested. I shut myself off from this killing event, as I did not want to see another animal sacrificc for the celebration of us people.

Being Sunday, the large garden was crowded with happy shouting people. This was an honouring party within this family for a little one-year-old person. Balloons festooned the trees, and lights glittered amongst the leaves, even in the bright sun. A large jamboree box, covered with coloured tissue paper and large tissue-paper flowers hung like giant jackfruit from one of the trees. I knew this from my childhood party days when no party was complete without this treat of a thin cardboard box filled with puffed rice, sweets, and toys. I remember our shrieks of delight as the box was pierced from underneath with a metal skewer or knitting needle and down would shower a rain of puffed rice over us, our hands reaching out to catch the assortment of treasures and we would all scramble on the ground grabbing for the sweets and toys. Suddenly we had become little animal children.

I wandered around, smiling and chatting, saying 'Hola' and checking out who could speak English, but none of them did except Norrie and Alex.

After an hour, the smell of roasting meat began to rise through the air, as spirals of the essence of the pig rose, entwined with the smoking banana leaves and charcoal. My stomach turned a somersault.

Wandering inside the house, I passed into an open kitchen which was well-equipped with all that I had in my kitchen. A bright and airy room, crowded with women of all ages and sizes, dressed in floral slim-fitting dresses, all looking a little like the fashion pages of a 1950s magazine. No one wore jeans and all had their hair coiffured and styled, some wearing high-heels or flip-flops. This was a woman's domain. Amongst the glitter and chatter, their eyes sparkling and their lips smiling, large plates of plantain fritters, fried chicken pieces, bowls of fruit, cut and sliced mangoes, bananas, and papaya, all so exotic and lush, were being carried to the guests outside. They all looked at me and uttered, 'Hola,' and I back to them and continued through to the dining room.

To one side of the room a table was laid, covered with a white tablecloth, upon which was set a rectangular cream-covered cake, about 60cm long, with tiny icing-sugar blue flowers edging the cake and in the middle, a space for one candle and Jonathan's name scrawled across its top.

The little boy was now being held in the arms of another woman. Again, in this room, mainly women stood chatting with each other. Most of the people here seemed to be related in one way or another and there were a lot of relatives. I did love the friendly chaos and strident laughter of these people. They knew how to enjoy their moments, their faces reflected joy and I felt caught up in it.

Sometime later, I needed to use the toilet and went out looking for Alex, but he had disappeared and so had my car.

I was directed to the place of the toilet. At the back of the main house, off to one side, sat an outbuilding which looked like a chicken coop. Its front door was made of narrow slats of wood, with a cemented gully between the house and the coop. Its roof was covered with corrugated metal, with the door opening exposed to the eyes of the party revellers. I hesitantly went down the gully. A group of men, women and children sat on low stools at its entrance.

I carefully pushed open the door into a dark space, crouched down and closed it, keeping one hand on the door to keep it shut and the only light came from the sliver of gaps in the wooden door. The place smelt of inhuman stuff and I gingerly squatted over a hole in the ground and once finished, noticed a tap on the wall which I knew would be the way to wash. Flashes of memory, thinking of the many times I had squatted over holes such as these in different corners of the world, remembering the sound of flies buzzing around the nether regions of my world. A thought came to me in that semi-darkness, of a day, of a disappearing allegorical world of the darkness of the heart set apart from the clamour and refinement of the upper shiny world. A shaft of sunlight struck the ground in front of me as I arose and left that chicken coop.

The contrast of the house, with pale creams, pink and blue interior walls, and a garden full of spreading Poinsettia and a couple of Magnolia trees and large-headed colourful flowers, and the cramped, dark, primitive toilet down the side of the house was allegorical in its context. I had no critical thoughts and was more interested in the priority given to their dwelling. I did not believe that the chicken coop was the main household toilet but, somehow, as a guest being shown this place spoke volumes to me of my status there. Or was I being oversensitive?

Although I was a guest of Alex, I was also a stranger without context.

The pig had been melted down to dripping hot slabs of meat laid out on platters. Jonathan had blown out his candle and the cake had been cut and handed out on trays. Cold bottles of beer were held in laughter-shaking hands, the children had poked the jamboree box and now puffed rice lay scattered like snowdrops all over the garden.

I wandered around, feeling restless and bored. I had had too many family functions to attend and where was Alex?

The afternoon was turning to early evening. The sun had begun to lay its head down below the horizon and a quiet air descended to an even more convivial atmosphere. I heard the opening of the small garden gate and he appeared, carrying bottles of rum which he handed to his father and packets of cigarettes were given to Silvana and Valeria.

Florencia stood chatting with Papa. Sister and brother, so alike in bearing, a regal air on their dark-skinned handsome faces. Alex strolled over and sat on a bench in front of them, drinking a beer. I suddenly noticed that all three were wearing red. Papa's arm around his sister, Florencia's hand resting tenderly on Alex's shoulder; he sat with a contented air like a little boy. Spoilt and much-loved by his family. A cameo I would never forget.

Who or what was Alejandro? What was his special place within his family?

I noticed, on many occasions, an indulgence surrounded him, more than his other cousins. Months later, I would discover what my place was within this family context.

By now, the children and most of the other guests had left. Jonathan had been taken off to bed and only a few family members remained. Papa plied me with large glasses of rum, while soft music played, and Valeria and I danced a fusion of salsa and drink-induced moves, together with Norrie and Mariana; our feet covered in dust, our bodies bending and swaying with the rum and the music and that ever-blowing evening breeze.

As the evening ended, he, who had disappeared again, returned to say he had gone to look for a taxi for the family but could not find one. I commented on the length of time he had been gone, over two hours. He shrugged his shoulders with indifference, and said, 'This is Cuba.'

A taxi did turn up around 10 pm and he came to me and asked for 50 pesos (about £50) for the taxi fare for the family. I felt my anger rise and told him that they could pay for their taxi. What reason did I have to pay for them to go home? This was not a party for me but someone else, so why was I having to pay?

I saw his anger flare up too, saying they had no money to get home. I stood there, shaking inside, knowing that I was being taken for a fool, but a fool in a country where I was on my own. I wondered how much he would keep for himself and how much for the taxi fare. Already I was distrusting him.

The five family members were standing at the gate, waiting to go and as I looked over to them, their heads averted to the front. I reached into my skirt pocket, took out the 50 pesos and gave it to him. I had to wonder if he did not understand the value of 50 pesos and what that meant to me as well.

We drove back in silence to the casa.

I heard myself saying, 'Alejandro, enough of being with your family. I came to spend time with you and, so far, you have dropped me off at your family in the late morning, left me with them, taken my car and disappeared for hours without any explanation of where you have been. Tomorrow, we go to Havana and if you want to stay with your family, you can, but I will drive to Havana on my own. I have four days before I fly home.'

He reached over and took my hand, putting it on his thigh.

He was passionate that night and as I drifted off to sleep, I doubted my judgement and reasons for being in this unbalanced relationship.

# 22

I can never be angry or disgruntled for long. My sense of adventure and love of life always get the better of me and drag me out of my darkest moods, as though being sucked out of a vacuum.

Almost 1000 km of fast driving through tobacco and corn-filled countryside, interspersed with faded-walled one-street towns, wooden stalls along the roadsides hung with strings of garlic, and small piles of avocados and potatoes; these all added to my new bank of memories. The colours of the countryside filled with watercolour landscapes of washed-out greens and neutral blues, cloud-reflected lakes, silver-green forested hills with steep roads cutting downwards into gentle lush, vegetated valleys and the constant "beep beep" of passing jeep taxis, with bronzed arms waving to us as they passed by.

Around Cienfuegos, about halfway to Havana, the conversation began.

'Gina, I'm thinking that a taxi business would be good here, between Holguin and Varadero or Varadero and Havana. Many tourists and people always need a taxi, as a bus is too long. Maybe I could get a taxi for business and when you come back, like you say you want to come and live here, there is car and money from taxi business for you. You think it a good idea?'

Along our journey, I had already asked him what he was going to do with his life here in Cuba. He said he felt at a loss to know what to do, again repeating that teaching salsa in Levisa was impossible and he would have to go to Havana to do that, but there were already many teachers there.

I'd also noticed that he did not have a settled place to live and when I asked him about that, he said he sometimes stayed in Havana, Cienfuegos, and Matanzas, as he had family and friends everywhere. Sometimes he would share a bed with someone or sleep on the floor or at his papa's. I'd noticed during the many times of visiting that house, that he shared a small room with his younger brother Raul, his bed being a metal stowaway folded bed, not big enough for a man. Returning from Switzerland seemed to have displaced his sense of stability and homeplace.

I was attracted to him but at the same time aware of the fission caused by money and his expectation that I would pay for everything.

Even so, I felt a thrill at the thought of owning a new business there. I was already enamoured with the country, its rawness; not forgetting its history which, my god, was always present, in every 360 degrees turn on my heel.

The idea of having a car to get around appealed to me and, of course, I loved the idea of buying an old American car. Starting a new and different business would be risky, but I'd already taken so many risks in my life, that this new idea did not overwhelm me.

The excitement began to rise as a stirring of a volcano which, unknown to me now, would erupt to proportions beyond my imaginings.

# 23

Entering Havana around midnight, with its streets quiet and mellow-lit, a softness of feeling and peace enveloped. He took my hand and led me through a narrow passageway, up a flight of worn cement stairs to the first floor of an old Spanish house, its rooms opening off a wrought-ironed balcony, which ran along the front of the casa particular.

The night was still young, so having changed, showered, and perfumed with Hugo Boss aftershave and Chanel's Rose replacing other night aromas, we drove down to Casa de la Musica. The atmosphere was not just electric, it was a power station of electrified energy. We became a part of those intoxicating pulsations, mixed with mojitos, daiquiris, and beer, and danced to every rhythm that filled the air. That night was ours to dance and be with each other, and every other irritating thought that had passed over the last few days melted away in a whirlwind of sensual attraction, music, drink and "abrazo lujurioso".

Drifting off to sleep as the dawn rose, for that blissful moment as the angel of sleep caught me, I had reached my long-sought sanctuary.

# 24

The day held us in its languorous hand as we walked down some of the old familiar streets. Early afternoon, when it had reached a climax of heat and buzz, we bumped into Jonnie at Café de Paris, the two men hugging in that Cuban way of friendship and camaraderie.

Jonnie embraced me warmly and we sat at a table ready for an afternoon party. I saw Alex beginning to withdraw into himself around Jonnie, as on our first meeting. They chatted but Alex's replies became monosyllabic, and he shut down, his face unreadable. The café's small band struck up a familiar salsa tune, and immediately Jonnie jumped up, pulling me off my chair and onto the pavement. I looked over at him, his face averted. I felt so shy to be dancing out in public, but Jonnie had this ability to drive away my shyness and, within a few minutes, a group of people were standing with video cameras in hand. Once Jonnie started, he could not stop dancing, weaving me around through the words of the songs.

At the end of one song, I remarked that he seemed supremely happy.

'Yes, marriage papers have finally come through after four years of waiting and I can leave Cuba and be with my wife in England.'

I had not known that he had married an English girl in Cuba four years earlier.

'So, when will you be leaving?'

'Soon, soon, I hope,' he said, as he escorted me back to my chair.

Later in the afternoon, Jonnie left as he was dancing at the Tropicana Hotel that evening. A shadow crossed Alex's face when he heard that. He was obviously jealous of Jonnie but still good friends.

I never saw Jonnie again after that, despite my many returns to Cuba and I did wonder if he was able to leave and live in England. I hoped his gilded cage door had been opened and he had been able to fly away and escape this island paradise.

That day in Havana was how I had imagined it would be with him. We were both relaxed and easy in each other's company, wandering around, visiting small churches, watching street artists outside Bar Asturias drawing caricatures of their sitters, guffaws from the customers, picking up a drift of music in the air, and watching others dancing the Tango which had just started to become popular.

Wherever we went, there was a hail of 'Hola' from fellow 'bici' riders (bicycle rickshaws) or jeep taxi drivers. He seemed very familiar with those streets and a multitude of people. I later heard that he had also been a 'bici' rider in Havana. Information which he did not share with me.

He needed new clothes, as that suitcase which he had brought with him was still empty, so we meandered through tiny doors in large, museum-like buildings, up rickety flights of stairs, along corridors with chipped terrazzo-tiled floors and handrails in various states of collapse, to tiny rooms, with paint and plaster flaking off the walls but bulging with every designer brand sent from Miami. He was very selective, trying on jeans, shirts, jackets, sneakers, trainers, and fake gold jewellery. Each garment had to coordinate with the other, and every pair of pants and jacket had to fit perfectly, with the pile around his ankles growing in height. I stayed in the background, knowing the awkwardness of the moment for me when I would need to pay. Some of the sellers seemed very comfortable with an older woman with a young Cuban man and chatted with me in good English, looking at me without any expression or question in their eyes. We left each shop with my fingers scalding, as my credit card slid into the card machine and my trips to the ATM became alarmingly frequent.

On our return trip to Mayari early the next morning, we stopped over in Matanzas for him to visit his old teacher who taught English and, of course, spoke excellent English, as well as her two daughters. We parked our car along the side of a metal fence and walked down a rutted track along a row of assorted dwellings of varying materials. As we walked, a group of small children ran up to him, hugging him around his knees; the dimples in his cheek deepening as he picked one of them up high into the air and swung him around, to the child's delightful squeals.

We must have visited at least six families, and at one family, we stopped for some time. Three women sat outside on chairs, one of them had her elbow encased in white plaster, which she rested on the table. Alex ran up to her and hugged her, seemingly asking her what had happened. She hugged him back, amid tears which rolled down her face. Again, I never found out the cause of her plastered arm. I noticed the indulgent look on their faces, a softening of their eyes, as they looked at him and stroked his arms as he stood near them.

He told me that that was the house where he often stayed in Matanzas and showed me the bed where he slept. It was a large double bed, with a toddler asleep, flat on his back, arms outstretched above his head. Alex gently leaned over him and kissed his chubby cheek. At that moment, I saw a future of him with small children of his own and I felt a light thunder in my heart.

We drank black tea and left after a couple of hours, with a train of children walking with us to the car and then running behind the car as we sped away.

We drove through the early evening, stopping off in Cienfuegos where his stepbrother Karl lived and worked in one of the local factories. Their house was down another dust-covered bush-filled lane with household debris littered all over. We stopped outside what I would have called a tin hut, no more than about 2.40 x 3.0 m sitting on a concrete foundation, with building rubble all around, a single silver metal door to the entrance, and a Papaya tree growing outside laden with small green budding papayas, all covered in creamy-brown dust.

Ana stood at the door, a warm and welcoming smile across her face. A petite chubby woman, with black hair pulled loosely off her face, and swarthy skinned. I walked through the door into the main room, one room, with a king-size wrought-iron bed, covered with a mixed-purple bedspread, and a wire strung high on the wall beside the bed for hanging clothes. To the left of the front door was a table, groaning under the weight of hundreds of small nail varnish bottles of every colour on a colour chart. It seemed Ana was a manicurist.

Through to the back, sectioned off by a thin red curtain on a wire, was a small dark area which led to a kitchen. Her son, Alfonso, whom I would meet on another trip, lived with her and slept on the ground behind that red curtain. I didn't allow my thoughts to even begin to form an opinion. I was offered a glass of mango juice and walked with it down to the end of the lane with Alex.

Looking across the bay, its bankside waters full of unimaginable debris, there rose a large cream building with window frames painted in post box red, and smoke curled out of several chimneys, creating their own toxic clouds. This was the factory where his brother worked, and he was due at Ana's house shortly. Karl had already arrived when we strolled back and, on meeting him, I felt myself slightly recoil. The hostility which glared from his eyes was palpable. A man of about thirty, and light skinned. His mother was Laura, Papa's other wife (I had no idea how many wives he may have had). We stayed for a very short while, after this emotionally loaded encounter with Karl, returning to the main road towards Mayari.

We drove through the night, stopping off at wayside diners for food or a drink, thundering down the motorways at 160 km, while music softly played. He held my hand for most of the journey, telling me about his short career in the army when he was 18, in which he hated and loathed guns and any form of killing. I asked him about Karl and his various step and half-brothers but he seemed reluctant to pursue the conversation. His affectionate behaviour towards them, when he greeted them, seemed in contradiction with his unwillingness to share his feelings about them in conversation. I was learning to not pursue details of his life.

As the dawn began to rise around 4.30 am, he asked if I had thought any more about the idea of a business in Cuba and maybe a taxi business. I asked how much an old American car would cost. He went quiet for about five minutes, took out his phone and made a call at that dawn hour. It would be about 22,000 pesos, the equivalent of just under £20,000. I blanched in disbelief, then remembered the conversation Ella and I had had with our driver on a tour around Havana on our first visit. He had told us his car had cost about $35,000.

'That is a great deal of money, I will have to think about it on my return home and let you know.'

He replied with silence.

The sun had risen far up the horizon by 7 am. I had shared some of the driving, not during the night but more towards dawn, while he dozed for a couple of hours. I knew that I could not cope with night driving and the piercing glare of the lorries, their full lights blinding oncoming vehicles, and the road edge falling into a sheer drop on either side.

We slept till about midday. My second last day and I still had not swum in the sea since my first visit to the casa near Emerald Beach, near Holguin.

As we went to get into the car, I noticed a huge dent on the passenger side, the side facing the road.

'Alex, have you seen the dent in the side of the car? How did that get there?'

'Oh, maybe you hit something while you were driving.'

Of course, I had not. I would have known. Then I remembered that we had parked the car at the side of the road in Matanzas when we visited some of his friends and family the day before, but I could not work out how that large dent above the wheel hub could have got there.

'Oh no,' I thought, 'I'm going to have to pay a lot for this repair work as per the terms of my car hire. I have no witnesses to this accident or any knowledge of how it happened.'

He seemed to be disinterested in the matter.

'Come on. We are going to a beach in Corinthia. It's a small village not far from here. You will like it.'

I rushed back inside, grabbed my bikini and a towel and sun lotion, not forgetting my large Cuban straw hat which I had bought at the beginning of the trip.

Our drive took us up into semi-hilly countryside, along winding roads, and red tracks amongst tobacco fields, where we stopped and saw hundreds of tiny crabs scurrying around the red ground. We came out into an area of cleared land, where there stood a small, deserted hut. We parked and I ran toward the beach. The water was warm and the colour of blue surf, and the bay was a coronet of sparkling blue jewels.

I swam while Alex sat on the white sand, drawing figures of hearts with a straw stick. He had picked up a bleached skull of a small animal and given it to me when I came out of the sea. I asked if he knew what it was, but he was unsure if it was a small deer or a dog. I had seen tiny dogs out in that part of southwestern Cuba and later discovered that they were called Havanese and reminded me of the furry Ewoks from Star Wars. I was not sure that it was one of their skulls, but I kept it for many years until I decided that a dead skull from Cuba may not be the best charm to have in my home.

'Will you not swim with me?'

He declined with a strong shaking of his head, saying he did not like swimming. Of course, I should have remembered.

That day, he had worn a red t-shirt and red chinos and I stood, my feet sinking into the soft sand, looking at him. So, he did not like to sunbathe, did not like to swim; what sport did he like? When I asked him, he said baseball and that we were going to a local baseball match that evening and then dancing in Holguin. Off to Holguin again, back the way we had passed through during the night.

'Here we go round the mulberry bush,' I hummed in my head, playfully.

As we left the beach, he drove through a conservation area, land which "belonged" to Raul Castro. He told me that deer lived there, and, through the low undergrowth and rocks, I saw what looked like iguanas. He surprised me by calling them 'rock iguanas' and, with a huge grin on my face, I said, 'Alejandro, how come only on my second last day you are bringing me to these places? This is what I came to Cuba to see. It's such a pity we spent so much time with your family and here, so close, is so much wildlife. If I ever return, I really would like to see more of the wildlife of Cuba.'

'OK, Gina, next time. When I have the taxi business and you have bought that small house next to Aunt Silvana.'

Some of the family came with us to the local baseball stadium, which was thronged with local youth, and piles of coke bottles spilt out of large waste bins and on the ground. Loud voices sang and chatted, and the stadium and grounds were buzzing. For me, it was thrilling to be part of the local games and community even though my interest in baseball at the time was minimal, although we had played rounders as children, which was the nearest game to baseball. We didn't stay for the whole game as it would be starting much later, so I was not sure why we had stopped off at the stadium. Norrie, Mariana and Valeria, who had come with us, piled back into the car and we headed out to Holguin for the last night of dance and song. A fun and light-hearted evening with their hands stuffed deep in their pockets, while mine were emptying as I paid for all that was required to allow the evening to be successful.

Driving to the airport early the next day, he surprised me by saying that he needed to go to the immigration office in Santiago de Cuba, to get his papers renewed and needed 360 pesos. Could I help him with this?

'I don't have enough cash on me. I have only 260 pesos. What are these immigration papers?'

'OK, that's OK too, no problem. I will ask another friend to help me with the balance. I can go today to the immigration office and the bus leaves in about 30 minutes.'

Arriving in Holguin, we stopped at the bus station to let him out and I took over the driver's seat back to the airport. He jumped out, clutching the pesos, said a hasty goodbye with a kiss, and crossed the road to the bus station, not looking back.

I drove slowly in the direction of the airport, slightly nervous that I would miss the turning, lose my way, and not arrive in time for my departure.

I made it and returned the car to the rental company. The gleaming Peugeot was no longer gleaming. The back seats were covered in spotted-red dust, with circles of humidity imprinted on the fabric seats. The passenger left rear side was dented and the floor of the car was covered in road debris and grit. I felt embarrassed returning the car in that condition. The rental guy came out of his office and was visibly shocked to see the state of the car and when I told him it had a dent, he rolled his eyes heavenwards.

'Why did you not phone me when this happened?'

'It happened a couple of days ago.'

'But the car hire terms say you must phone, and here on the paper is the phone number. Now you will have to pay the excess as per the terms of the car rental agreement.'

I stood forlorn and thoroughly dejected as I followed him back inside his hot cabin of an office.

Sitting across from him, with the room in shadows, and a fan hanging rockily from the ceiling. He said he would see what he could do to help. He picked up his phone and spoke rapidly.

'Wait thirty minutes, as the insurance assessor is coming to look at the damage to the car.'

I waited, feeling that it was a bad end to that rather strange holiday experience. A tall, rather lanky light-skinned Cuban entered and sat opposite me. He took out papers from a black synthetic-leather zipped briefcase, laid them out in front of him, took out his thin ballpoint pen, selected the relevant form and filled in the details.

The car rental guy whispered in my ear, in English, that maybe I could give the insurance assessor some money and he would settle everything. I asked how much, and he replied, 'About 40 pesos.'

At the end of the form-filling, I slid the pesos across the desk to the insurance assessor who took it without looking at me and the car rental voice said, 'OK, all OK now. No problem, all sorted.'

I thanked them both, got up and left the dark stifling office. I went out into the blinding sun, closing my eyes at the same time and then turned to glance back, one last time at that bright shiny red Peugeot, which at the beginning of the holiday had symbolised so much, but at the end …?

Once inside the terminal and through immigration, I called him but all I got was a persistent ringing tone.

# 25

Those piercing blue eyes stared at me intensely as we sat in Café Nero, sipping our espressos.

'So, do you remember our conversation before you left for Cuba a couple of weeks ago? Did you find what you were looking for?'

His eyes were challenging, with a hint of laughter.

Sometimes my son was just so irritating and acted like an investigative journalist, probe, probe, probe.

'It's only been a week since my return, and I am processing what happened out there. I loved returning to that island, as I knew I would, and would like to spend more time out there. That's nothing to do with the man I met. I don't see a future with him, and I'm not looking for that type of future, but I am aware of our comparative wealth to the people there and feel I would like to help in some way.'

'What sort of help are you talking about? Not financial, I hope. You have family here.'

'Yes, and my family are old enough to take care of themselves, are they not? Anyway, I had a thought to buy a small house out there, which could maybe be a holiday let, and it would be easy to market initially among my circle of friends. It would cost about £3000.'

'Hang on. I know that foreigners need a local to be able to do that and it must be in their name. That would mean …'

He let the rest of the sentence hang in the air, letting out a sigh of exasperation.

'It's only a thought. Don't you remember all the many ideas we have chatted about? Moving away from here, finding a different lifestyle, even for you. You want to live in a seaside town, a place for retirees, your continuing mantra …'

My mobile rang, it was him. For a moment, I ignored the call. Then a text message appeared.

'Gina, hola, como estas? Please could you top up the credit on my phone so I can speak to you? Te quiero. xxxxx'

That was something I had done a couple of times, via Cubacel, when we were together.

I found myself becoming secretive with my family. I didn't want them to know that I had already decided to buy the little house next door to Silvana, or that I had also decided to buy an old American car for him to start a taxi business so that there would be an income for him and transport for me on my return, as well as a base to stay.

This return from Cuba was different. I felt an urgency, as though my time was running out but based on what reasoning? What a mess. I found myself to be the most contradictory person I would ever want to meet.

While working, I researched how to get the money for the car to Cuba. There were not many banks that would transfer money, and my own bank National Westminster tried and failed.

Eventually, I found Havana International Bank, which transferred funds in a couple of days. It was the only bank which could do this and is now called the Havin Bank. I used it on a few other occasions as, later when the car had been bought, there were urgent requests for money for car repairs.

When I made the first transfer payment for the car, a 1956 blue and white Chevrolet, the index finger of my right hand hovered over the send button for at least ten minutes. I was apprehensive, putting my trust in God and him that I was doing the right thing. I knew that the car would be in his name, and I would have no recourse on anything if it all went wrong. £19,500 was a lot of my money going to an unknown person. I was a risk taker. It was a part of my life for a long time so, with trepidation, excitement, and a new adventure opening, I pressed the send button.

Of course, before sending the money, who would receive it, as he had no bank account? I received an email from a man called Domaso who, it turned out, was the husband of a good friend of his who lived in Matanzas. He politely introduced himself saying that he wanted to help Alejandro to buy this car and that I could use his account as he was a businessman. He ran a business helping people invest in Cuba as well as selling solar panels to Angola. Well, all that information was irrelevant right now.

Three days later, I received an email from Domaso saying that the funds had arrived, he had taken out the money and given it to Alejandro. There followed a phone call from him excitedly saying that he had received the money and he sent me a copy of the car paperwork.

So, my trust was being rebuilt in him. Photos were sent of this 1956 Chevrolet and, for whatever insane reason, I was excited and sent a picture of it to one of my cousins who had also visited Cuba and loved American vintage cars. He could not believe that I had bought a car out there.

April passed, with lots of phone calls, and top-up requests ensued. There were lots of midnight phone calls of 'Te quiero, I love you,' whispered down those long cables of connection.

'When will you return? The car is wonderful.'

'Are you driving it as a taxi?'

'No, not yet, but soon.'

'Is there a problem?'

'No, and yes, small problems with the engine, it's old but all OK.'

April tumbled into May, and I was restless to return, to see him, to see the car, to drive it through the Cuban countryside, along the green hills, down to the blue surf, to drink mojitos and dance.

I returned at the end of May. He was at the airport but not with the Chevrolet. He looked less happy to see me and said I would need to hire a car.

'What happened to the Chevrolet?'

'Many small problems, Gina, and I have no money to repair it to get it to work.'

'What sort of problems?'

To my regret, I wish I had paid attention to the inner mysteries of a car. I had basic knowledge. This was an old car, probably held together with bits and pieces of hope and borrowed parts to keep it on the road.

'It needs an alternator, tyres, headlight bulbs, and windscreen wipers are old and not working. I cannot drive at night because the police will stop me and make me pay money.'

'Did you not check all this before you bought it and handed over the money?'

'Yes, my friend Tajo and I, he knows much about cars, checked all before I pay money to the guy.'

I looked at him, with his brow furrowed, nose wrinkled, mouth turned down, miserable.

'OK, let's hire a car.'

I was there for just over one week at that time, arriving on a Tuesday and returning the following Thursday, but it was one of the worst trips and I would never understand why I continued to return.

# 26

From the airport, we drove out to a place which I vaguely recognised as where we had first met his uncle, Roberto, on my return visit in March. I was informed that we were going to see the Chevrolet. I felt a quiet excitement at the thought that it existed.

We left the main road, up a narrow winding stony track, down narrow paths lined with palm trees and others I did not recognise, and we drove through a small metal gate towards a wreck of a barn in the middle of an abandoned clearing. Drawing up at the side of the barn, we saw the Chevrolet. That was the first time I had seen it, other than in a photo. I was surprised at my lack of excitement, after all the build-up to seeing it and the thought of driving it.

Three young men sat in worn-out deck chairs, which had a leg broken here and there, and part resting on the earth amid dry dead grass. The few trees around were languishing with half-broken stemmed leaves, hanging dry, in the late afternoon heat. They continued to sit, their hands greasy, holding an odd wrench or two, overalls blackened with streaks of grease, and baseball caps turned front to back.

Their greeting to Alex was quiet and I was introduced to them, one of them being his friend, Tajo.

I asked if the car was working, as its paintwork looked well cared for. He said there were a few little problems which his friends were fixing, and it would be ready for us to drive very soon. I did a quick mental memory recall of our earlier conversation at the airport.

After a few minutes, we left. I turned, just before getting into the car, and looked at the scene before me. It reminded me of a movie I had seen years ago called "Deliverance" which was set in the Appalachian Mountains in America. Not too sure why, but there was a feeling of these young men waiting for deliverance, while sitting under the sun, with wisps of dried grass all around, the hum of insects, little work, little money, family and friends meshed together, fixing broken cars innumerable times, and fixing them over again.

At the beginning of that trip, I told him that I did not want to spend time with his family as I did back in March, once or twice but that was all. I asked him if we could revisit Havana, the beach and the national park in Corinthia.

The first couple of days were relaxed.

I was quite happy to visit Silvana, where we hugged on meeting with genuine affection. We chatted and drank a hot black coffee, then I went with him to the next-door neighbour, whose wife and daughter were in the kitchen.

I gave her the £3000 for the house and asked Alex when I would see the sale papers. He replied by saying that the owner would get them signed with a lawyer in the next day or two. I looked around at the small house, which could become a pretty and comfortable place to stay.

Leaving the family to their various daily chores, we went back to Casa Caraolina, dropped off my luggage, and drove to collect Valeria and one of her friends, Theresa, a gentle-faced, pale-skinned Cuban with a long black plait hanging down her back.

We bought food from a local store for a picnic and drove down to the beach at Corinthia, where we three girls enjoyed the isolation and seclusion of the beach. Swimming from one end of the bay to the other, generally being silly, splashing each other and talking quietly in halting English and Cubano, amid much laughter over a misunderstanding. Valeria had put extensions in her hair, looking very much like Medusa, with her hair piled high on her head. Her smile had become affectionate, her dark eyes brighter and teeth even whiter as her skin darkened in the searing hot May sun. Theresa was like a Mariposa flower with the sea reflecting off her alabaster skin. I had a feeling that, although the beach was so accessible to them, they rarely visited it.

He sat on the soft sand, dressed totally in yellow, as the Red-Hot Poker flower, drawing letters in the sand with a seashell, still refusing to swim. I remembered taking a photo, his face cast downwards, a small smile curling his lips, looking like a child.

We had brought some white rum and he climbed up one of the palm trees, knocking off a coconut which landed with a thud in the soft sand and then rolled steadily down to the beach. Theresa ran, screaming with laughter, to catch it before it rolled into the lapping waves. Alex took it from her and expertly cracked it on a sharp pointed rock, splitting it and pouring rum into each half.

The next day, he organised a family picnic, with eight of us squeezing into the five-seater car, with piles of bananas and pieces of chicken. More rum and, this time, a bottle of whiskey for me as they had discovered I liked whiskey. This was all bought at a local convenience store; cash having been given to him before we had set off in the morning. We seemed to have giggled and laughed the whole way down to a bubbling river which flowed under a small bridge.

We parked the car, carried the food along the grey sandy-coloured river beach and sheltered under one side of the bridge. Papa collected firewood and made a huge roaring fire. Silvana sliced the bananas and Norrie boiled the chicken pieces over the fire until they were soft enough to then fry. Those chickens were tough and needed to be softened before frying.

Valeria and I waded into the rushing cold water of the river, our breath catching in our throats, and our bodies numbed for a few minutes. As we sat, semi-submerged on underwater rocks, chatting in broken English, so desperate to talk and share, young Raul walked along the riverbank with a glass half-full of golden whiskey. He waded into the water to where I sat and handed it to me. I looked up into his large limpid brown eyes, softly shadowed by his long dark lashes, while his golden-brown hair, with a hint of curl, glistened in the sun. The cooling water rushed softly over my thighs and stomach. Along came Norrie with my camera and he began to video us, while Valeria shouted, objecting to being filmed. Her shrieks were ignored. Although fiercely hot, sitting in the cold river water, hot skin cooling, this was just the right place to be. A balminess swept over us and, once again, that wonderful afternoon lethargy descended.

The world was just as it should be. Our group, so disparate, was as it should be.

My camera was stolen on my return home. A great pity as it had recorded one of the happiest times of my sojourns in Cuba.

Silvana's lightly booming voice called us over. We rose a bit unsteadily, walking over the slippery underwater rocks, and gingerly climbing up the sides of the river. Dripping wet, we sat on the pebbly sand under the bridge, watching the chicken and bananas being fried, with reggaeton softly playing from an old radio, and the occasional loud laugh from Silvana.

The food was delicious, their company warm and indulgent, and it was a perfect family picnic. Another opportunity for me to get under the skin of Cuba. I sat quietly, looking at each of their faces.

How many times had I sat, in this way, intrigued by my family's mixed heritage and at the myriad results of their coupling and bonding?

Dear Silvana, with her big round face, dark skin shining with light perspiration from the heat of the fire, her eyes bright, straight black wig caught in a white plastic clip at the back of her head, shorts too tight for her ample hips (she so loved wearing shorts), and generosity oozing from every pore of her body. She's my kind of woman, a warrior who could mow down all adversity with a big laugh and a backpack full of resolution to keep moving forward and never look back.

Papa, sitting with his legs drawn up to his chest, his bony hands clutching his knees and holding a full glass of white rum, caught between his bony fingers (I remember the bloody knife in his hand), big toothy smile, the whites of his eyes bloodshot, and ebony skin stretched tightly over his bony skeletal face. His smile showed kindness, curling around his lips, with a giggle escaping his throat. During an earlier conversation, he had told me that he was of Portuguese descent, hence his surname Rodriguez. I guessed this was from the old plantation days when former slave plantation workers would have taken their master's surname. My mother's family surname is Silva (of the woods), a true Portuguese name from the traders who plied the coast of Goa a few hundred years ago. My mother was of a swarthy complexion but with Aryan features, while Papa was of a defined African ancestral origin.

Norrie, sitting next to his uncle with their bodies touching in familial friendship, had bright eyes of shiny pools of light, and he still had my camera in his hand as he clicked away. The sort of man to whom friendship meant a great deal but, at the same time, he always had an air of caution surrounding him like a halo.

Valeria sat next to me, and the skin on her arms was still a little damp, as she gently leaned into me. With droplets of water curling in between the coils of her Medusa-like extension plaits, tied on the top of her head, her profile looked like Nefertiti. I felt the sharing of a bond. I often sensed that she carried a sadness. Maybe it was the gentle smile that played around her mouth and the corners of her eyes that whispered to me a secret she kept close.

Raul, wandered around, kicking the sandy dust with his bare feet, toenails ingrained with dirt from always walking around barefoot. Should he not have been playing with friends rather than being here?

And Alejandro, for once, sitting with us in a circle around the fire. His face was relaxed and gentle. His eyes smiling, legs crossed, feet bare, with his papa talking to him quietly and, every so often, he cast his eyes to the ground, with an amused laugh emanating from him.

Of the little I knew of him, that was the first time since we met that I saw, on his face, the look that had attracted me to him. It was the look of a man, with the vulnerability of a boy, which had touched my broken heart.

Our day ended with the whole family dancing late into the night in a small club in the back streets of Santa Rita. He danced with his sister most of the night. I decided that it was not important enough for me to get upset about.

The next morning, I woke up to find myself alone in the room. It was around 7 am. I pulled on jeans and a t-shirt and walked along the darkened corridor of the house, bedroom doors slightly ajar, and the family still sleeping.

I opened the front door, and the car was gone. I continuously called him till about 10 am.

'Where are you?'

'I'm in Santiago de Cuba. I had to return to the Immigration Department to get my papers. You remember that you gave me 260 pesos last time and now the papers are ready.'

'You could have asked me to go with you, as you know I would like to have visited Santiago.'

'Sorry, you were sleeping. I tell you to call my sister. I told her to come if you call and stay with you. Sorry, little credit.'

He hung up.

I sat down on the bed.

Stay with me, what does that mean? I did not want to spend the day with his sister.

The heat rose, and my temper rose. I lay back in the bed, in a room which I truly hated, my inner body drawing itself up in a coil like a snake and I waited the whole day for him to return.

That casa had an unusual layout, with a makeshift bathroom on one side of the bedroom, with a large veranda on the other side. The bathroom was enclosed by a glass panel and the toilet seat was visible to all occupants. This made using it very uncomfortable for me with its lack of privacy. When I mentioned it on our arrival, he said there were no other rooms available at that time.

I had no transport to get out of the area and find my way back to the beach. I walked out on to the covered verandah and sat on the rocking chair, reading my Kindle, a story by Andrew Marr (A History of the World).

I rocked back and forth, back, and forth, getting hungry and angry, and knew that I was on a short fuse. There was nowhere to go in this place without my transport. I attempted to lift my mood. I jumped out of the rocking chair, grabbed my straw hat, camera and purse, and stepped out of the house, breathing in the humidity, and I was soaked within a few minutes.

There was a vegetable and poultry market down one of the side streets. Middle-aged and elderly folk wandered up and down with cloth shopping bags, some pushing worn-out cycles. Vegetables and fruit were limited in their variety of choice and quantity. Onions, potatoes, strings of garlic, always strings of garlic, hanging off one side of a stall or cycle, and fruit lying in small piles in wooden carts which were drained of their original colour.

The clacking of live chickens in mesh baskets pierced the fetid heat of the day, while some hung upside-down, by tied feet, from cycle handlebars, dust forever hanging in the air and covering leaves on trees. It was an arid heat, and relentless.

Despite wearing oversized black sunglasses, as well as my wide-brimmed sun hat, I felt my forehead in a deep crease, my eyes screwed up small. How can there be so much heat in the middle of the day? "Only mad dogs and Englishmen go out in the midday sun." I decided that I was that mad dog, becoming madder as the heat intensified.

There were no small cafés or cool drink stalls around that street. I remembered seeing a couple more towards the middle of the town, so I took a 'bici' ride, only to find one closed until 3 pm and the other without ice to make cool drinks. I was in rural Cuba, totally off the tourist grid; the place where ordinary Cubans, lived, worked, partied, and died.

I began drifting and wandering in my mind. I was the only European woman in that place, so I did stand out and wondered what the locals made of me, strolling around, seemingly aimless. I felt that I had entered an old American western movie, walking along the side of the only main road in town. Wooden clap-trap buildings on each side, with the sound of the clip-clop of horses' hooves, the drone of the local bus, a hail of laughter, and a chittering of chatter. The locals' large straw hats, similar to mine, like the cowboy hats of old, pulled low keeping off the piercing sun. Old, sun-wrinkled, wizened men sat on the bare-stripped wooden floor of a building's patio, with their backs resting against peeling painted rails, eyes half-closed, and heads nodding and bobbing.

I removed myself from that scene and remember thinking that I had walked into an old painting hanging on the wall of a public salon, a street scene named "Forgotten in time." The colours faded of their first blush of vibrancy, gradually lustreless as the memories of that place, once bright and alive, sunk back into a long-ago time.

I wandered back to my casa, to the relief of the cool of the room, and resumed rocking in my chair on the verandah, pretending to myself to read. Early evening approached and I saw, once again, long shafts of mellowing sunlight streaking across the floor.

I heard the door open and looked up from my Kindle as he stood, relaxed in the doorway, dressed in lilac, the clothes I had paid for in Varadero on a previous trip. He looked at my face and asked if I was OK. I found it hard to find my voice and quietly said, 'Don't you ever do that again. Taking my car without telling me and leaving me stranded in a place I do not know and where there is nowhere to go. You are not insured to drive that car, nor are you legally allowed to drive it.'

'Gina, why angry? I told you this morning to call my sister, she would come to you.'

'I did not want your sister. I saw your family yesterday, and today I have spent the whole day on my own.'

I felt angry and drained and then realised that it was all my fault.

My fault for being here a second time with him, for some romantic, ridiculous reason; my vanity. I was beginning to see myself as ridiculous. The older woman, lucky or not, who did not look her age, believed that she would find something in coming here.

What did I know of Cuban men, their culture, their attitude towards women, their needs, and their desires? I had been loyal to two men in my life with whom I had had long relationships, so my physical and emotional experiences with a variety of men were minimal.

I came here, finding many of the men undesirable, my aim was more to find a new life and lifestyle, to start again far away from my past.

So, what had drawn me to this man on my first trip? Was it his wide-eyed smile, that sidelong glance, his gentle demeanour as he stood in front of me in Casa de la Musica, or that first salsa dance and his gentle hold of me? Or was it the memory of my ex telling me that I was now too old for him, and the hurt and anger needled itself so deep in my mind, that I was playing this out to prove that I was not yet too old to captivate a man.

Was I being honest with myself? Did it matter?

Whatever it was, I had stepped into a bed of curled vipers waiting to fully strike. In a few months, they had begun to bite. The early onset of madness, with its red line of venom, gradually crept along to my maddened senses.

It was a heady mixture of all that and my past, draped around my shoulders like a heavy fur mantle.

And yet, there was that age-old animal magnetism, that age-old vanity that pulls and tugs, and beckons and challenges that narcissistic desire to believe one's reflection. It floods the mind and closes it to any dangers of self-preservation. The poisoning and drowning begin slowly, slowly down that hallucinogenic helter-skelter.

I heard his muffled voice in the background as I surfaced to the heat of the early evening.

'Vale, vamos a Habana ahora.'

'Que, ahora?'

'Si, you drive me crazy.'


Picking up an overnight bag, changing my dress to my favourite white and pink floral 1950s-style halter neck dress and my espadrilles, we left in silence, travelling along the motorway as the dusk deepened and the few streetlights began to flicker through the small towns, crossing a railway line, with the sound of a train whistling in the distance. Flashbacks to my early childhood, walking along coal-dust tracks with my mother and brother, hearing that same sound, wondering if it would be our father's train coming home.


Approaching Las Tunas, we had to stop as there had been an accident on the outskirts of town. A 'bici' and an old Lada were badly damaged, and two women sat in the back seat of the Lada, both with head wounds. A crowd had gathered around, assisting the drivers. We stopped and he jumped out and walked quickly to the car, opening the back door. He helped them both out and guided them to the rear of our car. We drove quickly to the local hospital with a large red sign "Hospital General Dr Ernesto Guevara de la Sarna", and we helped the women up the stairs to A & E. We waited in the yellowed corridor, while their wounds were dressed. There was an air of quiet efficiency all around, nurses in crisp white uniforms, cleaning staff in pale green overalls, and doctors in their usual white coats with stethoscopes hanging around their necks.

They were both still in shock but able to walk back into the corridor. He chatted with them, making sure they were OK, and lent them his phone to call family or friends.

We left them there, continuing our journey as it would take us a further six hours to get to Havana.

'We stay in Camaguey. I am tired and feel sick. In the morning we take some family with us to Havana, OK? In Havana, I go to meet my friend Vicente, he is important policeman in traffic department. I must collect a picture from his house to take back to give to my mother.'

In the morning, we picked up three family members, his brother Karl's wife, her son Alfonso, and his cousin, Celestina. They were all very excited to see him again and there was non-stop chatter all the way to Havana, with shrieking music playing, windows down, and a carnival atmosphere. Those were the occasions when he could not stop talking. Hard to ignore it, best to become a part of the mood. It was infectious, uplifting, and raw.

By mid-afternoon, we dropped off the cousins on the outskirts of Havana, around an estate of high-rise flats. The weather had changed, the rains had become torrential, and the streets were flooded, almost ankle-deep, judging by those caught out in it. The skies above the Malecon were darkly thunderous, the road along the seafront awash with high-running water. The windscreen wipers struggled as the heavy rainfall drowned the windscreen, straining to clear the screen and visibility was a fog.

And just as quickly as it started, it subsided. The sun blazed out of the clouds, with steam rising from the streets and caught in the middle, was an overpowering humidity. The jungle of his garden had returned, the steam rising like snakes uncoiling.

We arrived outside the police station, one of many but, which one we were at, I did not know. He parked outside and went through a metal-gated fence up to the station. I got out and walked along the street that resembled a few I had seen in small corners of Seville. Remnants of old Spanish townhouses, dark leafy-green canopy trees lined the surrounding streets and overhanging, the small mariposa bushes lay beneath them, a soft trail of their perfume in the stewing air.

I stood for a moment opposite a small fuel station, noticing some of the men staring vacantly at me. Entering a small general store, I bought an ice-cold orange Fanta. He must have been gone for over 30 minutes. Standing by the car, drinking my Fanta, I saw him returning slowly with his friend who he introduced me to as Vicente. A slender light-skinned man, with brown eyes and hair and an easy smile. He greeted me as though we were old friends and kissed me on both cheeks, then jumped into the back of the car. We drove back out of Havana to the same estate of high-rise apartment blocks.

By then, it was early evening and we had not eaten since around 8 am. Pulling up by the corner of a road, a group of men and women, some lounging on their cycles, stood by a makeshift wooden food stall, hands outstretched for what looked like pulled pork sandwiches, a favourite throughout Cuba. The memory and smell of that little pig, roasting over the spit on my first return visit to his family home, lingered in my nose and heart. A small golden-brown creature was being turned on a mechanical spit by the side of the food stall. Alex looked at me enquiringly, but I declined, preferring the now-warming Fanta in my hand. Both men jumped out and disappeared into the small crowd around the stall.

They returned, one arm around the other's shoulders, pulled pork sandwiches in the other. We drove to Vicente's apartment. He jumped out, going in alone, and a few minutes later came out with a long brown paper roll, about one metre long, which was put into the boot. I had no idea what it was.

Farewells were long hugs and fist punches.

Returning to central Havana, by then the sun beginning to dip, the skies stormy blue, shards of illuminating light streaking the sky, the roads and streets were glistening wet, small spirals of steam rising into the air, with only a few people around.

'I want to go to Cuba Street for a few minutes, can you take me there?'

'Porque?'

He often dropped back into Spanish, and I think he got tired of speaking in English as he was not fluent.

'I want to visit someone I met on my first trip; please pick me up in about 30 minutes.'

The tarot card lady, Beatriz (I remembered her name from my first trip), lived on the corner of Cuba street, that same small white house with its iron-railed door which Ella and I had visited. Pressing the bell, I pushed open the gate, entered, and walked past two black dolls in long white lace dresses, hanging on the narrow corridor walls. I was greeted like an old friend as I sat down at that same small table. Her slender brown hands began to lay out the cards, one at a time in that tarot sequence. Neither of us spoke for some time.

She whispered softly, 'You will find love, but not yet. Be careful not to give him any money. He not bad, but not good. He is kind and wants love. You must be careful. You do not know of this kind, be careful. One day, good love come, but not yet. You, strong woman but sad.'

She apologised for her poor English.

As we both stood, I'd forgotten how tiny she was, like a fragile flower, like one of her dolls. Streaks of grey showed through her lightly waving black hair, her body was narrow, candle-thin, but shapely. Her white sleeveless dress hugged her body, flip-flops on her feet, bracelets on both hands, hanging loosely over her wrists, a little Mariposa flower. She smiled and her eyes suddenly sparkled.

I held the fear of a groan, as my mind raced with the amount of money I had already parted with.

She looked up at me and took my hands in hers and gently squeezed them, walking with me to her front door and pointing to the two dolls hanging on the wall by the entrance. Her brother, whom I had also met on our first trip and who spoke excellent English, stood at the front gate. We chatted about the dolls and the religious origins of Haiti; I was aware of the religious Vodou culture brought by the French refugees of Haiti and their coteries of slaves to Cuba after the Haitian Revolution. The slaves helped to build the coffee plantations in Cuba and, with Haiti's sugar market being abandoned after their revolution, gave rise to the success of Cuba's sugar production.

Vodou brings up so many images. I must have a superstitious side to my nature for, as I stood there, looking at the dolls, I remembered putting 20 pesos in the lap of Theresa, the doll that sat at the back of that house. Theresa, a doll, offered her money in exchange for giving or finding love.

I left, my mind quiet and pensive, with my head bowed and, as I looked up, I saw him standing against the red brick of an old building, one leg bent and propped against the wall, with his hands in his trouser pockets. He looked at me and smiled and, walking over to him, I kissed him on the cheek.

'Thank you.'

'OK, we go now and collect Norrie.'

'What? He is in Havana? When did he get here?'

'This morning, he took the night bus from Holguin, and he come back with us today.'

The distances people travel around Cuba by bus are quite phenomenal. It's almost like just hopping into a car and whizzing around like the skittles of a child's game.

We saw him, standing at the foot of the steps of El Capitolio (National Capitol Building) on the Paseo del Prado, which resembles the Capitol in Washington DC. The sunlit sky, melting behind its dome, with its diffused rays of light creating waves of sunsetting colours. He waited, darkly outlined against the stark white of the building, holding an enormous brown box, almost as tall as him.

Alex grinned, 'Present from his brother in Miami. He collects from a friend here and we take him home with us.'

I was so pleased, as Norrie was light-hearted company, and the journey back would be full of conversation and easy laughter.

We hugged each other tightly and he crawled into the back of the car, pulling in the large box which almost hid him from view. This was not a convertible and I thought of the 1000-odd kilometres he would be sitting in the back, through the night. The box contained a large loudspeaker, those desired by the Cubans. More loud music back at their house. Silvana would be so pleased, as she was such a party person.

Norrie must have been completely cramped but he retained his good humour throughout the journey to Levisa. We stopped a couple of times at small restaurants down little side streets in small backwater towns, paying 10 pesos for the three of us.

At one service station, I was asked to buy windscreen wipers, lightbulbs for the front and back of the Chevrolet, oil, car wax, and two new tyres, which were all bundled into the boot of the car. There were no alternators and he said we would have to go to Holguin later the next day to get a cheap one.

Many cold beers were drunk through the night journey and, as the dawn gradually approached, we drove straight to another area, near Levisa. A place I would get to know later, in circumstances that the tarot lady did not foresee.

Alex jumped out of the car without a word, opened the boot and with the paper roll, ran up the garden path to a new-looking wooden house.

I got out and stretched my legs, and Norrie, who had crawled out of the back, his back a 'C' shape, stood next to me.

'It's a photo of his wedding which he wants to give to his mama to hang in her house.'

So many random events seemed to be happening. Nothing seemed to be flowing or fitting together. My curiosity piqued. I looked at him, but he averted his face away, looking straight ahead.

I turned on my mobile and went onto Facebook, only for a few minutes. The cost of the internet there was exorbitant, and I had to be quick.

I scrolled through his page which had a few posts and there, recently posted, was a photo of him in a wedding suit, holding the hand of a blond-haired girl. I stood looking at the photo. He looked so happy but seemed to be pulling her by the hand as she was slightly behind him.

I nudged Norrie, who looked down and whispered, 'Elena. She is Swiss. He married her two years ago, in Cuba, here in Levisa, but now they are divorced, before he came back from Switzerland.'

'So that rolled-up picture is of their wedding day? Why does he want to give it to his mother now? And which mother, Norrie?'

He returned then and dropped Norrie off in Santa Rita, the house still in sleep.

I didn't feel anything. A little surprised, but more surprised by the way I had found out. Not once had he suggested that he had been married in Switzerland, but through the clothes and jewellery that he wore in his photos on the FB page, I began to understand how he could have afforded them.

Later, after we had slept and had lunch, we were driving back to Holguin to buy an alternator when I mentioned that I had seen a photo of his wedding day on Facebook. The widest grin crossed his face and then he said that he had just given his mother a photo of his wedding. He then said that if he ever got married again, it would be in Havana. There was a castle on a hill which was a beautiful place for a wedding.

'Are you OK I was married?'

'Of course, why did it end? She looked your age, and you could have lived in Switzerland.'

A dark shadow enveloped his face, and he remained silent for the remainder of the journey.

We bought a second-hand alternator from a local market. I stood outside a fenced area of what looked like a disused basketball pitch. Groups of young men sat huddled together around bits and pieces of car parts and he went from group to group, bending, picking up various alternators, until he found the one, he needed. He came back out asking me for 50 pesos. I watched him as he returned, stuffing some money into his pocket, and then handing over some to a dealer. Well, the cost of the alternator was a lot less. Some for me, some for you.

'OK, now we fix the Chevrolet and tomorrow we go for a drive.'

'Alex, the £3000 I gave to the owner of the house, when will I see the paperwork? I know, for now, it will not be in my name, but I would like to see the sale documents.'

'You don't trust me?'

'It's a lot of money I have now given you, for the house, for the car, for all the repairs and spare parts for the car. I want to see you make the taxi work profitable, so you have money to live.'

'Gina, I would like to go to England. Maybe I will apply for a visa next time in Havana at British Embassy. I can come to stay with you and get work in England.'

My stomach turned over with a tremor.

What now, now this? What was the purpose of buying the car and the house? I realised that the snakes were unfurling and curling around me, lightly creeping up my legs, stroking them. I didn't feel overanxious, just cautious and observing the events as they continued to unfold.

# 27

Two days before I returned home, another hot day arose. A glorious still blue sky with a dry Sahara wind blowing gustily. The Chevrolet stood outside the casa. Long-finned, summer-blue and cream paintwork washed and polished. Tajo stood against the passenger door, a slight smile across his lips but not his eyes.

'Vale, vamos. We go for a ride as promised. Come, Gina, you want to drive?'

I sat behind the wheel. Yay, "Grease" flashed through my mind, with that wonderful car chase along the river basin between Danny and Leo. I looked at the gear stick, on the side of the steering wheel, and never having driven that type of car, declined laughingly, and let him take over.

Tajo stood on the pavement. I caught his face in the wing mirror, looking at the car as we sped away from him. I had a sense that, although he and Alex were good friends, he had stronger feelings than just good friends. It was only a sense.

But nothing was going to daunt my mood that day.

We drove along towards nowhere in particular, meandering through the countryside, just enjoying the morning sun, the wind rushing in through the open windows, jeep taxis tooting as we went by, with shouts and laughter from his friends. Windows down, music blaring, impossible to talk above the music, companionable silence as he took my hand in his, peace in our world for those moments.

He stopped and there, on the side of the road, stood two young women. They jumped into the back, Celestina, and her friend Rosario. They had both arrived back on the night bus from Havana to Holguin and I had no idea how they got back from Holguin, but all seemed to traverse this terrain as though in time machines. Distance meant nothing to them. Amid laughter and constant chatter, we drove them to a spot about 20 km down the road. I had no idea where we were. They jumped out and, several kilometres later, we stopped again to pick up his uncle Roberto and his family, who needed a lift to Papa Luis's so, turning the car around, we headed back to his papa's house, by now mid-afternoon.

Great surprise and compliments were bestowed on the car. Papa sat behind the wheel, his face brimming as though his smiles would fall off the edge of his face, laughter lines deeply creased, and little Raul, barefoot again, hopping into the back of the car, putting his hands behind his head, lounging feet up on the back of the front seat. A large bulbous water tank on the back of a long wooden barrow, pulled by a water buffalo, came trundling along the rutted path behind us. Silvana appeared from a neighbour's house with a bucket in her hand and filled it up from the water tank. This was almost like a game of "Pop-up".

I loved their all-embracing and simple enjoyment. This car, in this moment, seemed to pull them together in a family moment of excitement of a new and different acquisition, a symbol of a bound past. A stranger had come into their lives and new possibilities could happen for them.

That afternoon, in the small, darkened living room of Papa and Laura's home, Alex and Norrie danced salsa while I stood outside, looking through a window taking a video, capturing a scene, a memory of 'I want to dance salsa like Michael Fong' as, for over five minutes captured on video, they were both on stage and in a happy place. They moved with grace and ease. This was Cuba, this was country life, family life, and moments to be treasured. The afternoon wove its way into the evening, when neighbours and Valeria descended on the small hearth, all dancing and weaving like musical snakes to whatever music was on the CD player.

Again, I videoed those dance scenes as they sang loudly, mostly out of tune, but bubbling with laughter. While the dancing was danced, in the front of the house, a small table had been set up under a canopied patio in the front and the men played cards, with bubbles dripping down the sides of cold beer bottles onto the table, lightly mixing with resting sweating elbows. The men's soft chatter and laughter, a gentle simmering and bubbling of simple and contented country life.

And there amidst the countryfolk, Che Guevara joined them for a game of cards, tattooed on the muscled upper arm of one of the neighbours.

A couple of months later, I had a conversation with my salsa teacher during a lesson and, while talking about Cuba and Alex, he said to me, 'You know that you are now a family asset, and they will not let you go when you are in Cuba.'

He said it with a smile. I listened with a half-smile on my face and an insinuation that, to this day, seems to be true even across the distance of time and country.

I had the pleasure of two days of driving around in the Chevrolet. My cousin, Ella, would have loved to have been there with me. I felt I had begun to see many new parts of the Cuban way of living, a living which I would be happy to be a part of if I had enough clairvoyance of its outcome.

On the day of leaving, as we drove through Mayari, we drove down a small lane past old wooden houses, framed by gardens, and in one drive, stood the Chevrolet. We slowed to a stop.

'What's happened? Que pasa? What is the car doing here?'

'This is the house of a mechanic friend of mine, he is fixing something else in the car, which is again not working.'

'I bought so many new parts for it.'

I put my hand to my forehead, rubbing my furrowed skin and knowing, somehow, that I had to stop all this. I had a sense that the car was a coverup for something else, but something I did not know, just an intimation of a feeling which was ferociously rolling around inside my head at an uncontrollable speed. Much like the circus act of the "Wall of Death", where a car starts at the bottom of a wooden pen, circling the base, gathering speed, rising higher and higher to the top until it is almost touching and shooting over the top rim of the wooden pen.

'So, this car was not a good deal, ugh? All the time, in so short a time, so many breakdowns and so much money spent. Maybe you should sell it and give me back the money and we can think of something else for you to do for work.'

'No, no, no problem. We fix the car, and I will do taxi work, as I said before. Once all fixed, it will be a good car, but you know I have no income so I cannot keep repairing the car, and my friends are good, they help me lots.'

I looked once again at the car as we slid by, the sun glinting off its old but shiny paintwork, sitting there hopeful and broken again.

He remained silent for over half the journey, looking straight ahead, despite the constant cheering and honking from jeep taxis, many of whom I now recognised as his friends.

He reached his hand over to mine, holding it.

'Don't worry, I won't sell the car. It will be fine and next time you come here to Cuba; I pick you up at the airport in this car.'

Once again, we drove to the bus station in Holguin, and exchanged seats. He stood at the edge of the pavement, bending back into the car to give me a light kiss on the cheek.

I gaily said, 'Thank you for the kiss,' at which he grinned that impish grin.

'Ciao, Gina. See you again in Cuba, Carina.'

I did not ask how he would get back but, looking through the rear-view mirror, I saw a black taxi jeep pull up beside him.

There had been little affection, long days of being on my own, my credit card in constant use, the car repairs making no difference and a sense that all the money given had not been used on the car, but it was patched up sufficiently for a few miles of driving around.

As I drove away, I had a sense that I would not return for quite a while.

# 28

Whispers in my head.
'What now?'

My head and heart were polar opposites.

Whatever common sense I had was no longer aligned with any part of my life, whether of a practical or emotional reference.

My son and his family were living with me, and I think that they had a tough time not knowing what was going on in the whirlwind of my mind. My partner of twenty-three years leaving me for a younger woman, a year before the death of my mother, left me feeling unstable without her around and rejected by his departure.

Whatever was happening, I remember feeling at times in a happy state of dream time and other times embarrassed with those feelings for a younger man and remembering his behaviour and long absences, leaving me stranded with his family in the heat, and returning breezily without explanation.

Yet the overriding memory for me was that I had fallen in love with Cuba, the country, the café music, sitting in the warm evenings outside Café Paris, and the fibres of my body soaking up every particle of life surrounding me. The country's memories of another eon are held in a time warp. A place where I wanted to return to. Maybe it was that yearning to have my mother and Jack back in my life. The missing of them was unbearable, always in my thoughts, a choke away from tears. I was out of my body and my mind with despair, longing, hurting, yearning, needing to be loved, held, my hair stroked, and my bare skin stroked to ecstasy. I felt fragile, like a blooming flower whose petals had been crushed, torn asunder, hanging on to the remnants of being a whole bloom.

Many nights, I fell asleep to the sounds of Andre Bocelli's "Besame Mucho" and the thought, 'let it all go'.

# 29

Over eight weeks had passed, and I did not feel the need to call or text him often. He too had become quiet, with the occasional text saying that the Chevrolet had broken down again and he did not know what to do with the car. He needed money to repair many problems, at least £2500. His friends could no longer help him as it needed to be fixed by a proper car mechanic since the problems were getting bigger. Could I send him the money?

I had decided not to return for a while. I knew that the money spent buying the Chevrolet and the constant repairs needed to be resolved, and quickly, so that I could make him sell the car and return the money to me.

The weather had warmed up and, although I had picked up the daily rhythm of my life of work and socialising, a heaviness weighed on me.

The summer months were passing. May, June, and then July, when holidays had begun, and the beach was crowded with out-of-towners, grabbing whatever chance of sun, sand, and pebbles they could get on our beaches. On Sundays, a mass of bodies lay prostrate across almost two miles of pebbled beach, covered with towels and bare-skinned bodies. The white and blue clouds scurried across our seaside skies, and murmurations of starlings circled and weaved around the old burnt-out pier, its iron pilings still standing deep and strong in the English Channel's basin. Tail-wagging dogs of every shape ran crazily across the ins and outs of tides, barking and laughing as they plunged headlong into rolling waves, retrieving colourful balls. I had to laugh out loud at their wonderful crazy happy behaviour.

I continued running along the front, keeping fit, keeping my sanity and my doubts under control.

With those thoughts in mind, I decided to return and booked my flight to Holguin for five days, as that trip would coincide with a swimwear trade show in Miami. I had been thinking of ways to extend the business and my swimwear cover-ups, kaftans, had been selling very well for the past two years, all made in India. I felt that I could extend into the American market, but first needed to get to know that market more thoroughly.

It was going to be a quick trip.

My family were stunned at my pending return, and I felt they had given up trying to help me be rational.

I had a choice in this. Let it all be and lose the money given for buying the car and the repairs, which totalled up to no longer a small sum, or return and find a solution to retrieving as much as possible.

I searched the net for a casa particular in Holguin, unable to remember the one we had stayed in for one night on a previous trip. I found it, texted him and gave him the name and phone number of the accommodation, as well as my usual arrival time in Holguin. I asked him to collect me in the Chevrolet as I did not want to pay for another hire car.

The plane touched down, its small wheels bouncing tremulously on the hard tarmac to the sound of tourist cheers and claps. The droning and whining of the engines reverberated in my head as I glanced out the small window and saw the bright blue sky. My eyes closed, already feeling that blast of hot air that would engulf me the second I stood at the top of the stairs of the Thomas Cook plane which had landed at Holguin Airport.

I could not bear the piercing heat in July, which made me nauseous. I automatically walked down the plane's steep metal steps, across the now familiar tarmac, through immigration, and out the glass doors of the airport terminal. I would usually head to the Ladies, change my clothes, reapply my makeup and emerge fresh and excited.

Not this time.

I was no longer that same excited woman from my first return trip.

I headed straight out through the arrival's hall. There was no sign of him standing outside. My bare arms quickly burned under the mid-afternoon sun. I waited for data roaming to connect.

I called him, feeling angry at his non-arrival.

His voice was edgy as he spoke to me, 'Gina, this is a surprise. What are you doing here? You didn't tell me you were returning so soon. I am in Cienfuegos, with my brother Karl.'

'What? I texted you to say I was coming in today and to meet me at the airport with the Chevrolet.'

'Sorry, my phone had no top-up only one hour ago, my brother Karl topped up for me.'

He knew I was angry. We arranged to meet the next morning at my casa, texting him again with my details. He said he had no money and would have to take many buses to different cities to get there. I heard his chattering; I couldn't care less!

I asked him about my car, my Chevrolet. He said it was fine but needed repairing again.

My fingers tightened around the handle of my pull-along and, dragging it in anger, almost tripped on a kerb stone as I headed to the taxi rank. Large droplets of hot humid sweat rolled down the back of my neck and legs.

A taxi took me to my pre-booked casa particular in a street in Holguin City. A twenty-minute ride along the highway, past dishevelled pink low-storey buildings, stark shapes against a barren blue sky. The scenery, once seen as charming and delightful, was now a nightmare of remorse. I sat silently on that ride, thinking of the mistakes I had made, and the money I had spent and lost. The vanity, the insanity of the whole experience, and I wondered what had happened to me during that time. The taxi driver asked in a heavy accent if it was my first time in Cuba. I ignored him. He was invading my thoughts. He looked at me in the rear-view mirror and a surge of prejudice rose within me.

It was 4 pm by the time I arrived at the casa, the sun beginning to slip down to its now familiar orange horizon, the air slightly cooler, already a breath of relief. I knocked on the kitchen door and entered, greeted by Maria, who recognised me, with a gentle look on her face as if she already knew something I did not. I told her that I would be staying for two nights as I was going on to Havana and was waiting for my "friend" to arrive the next day.

She led me to my room, brought coffee then left me alone.

I felt alone.

I barely spoke a word of Spanish, the few usual hola, como estas, gracias, por favor, café con leche, uno mas - a few simple words to get me around, as my Spanish had not improved.

Lowering myself onto the double bed, I looked down at the cement-tiled floor, the windows covered with pale buttercup-yellow satin curtains, and white towels, folded like kissing love-heart swans, were positioned in the centre of the bed reminding me of cheap honeymoon suites. I hated those swan towels, so I picked them up and flung them to the ground.

Moving automatically, hanging up my clothes in the single wardrobe to air and then, out of habit, locked the pull-along travel bag, as on that first stay there, when I had come out of the shower and found him going through my bag, looking up at me sheepishly.

And then I waited, not knowing what I was going to do until the next morning. Having been to Holguin four times. I was familiar with the sparsely populated and semi-deserted central plaza, with its arched three-storey high brick, red and cream walls screaming to be repainted and smartened. It's a provincial Cuban town, without any real cultural relics of a bygone Spanish era. Like so many Cuban towns, there were always those heavy, blocky Russian architectural buildings, Lenin's pride, utilitarian apartments, and flat-roofed, low-lying houses, with the saving grace of pastel colours, intricate metalwork balconies, and palm trees.

I suddenly grinned and felt like a travel writer recounting one of my many travelogues for the next edition of a travel magazine, which had to be "Vogue Travel".

At least I could still laugh at myself.

The fan whirred overhead and, kicking off my leopard-print ballet slippers, I curled up on the bed under the spinning fan and dozed, swimming in and out of disturbing anxieties.

Waking, I was hungry and restless, so I left the casa, caught a passing taxi, and went into town. Seeing a café on one side of the plaza, I entered. Its walls were filled with framed sketches and charcoal prints, cartoon images of famous revolutionary generals and reverent images of Che, Fidel, Raul and of course Venezuela's Chavez. I sat on a high wooden stool at the bar and had numerous coffees to kill time and keep me adrenalized.

I knew it was insane to give him more money to fix that old car, more than fifty years old. It was like trying to hang on to dated ideologies which had lost their original identity and were now held together for the sake of memories kept alive because there was no alternative.

He had taken so much money from me. Correction. I had foolishly given it to him thinking I was doing some sort of good. I had been desperate to change my life, but the one I was now experiencing was unexpected and I knew would have serious repercussions.

Early evening drifted into the early night and exhaustion forced me back to the casa. I chatted with an elderly Cuban man for over two hours. I think he was my age but looked so worn and weary that chronology was assumptive. The man spoke in a tremulous voice, maybe caused by illness or an emotional inability to express himself. A mix of the local dialect, words of indecipherable English and several nods of acknowledgement from me encouraged him to continue. I had by then drunk copious amounts of caffeine, leaving behind a very happy barista. As I slipped off the high stool, one foot on the ground, I felt a gentle hand on my shoulder and looked up into his kindly blue eyes and a whisper of 'Cuidate, take care'.

A phrase I heard repeatedly, a mantra of concern or warning.

A thin line of sun peeked through a rift in the curtain. I had fallen asleep with the phone in my hand and pressed the recall button. No reply.

I was determined to dig out the rot that had set in. My resolve to find out the truth was burning me up. My sane self told me to forget all of this, put it down to my lack of truly knowing men. I was not as smart as I thought I was and no match for the wiles and determination of others more desperate than me, who understood the art of manipulating emotional and vulnerable women, such as I had become.

I lay in bed and waited, the hand of the clock in my head moving at an excruciatingly slow pace. Maria called me for breakfast. I ate it, went back to the room, lay on the bed, and waited.

I must have drifted off to sleep. Somewhere in my crazed unconscious, I heard knocking at the door. Waking drowsily, Maria told me there had been a phone call to say that he was almost at the casa.

Early afternoon arrived, and so did he, bouncing in with a broad smile on his face showing off his brilliant white teeth. His light, brown-skinned handsome face had a gentleness to it until one looked deeply into his slightly slanting brown eyes with needle thin plucked eyebrows.

He had a Nike trainers cloth sports bag flung loosely across one shoulder. He always travelled lightly and, by now, I had learned the reason for that. He greeted me with, 'Hola, Gina, how are you?' and apologised for taking so long as he had to change many buses and taxis to get there.

I looked at him and wondered what he had done with all the money he had been given and what had happened to the Chevrolet, my car, which needed another £2500 to repair. I had wanted to drive it instead of hiring yet another car but could not unless I paid for the Chevrolet to be repaired, again.

He threw himself on the bed, with his eyes inviting me to join him. I sat down, unmoving, and he instantly fell asleep.

Sounds of clatter came from the kitchen and Maria called us for lunch.

Then the strangest series of events began to unfold. I found myself drifting off into a light drug-induced dream, subtle, as though I was being taken by the hand like a little girl and led down a pathway that all seemed very normal but around every corner lurked a puppeteer.

I looked at the scene that was playing out in front of me. Maria's ease in preparing his lunch, the phone call she received from him, their chatter as if old friends. Or was that the Cuban way? That the whole of Cuba is connected as one big family, and everyone knows everything about everybody and has secrets from "extranos".

He sat at the table, chatting easily, with her smiling or laughing. She leant towards him, laying a plate of chicken and rice, and setting a Bucanero beer in front of him. I was invited to join, sat at the table, and drank a cool mango juice as my stomach turned like an organ grinder's manipulations.

Finishing, we left, as the early evening sun softened and the heat with it. As we walked out into the courtyard, I noticed a huge black Kawasaki motorcycle parked against a wooden shed. I slowed my walk and looked quickly but carefully at it as it was unusual to see such a magnificent machine in Holguin. He walked on looking straight ahead. I also noticed the visored helmet resting on the front seat and assumed it belonged to Maria's husband.

We took a taxi back to Holguin Central and barely chatted, my tension mounting, my need-to-know churning inside me like a butter churn, my emotions like a molasses of butter. I avoided using the phrase "que pasa?" as I knew that irritated him.

I asked him about the car, his answer was that it needed a lot of money to repair it. Did I bring any money with me? As well as some extra money for his visa and lawyer's fees? I confirmed saying that it would be the last time I would give him any money for the car and, once repaired, he had to sell it. I told him that I had to be in Havana the next day as I was flying to Miami for a trade show on Friday.

Out of the blue, he suggested that we went to Havana that night, as it was more fun there and we could take the overnight bus which left at 9 pm. We would have to go then and buy the tickets. He asked again about the money, as he had to give it to a friend whom he was meeting at the bus station. He told me that the Chevrolet was at his papa's house in Levisa, which I knew was about 129 km from Holguin. At the bus station, he left me by the roadside and walked towards a red car, an old dusty Russian model, a Lada. I saw him pass the money to his friend and recognised Tajo, his surly best friend, whom I had met on earlier trips. Tajo glanced at me and then quickly averted his gaze. I stared at them both and their exchange looked furtive.

He returned, took my hand, and walked towards the ticket office where we queued for a while at the special counter for tourists, to buy our tickets. I handed him $70 for two tickets, which he took, and brought mine back and when I asked about his, he said he could not travel with me, as he was Cuban and would take the "Cubans only" bus, which would leave shortly after mine. I was doubtful about this but did not question it.

Returning to the casa, I informed Maria that I was leaving a day early but paid her for the two nights, packed my bag, bought food at a local shop for the journey and returned to the bus station. He stood with me at the bus stop, silent, until the bus departed. We did not kiss or exchange any embrace, but he told me not to worry and would meet me at the bus station in Havana, at 9 am the next day.

Travelling through the night, looking out of the window at a black sky for a long time, my body felt like a tightly wound-up spring. The sound of the engine humming gently, an occasional rattle of metal on road, the seats soft and enveloping, the lights dimly lit, seductive, embracing and the passengers mainly local Cubans. I called him once and he said he was already on the bus following behind. My bus was full of Cubans, no overseas foreign travellers.

My eyes closed, fingers knotted like a tight rope, my engorged veined hands pulsating, realising I had just been led through a forest of lies and deceit and that the Kawasaki that I had seen parked at the front of the casa was his, and my Chevrolet had been sold. Snippets of memories of information about him riding a black Kawasaki in Matanzas, started to make sense. The blatant parking of the Kawasaki in the casa forecourt was audacious. Not for a moment when I saw it did I think it was his until I sat on the bus surrounded by local Cubans and knew that I had been outmanoeuvred, outflanked, outsmarted, and duped. From the moment of my phone call to him at the airport the previous day, he had planned this duplicity. I felt like an old fool and could not bear to reveal my thoughts to my conscious self.

I must have fallen asleep, waking just as the bus pulled into Havana Bus Station, under another hot July sky.

He had put 745 kilometres between us.

I hated Havana. To me, it had become a writhing snake pit.

Getting off the bus, I looked around for him. Of course, he was not there. Again, I phoned, and he answered, asking him where he was. His wheedling reply was that he was in Camaguey, 547 kilometres from Havana, saying the bus had broken down during the night and he would have to take another and meet me the next day.

The searing morning sun, already burning the air with its added fierce humidity, made me hot, sweaty, dirty, and angry. I felt overwhelmed. The helplessness enraged me, with no idea of what to do next. The roar of buses bounded past, heat rose from the black tarmac roads, the smell of fuel crushing the air, my pull-along felt like an iron road roller and, dragging it behind, I found a waiting taxi and crawled inside its dark worn interior.

I could only think of one place I wanted to stay at and that was Hotel Beltran in Plaza Vieja, Old Havana. Once inside the cool vaulted ceilinged lobby, I could pretend to feel safe. I remembered my first time there, uncomplicated, unsoiled. I hadn't listened. I'd refused to see the warning signs from the beginning. I had seduced myself. Inside that darkened room, I knew I would have to crawl into a pit to make sense of my shame and stupidity.

I should have stopped. I should not have answered that phone call back in January when I returned from my first trip with Ella. That old saying, "If I had known then, what I know now".

# 30

I could not remember how long I sat on that stone bench under the dark trees but, when I did finally stand up, my watch glowed midnight. Sitting for hours, waiting for him to arrive as he had promised when I got off the bus that morning, had dissolved away my anger. I felt oddly calm, almost numb.

The plaza was deserted except for a couple of nightlife opportunists.

It seemed strange to look around and see a lack of vibrant nightlife. The plaza had taken on a conservatism which I found odd but, on reflection, I remembered its socialist history of austerity. Even though my numbed brain thought that there would be a night bustle, it was quite the opposite. Hotel Inglaterra across the plaza, its front veranda caught in pools of shadowy light where tired white-shirted waiters sat at tables devoid of customers, their heads propped on tired hands. The urgency and verve of the daytime bar had lost its allure, when the throb of its four-piece salsa band had played to the delight of enchanted overweight couples of no fixed nationality.

Crossing in and out of quiet back streets I made my way to Plaza Vieja, staying at El Meson de Flota, an old Spanish-style five-roomed hostel in Mercaderes Street. Although the taxi had taken me to Hotel Beltran on my arrival in Havana, they had to book me into El Meson de Flota, its sister hostel.

Walking back, I quietly slipped through shadowy potted streets getting lost, turning down the wrong left and right. In the quiet of those shadows, I felt no fear of unwarranted attention. Throughout Cuba, there is a code where foreigners have safe passage and, experiencing the lonely walks through those night streets, I was grateful for that.

I moved in a trance. Now and then, I picked up on a familiar smell, a smell from childhood, a hot, sweet, sticky, fruity perfumed smell. It reminded me of the experiences of the last few months. For me, Cuba was beautiful to look at, rich and warm like the deep-orange mangoes of June, hanging ripe and lush, but reach out, pluck them, cut them open and you will find that in the soft perfumed engorged flesh lies the deepening black, the beginnings of decay, its flesh tasting bitter, even poisonous. Its perfume reminded me of dark unfathomable eyes which hid secrets that I had begun to uncover. It was all beautiful and now part of my disillusioned soul.

The lights of the hostel shone brightly in the darkened street, and my weary footsteps dragged me forward to the entrance. I still could not believe that I had been played for a fool. It was not so much that my pride had been lacerated but that I had acted so stupidly, that every one of his family and friends I had met in Mayari, Levisa, Matanzas, and Cienfuegos, knew that I had been played for a fool.

I felt I was walking through the streets of an old Alfred Hitchcock film where the audience sat watching with wide gaping mouths, teeth-bared, eyes wide open, then roars of laughter at this most stupid protagonist.

The hotel manager stood behind his desk, and I asked for his help telling him that I needed to contact a man whom I was friendly with but unable to reach by phone. He looked at me for a while then nodded his head. I told him that I needed him to ask his family if they knew where he was and what was happening with him. I took a piece of paper from my passport holder which had Silvana's number on it and handed it to him. The manager called her, a long-distance call to Santa Rita near Levisa, and, after several moments of chat, confirmed that Alex was in Santa Rita having travelled from Holguin to her home on his motorbike the previous day.

My anger screeched at me. My head pounded from sitting out in the sun all day and, looking at the manager, I asked him to call the police as I wanted to make a formal complaint that a man had taken £2500 from me under false pretences. The manager stared incredulously, his face blanching, as I mentioned the sum of money, which was equivalent to many years of a man's salary in this country.

Three police officers arrived within minutes of the phone call, and I explained to them what had happened. They stood solemnly, expressionless, and one of the three, a young woman who spoke excellent English, told me that if I made a report, I would have to stay in Cuba for one week so that they could investigate the serious allegation. I gave them his name and address in Levisa.

I tasted the thought of bitter-sweet revenge.

Again, I was informed that I would have to remain in Cuba for one week.

Waves of tiredness overcame me. I told them that I could not remain as I had a flight booked in three days to fly to Miami for business and my flight could not be cancelled. A hot trickle of tears gathered behind my eyes. The police officers appeared genuinely concerned about my story. I guessed that maybe it was another part of a code of care, or law, to protect foreigners but more so for locals stepping out of line and misbehaving with "extranjeros".

They left.

The hard metal room key dug into the palm of my right hand as I walked up a flight of cold stone steps to the room. As I opened the door, a rush of hot dry air enveloped me. I let my head bend backwards as it swept over me, closed the door behind and stood in the middle of the room, looking out to the balcony with its doors half-open. I felt a surge of self-pity as I looked at the long diaphanous white curtains gently blowing inwards. I stood and stared at the huge double bed under its high cathedral-domed ceiling, feeling small and fragile. At another time I would have felt a thrill of delight to be staying in that famous old hostel, with visions of making love.

I called him again. No answer, of course. There was an unfathomable part of me that, although I had reported all his details to the police, was still reluctant to have their involvement and I wanted to resolve it myself.

Exhausted, but restless for the remainder of the night, I called him a further dozen times, with no response until, finally, I knew he had turned off his phone.

As the clock wound its way around to the early hours of the morning, sleep overtook me, and I finally woke, hot and dehydrated. The fetid heat in the room was suffocating, with the overhead fan whirring warm air. Having left the balcony door open, I heard the relentless hum of outside traffic and noisy passersby.

I suddenly caught the strumming of guitars and the stamp of rhythmic feet from the bar below. I jumped out of bed like a tight spring uncoiled, remembering from a previous trip that superb flamenco dancers and guitar players played there daily. A leap of joy burst forth because I loved the raw sensuality of Flamenco, with its Cuban origins rooted in the early Spanish settlers.

I phoned him again and this time he answered. He was quiet at the other end. I waited until I could find my voice.

'I've reported you to the police here in Havana, giving them your name and address in Levisa. Silvana told me that you were staying with her. You rode your black Kawasaki from Holguin to her home yesterday, after you dropped me off at the bus station in Holguin last night.'

Quiet.

Controlling the anger in my voice, I querulously demanded the return of the £2500 I had given him the previous day, which he said was for his car repairs, visa to England and lawyer fees, which I knew was a lie. All the money had been taken under false pretences. He had to bring it all to Havana by the next day, Friday, as I had already told him I was flying to Miami on Saturday. If he did not, I would further report him to the Immigration Department and, as a foreigner making this serious complaint against him, he would suffer consequences and could be imprisoned.

He finally spoke, sighing heavily, 'OK, Gina, I'll come to Havana tomorrow morning with the money, but the car has given me many problems, too big a headache. The car is in Matanzas.'

His words sent a bolt of lightning through me, making me feel as though I had been scorched by one of those bolts. I let the phone slip through my fingers and fall to the ground, knowing I would not succeed at recovering the money, but I would keep on trying.

The thought of the day ahead on my own, in a city in the July heat, was unbearable. Having been to Havana, I had seen almost every tourist attraction and walked those worn-out streets of Havana Vieja. I no longer felt the sense of marvel or desire for further cultural delights.

My breathing eased as I left the hostel. I entered Plaza Vieja, bought a café con leche from a corner stall and sat on one of the many steps against a Delphic column, where I gathered my thoughts. I waited, wanting my old self to return.

A further café con leche and I found my old self, rising through the shadows of self-doubt. As I sipped my coffee, I decided that I was a strange creature.

I had put myself through an experience which was unfolding into someone else's story. It couldn't be happening to me. I'd always been sensible and disciplined and thought things through while travelling and passing through unfamiliar cultures.

But the new story had turned into a burrowing worm, into a Dantesque soliloquy. I no longer wanted to stand on that podium of hellish self-vindication.

Another coffee and my old humorous, adventurous, curious self slowly percolated to the surface. My constant sense of optimism and hope, which I carried like a mantle around my shoulders, began to whisper words of comfort.

The sun-drenched plaza, with its bleached flagstones reflecting its dazzle, created a theatrical illumination as people sat in small groups under large white umbrellas or strolled across that vast space. Children ran around, with ice creams dripping over the tops of cones, leaving colourful trails of spots as they weaved in and out of each other. Their laughter was infectious.

Waiting until I boarded the plane to Miami was going to be long and hot. In my heart, I knew he would not come, and I knew that I would never really know what had been done with that accursed money. What a mess money creates. Those of us who have it think we can do good with it, then we try to do good with it but cause problems of Olympian proportions.

A swaying movement, a distraction from my thoughts, and I noticed a group of Cuban women walking closely together, their hips bumping and brushing each other, carrying baskets of colourful paper flowers on their heads, radiant white blouses slipping off their shoulders, tiered skirts gathered at their waists, with flip-flop adorned feet. From around another corner, a troupe of young girls and men emerged, some walking on high wooden stilts on the cobbled stones, dressed in tight-fitting, brightly coloured long flowing pants with contrasting rainbow ruffles at the bottom hem, their mid-riffs bare, and their painted faces with masked clown-like features. Slender girls wearing the "Bata Cubana", a traditional Cuban dress resembling a Spanish flamenco dress, all tiered and ruffled and tight-waisted, walked alongside those stilted walkers.

The carnival of smiles and laughter was shared with passing tourists, as they stood tiny next to the moko jumbie, having their souvenir photos taken. A Mardi Gras style of infectious gaiety had arrived, uplifting my spirits. Their fresh vigour infused me, and, for the rest of the day, I was able to find that part of myself that others found attractive and magnetic.

As I sat, one of the moko jumbie girls came over to me with a black top hat but, instead of asking for money, sat next to me. She looked at me, her eyes soft and childlike, startlingly blue, her skin a soft buttery caramelised brown, a young girl of about eighteen. I noticed how she had balletically walked and settled next to me. I asked if she was a dancer and, of course, she attended the Alicia Afonso School of Ballet near the Jose Marti Square, which was named after the foremost Cuban ballerina.

Without prompting, she told me that every year she and her friends took part in the Moko Jumbie carnival. They loved dressing up and soon she would be able to walk on the stilts. She smiled, saying she was afraid of heights.

She asked what I was doing in Havana, and I briefly said, 'Touring and waiting for a friend.' At that, she looked at me curiously.

I asked what her father did for work, thinking that to go to the ballet school her family must be quite well off or she had entered on a scholarship. He worked for the British

Embassy in the administration department. She was quite coy about the statement, and I did not pursue it. We chatted a little longer, and she asked if I liked Havana, and how many times had I been.

Suddenly, she stood up, hearing her name called, but then sat down again. Turning to me and, to my complete surprise, said, 'Cuidate, be careful, Cuba can be dangerous. Many foreign women get hurt.'

With that, she lithely stood up and walked away, top hat in hand, turning briefly to wave. I sat, perplexed, wondering what that brief episode had been about.

The afternoon wore itself into early evening as the sun began to lose its intense heat, casting spikes of everchanging deep indigo shadows across the rooftops. Further above, huge white cotton balls of fluffy cumulus clouds scudded across the changing blue of the sky. I wandered back down the length of Obispo Street, which was always crowded with tourists, as it was the street of restaurants and bars. The party atmosphere reminded me again of Havana's enchantment and hypnotic allure. Walking slowly, allowing my feet to feel the consciousness of other travellers' feet, their global steps, mine was then added to theirs. Continuing down, I arrived at my favourite restaurant, Café Paris, with its Latin band still playing classic rhumba, salsa, and American-Cuban jazz.

I stopped a moment before crossing over and, like a rewind video, saw myself dancing salsa on the pavement by the café with Jonnie. Later as we sat drinking coffee, he had looked at me and, with a small rueful smile, said, 'Do you know what it is like to live in Cuba? It's like living on a beautiful paradise island, but I am caged and cannot fly away. I am a prisoner here. I dance at the Hotel Tropicana every evening for so little money. I am young, but what will become of my life here?'

I knew what he meant.

I smiled at the memory of dancing with Jonnie as tourists stopped to take a video. I had felt carefree and realised the attraction of the island called Cuba.

Café Paris's culture allowed me to sit till late into the night, and none of the waiters disturbed me. Fresh diners came and went, laughing, chatting, arguing, drinking too much, unsteady as they arose and left with their bodies swaying like musical serpents. I spoke to no one, swallowed ice-cold mojito after mojito, daquiri, mojito, coffee, then daiquiri.

More time passed. The evening began to wear its sultry cloak of soft darkness and I felt it wrapping around my bare shoulders.

I had not called him all that day or evening.

I slept deeply that night. The events of the last three days had siphoned off my energy, the oppressive heat draining me of my usual abundant effervescence. Embarrassment and shame had eaten to my core, and, for a few hours, oblivion hid me and healed me.

In the morning, the phone remained silent, and I had to let go. Months later, I discovered what had happened and, if I had known at the time, I do not believe the later events would have been prevented.

Saturday morning arrived and I received a phonecall.

'Hola, Gina. This is Domaso, I am in Matanzas and can come to Havana in about two hours. I am sorry for you and the Classico, maybe I can help? We can go to the police, and

I can help you. We can meet at Hotel Inglaterra at 2 pm. It is a very old hotel.'

'OK.'

I heard a muffled voice reply from far away.

What did he know about the Chevrolet?

I found myself sitting in a large easy chair, in a corner of the hotel lounge, facing the entrance, with a large mirror in front of me. I caught myself in the mirror looking as though in a trance as did the others walking around, also in a trance, or so it seemed to me.

A stylish light-skinned Cuban walked towards me. I recognised him from his profile picture in his email signature strip. Crisply dressed in a sharply tailored light grey suit, white shirt and striped tie, hair glossy and slicked back off his face, he had a briefcase tucked under his arm. I could not help but smile as he was very much how I imagined "the man from Havana". He seemed ready for business, of some sort, and as he approached, I felt the crease in between my eyebrows furrowing, wondering what his agenda would be.

Standing up, I shook his hand, which was warm and slightly sweaty. As he sat opposite me, he asked how I was.

I could barely speak. My anger and shame rested like a boulder on my shoulders.

'Gina,' he began, 'I am sorry for what this young man has done. He is a good friend of my wife, … too good a friend.'

His implication was clear.

'She and I have many problems. She is much younger than me, and I love her.'

I frowned again, at the same time understanding his inference.

'I hear him on the bike, very noisy, riding past our apartment at different times of the day. It is very bad he sold the car and bought that bike. It is more expensive than the car. First, you must text him and tell him that you know about the car and that he must return to you any money.'

I replied saying I already knew about the motorbike, as his Aunt Silvana in Santa Rita had told me he had ridden it to her house from Holguin a couple of days ago. I told him that I had already contacted the police the previous night and reported Alejandro taking money from me for the car.

He raised his eyebrows in surprise at what I had just told him.

Domaso urged me to text him again, telling him that he had to return all the money to me. He helped with some Spanish, although that was not a good idea as some of the words caused inflammatory outbursts from the other side.

Over the next two hours and several coffees, texts were exchanged with long intervals between answers.

I remember cajoling and threatening him with the police and the immigration department. In some replies, he denied selling the car, in others he was contrite, in others he was angry and aggressive and accusatory of me not believing him when he said he still had the car.

In one phone call, I told him that Domaso was with me in Havana and had told me he had seen him riding a black Kawasaki. At that, he started to shout down the phone saying he was a liar and was jealous because of his friendship with his wife.

'We are good friends since we were in school together.'

'I want you to bring the £2500 I gave you a couple of days ago in Holguin, and to be in Havana by 6 pm tonight or else I will go to the police again with Domaso, who will confirm that he has seen you riding a black Kawasaki.'

A long silence.

'OK, I come with the money, but I did not steal it from you, you gave it to me.'

'Yes, to pay for repairs for the Chevrolet but you do not have it and sold it a few weeks ago, so what did you need the money for?'

Another long silence.

'Also, I am sick and far away and do not think I can come for 6 pm tonight, it's big problem.'

'Then I'll see you outside Hotel Inglaterra tomorrow at 2 pm.'

Domaso was not convinced and said we should go to the police station. He had a friend who could help.

Stepping outside the lobby, I walked straight into a heat wall. It took me a while to adjust to the sunlight. It was a quick taxi ride to the local police station where a short queue of locals stood, all with bits of white paper clutched in their hands.

Being foreign, we walked past the queue into a small darkened and cooler lobby, with a hole in the wall for enquiries. Domaso led the way and spoke rapidly to a voice behind the wall for quite a few minutes. A hand appeared with an A4 piece of paper and handed it to Domaso, who in turn handed it to me.

'You must fill this in. It's in English but he says once you fill it in you must stay in Havana for a few more days.'

'I am booked for a flight to Miami on Sunday and cannot miss my connection back to England.'

I bent my head low to my chest and let out a constricted deeply held breath.

'Forget it, Domaso, thanks for trying to help me but I will wait for him to come to Havana tomorrow and see what I can do myself.'

As we left, he turned to me and asked me for fuel money to get home as he did not have enough, and it had cost him a lot to come to Havana. I looked at his smart suit and air of prosperity and held my tongue, wondering whose suit it really was. I gave him 30 pesos and hoped that I would not have to see him again as I knew there was more to this than trying to help me, as he constantly peppered his speech with 'my friend'.

Of course, Saturday came and went without sight of him and I spent the day visiting the large cemetery on the outskirts of Havana. On Sunday I flew out of Havana to Miami, staying in the Art Deco area near South Beach. I could not relate to Miami, despite walking around admiring the superb street art, taking a bus out to Key West, visiting Ernest Hemingway's other home, and driving over to Little Havana, which had no resemblance to the original Havana from where those Miami Cubans had emigrated to.

I stood on the beach of Key West, looking out to sea in the direction of Cuba, ninety miles away. I hoped I would not have to return to Cuba, as I had had enough.

Numbly I visited the swimwear show only to discover that, as I was not exhibiting as a retailer, I could not visit the show itself. I argued that nowhere on the show's website did it state that information. The organisers were adamant but relented as I had travelled from the UK and arranged for a staff member to escort me around the showground for a very brief tour.

In Miami, I visited another tarot card reader, who for $100 told me the same things that the diminutive lady in Havana, Beatriz, had told me. I must wear my heart on my sleeve or else we as human beings re-enact the same patterns of behaviour, universally known and therefore not impossible to foretell.

A few months later, when my world had exploded, I had a conversation with Vicente and discovered that, while standing at the security gate to exit Havana with my dark glasses hiding swollen red eyes, I had been watched on the airport's CCTV and filmed. Later he showed me the CCTV footage of my exiting Havana. I looked at the image of my so-called self and could not recognise myself. I seem to have shrunk. What really affected me was knowing that I had been 'tagged' on CCTV (and it turned out that Vicente was in charge of security at the airport), and here he was showing this information to me. What other information was now on record in Cuba?

# 31

So now what?
What had I got myself into? How was I going to get out of it?

On that last trip, I had given him £2500 to repair the car, sort out his paperwork for his visa, and pay for legal costs. A visa that had not yet been applied for nor any lawyers' fees involved.

It was all lies.

Sitting on the warm stone patio at the back of my apartment, with work over for the day, my son and I chatted, with a glass of white wine for me and water for him. He had given up drinking a year earlier and looked much more relaxed.

'So how are you feeling? You look deeply troubled. Tell me, are you in love with him? I truly hope not.'

There was a steely edge to his voice, yet his eyes were full of concern.

'You must find a way to get this money back from him. You know he has sold the car and he must have got a good return on it. You cannot let him get away with this, You have to return as soon as possible and I'm going to come with you this time.'

His voice was full of emotion.

'OK, OK, but this must be the last time. I don't think it will help. I think he took all the money to do something else with it.'

My son was stunned angry and concerned that I had been duped. No other word for it.

He too had had a similar incident in Africa around buying gold and losing $30,000 to a couple of African gold merchants, so he was overly sensitive and angry around this type of loss of money and situation.

'How much money have you given?'

Just then the mobile rang, and it was Domaso from Matanzas.

He asked me how I was and had something further to tell me but first asked if I could top up his phone via Cubacel as he had little credit left.

I topped it up with £10.

'Gina, Alejandro has got back the money from the house you bought.'

My heart froze for an instant and then I caught my breath, holding it while the racing slowed down.

'How do you know this?'

'Here, it is easy to know everyone's business. I think he took the money for the house to pay also for the Kawasaki. It is expensive here. I tell you this because I think of you as a good friend.'

I'm not sure on what basis he assumed that.

The phone went dead, and I did not top it up again.

My son looked at me quizzically and asked, 'What are you going to do? You need to return now and recover the money. You cannot let him get away with doing what he has done. You are not wealthy Mum, and have had to work hard for everything you have, and it seems that with this guy, you have lost your way entirely. What's happened to you?'

The tears just spilt over, wracking my body to a place of deep aching. I sobbed, and he took me in his arms and held me.

I had memory flashes of waiting for him to return, saying he was fixing the car, hours spent away, while I waited in the searing and punishing heat.

Remembering one of the days, when he had crept out of bed around 7 am and did not return until 2 am, having climbed up the drainpipe onto the balcony of Casa Carolina. Phone call after phone call with him saying he was with friends fixing the car and I was alone again in that hot dusty provincial town.

Memories of sitting in a taxi in some in-between town, in the rain, with Tajo listening to Ana Belen sing Amigas, as he had gone off again with another friend to fix the Chevrolet and we were waiting for his return.

Surreal memories of a man washing his flip-flop feet in a puddle of rainwater in the broken road in the middle of an open tenement area in Levisa. Moments before, we had stood in that self-same spot where the bonnet of the Chevrolet was up, a torchlight shining into its engine, and Alex and friend were peering over into its mechanical heart which was broken again.

Domaso sent me an email, unrequested but helpful, of a private detective in Miami who could help trace who the car had been sold to. I emailed the detective, told him my situation, paid his $300 fee, and the next day an email came back with photographic proof of the deed of sale, including the date and the name of the new owner, but not the resale price.

Coincidence, but a while after Domaso's emai I received a phone call from Alejandro asking how I was, his voice soft and gently, asking when I was returning as he missed me.

The next morning, feeling exhausted as I had not recovered from my trip to Miami, and informing him that I was returning, I booked another flight with Thomas Cook for five days to Holguin, this time returning via Manchester, not their usual return route but a special flight, my son insisting that he accompany me and I desisting.

# 32

It was now August, my Miami trip still fresh in mind and I was back in Holguin again. He was waiting for me, dressed in white, with his hands hanging by his side, a calm look on his face, and expressionless eyes but he greeted me with a kiss on each cheek.

'Hola, I book a cheap car for you, and we go to Mayari. The Classico (his other name for the Chevrolet) is in Matanzas and being repaired by some friends. I do not have the money you gave me because I spend it on the Classico and on lawyer's fees for the visa to come to Inglaterra.'

I stared dumbfounded at his blatant lies. He had not yet applied for a visa to England.

I knew that returning was a necessity and a mistake and the following days could possibly have been written by a Hollywood scriptwriter.

My memories of that trip played out like single frames, each vividly articulated, with the characters and events drawn sharply with a knife dipped in black ink on a landscape white canvas, each movement as though watching a Tai Chi master slowly draw out each movement with precision and impeccable timing.

There became a sense that the weeklong events seemed to have been planned in unison with several players.

We drove a black Renault from the airport to Mayari, staying at Casa Carolina again. Seeing Maria and her husband was a relief, they seemed to be the watchful and innocent, yet intimate, players.

This time there was no sex at all. I had no desire, especially as several times in earlier trips it was a continuance of "don't pull him, don't push him", even in play. In public, "don't be over demonstrative". In private, "don't pull him down to the bed, no seduction, and don't make an advance to arouse" because it did not work. Two days would go by with a mere brush of a kiss on the cheek. No making love if there were a couple of hours of languid lying in each other's arms, no foreplay, no stroking or touching. That all felt like prostitution.

Once inside the room, we sat on the bed.

'I've returned because you took a lot of money from me on the last trip under false pretences. I know you have sold the car. I hired a Miami detective who sent me evidence of the sale, yet you are still saying that you have the car in Matanzas. That is not possible. You must return the money to me. I am not wealthy, although you think I am. I came to Cuba in June to give you the money. I saw the car, and I saw that it needed many repairs and spare parts.'

I drew a breath.

'I also checked the cost for a lawyer to sort out your visa if you come to Inglaterra. But how can you come to England and stay with me, when you tell me so many stories that are not true?'

At that, he looked up at me and I could not believe it, but a single tear rolled down his cheek.

'I must leave Cuba, Gina, there is nothing for me here. I cannot get a job. I have no qualifications. After I divorced my Swiss wife, she gave me a lot of money but that is all gone just to live here and help my family. We must go to Havana, to the British Embassy, to get my visa. Please.'

With that, he got off the bed and left the room.

An hour later, I walked down the spiral staircase to the back of the outside restaurant. Across the low wall, a group of youths were playing football with him. I walked into the kitchen to get fresh juice, where Maria and her assistant Rena were washing dishes and clearing the room.

In slow Spanish and a few words of English, Maria said, 'Gina, Cuban men no good. They like nice clothes, go out, drink, and stay with friends. They are no good at sex, and not much interested in sex with wives.'

That was the gist of what I understood from what she said. Rena laughed loudly at this, as well as Maria. I too laughed. It was an infectious laugh without malice but resignation. I looked at her leathery hands, the weariness in her face, but still with laughter in her eyes. I reached over and hugged her, and she put her arms around me and gently returned the hug.

I took my juice outside, sitting under the overhead fan, washed over by a gentle stirring of an early evening breeze, soft on my face, soft on my body, ruffling through my hair. I turned my chair towards the back of the restaurant and continued to watch the men and young boys playing football, a faint sound of shouts of victory and laughter drifting down towards the casa.

Suddenly Valeria appeared, her hair extensions piled high on top of her head, a thin green satin ribbon woven through. She looked, for a moment, like Nefertiti, regal, royal, perfect bone structure, the wife of the ancient Egyptian King Akhenaton. My mother had a tiny golden alabaster head of Nefertiti, which she had brought back in the 1960s on our way from India. Our ship stopped off at Aden as we passed through the Suez Canal, and she disembarked on a journey to see the Pyramids, a birthday gift from my father before we came to England.

'Ola, Gina, como estas? Que tal? How are you? I am so happy to see you again.'

'Ola. Que pasa con Alex?'

'No se, Gina, no se, no nos dice nada de su negocio. I hear you have arrived, so I take a 'bici' to come to see you.'

'So you have been learning some English from the book I left you.'

She laughed, her white teeth shining and perfect.

We sat for a few minutes in companionable silence and then she got up kissed me on each cheek and left.

Lying in bed the next morning, the notion of not retrieving the money played around in my head. I had to stay there a few days, in fact until the following Tuesday, having arrived yesterday, on a Tuesday.

He woke up and turned to me saying, 'Gina, you here for a few days, let's go to Havana, my cousins, Celistina and Alfonso, want to go and I say OK. On the way, in Cienfuegos there is a big baseball game, so we go and see it, is a big stadium, and lots of fun. In English, the name of the stadium is "5th of September". Maybe arrive in Havana at eleven o'clock this evening. The money is all gone, I do not have it. I help many people with it.'

That last comment hung in the air like the Sword of Damocles. I didn't feel powerless. I just knew that I had dug my grave and had to crawl up its muddy, slippery sides and out.

By 10 am we left, and there, outside Casa Carolina, stood Celistina and Alfonso. I'd heard about Ana and Karl's son, Alfonso, at their house in Cienfuegos. I did not ask what he was doing in Mayari as I'd reflected earlier that Cubans seemed to move effortlessly, or so it seemed, on buses and taxis as we use our cars.

They both spoke fluent English. Celistina sat behind me, an attractive, pouty young woman. I felt her eyes boring into the back of my head.

Alfonso must have been about fifteen, full of good humour and laughter, with slender, light curly brown hair and eyes, those same brown eyes of Raul. Of course, all the people I met were related in some way or the other. The vines of relationships weave like a textile-weaving loom throughout Cuba. Their threads are tantamount to their survival and fortunes.

The green and cream-painted stadium was bathed in the golden light of the late afternoon, crowded with youth, and older men and women. Beer cans and bottles were already littered across the circumference of the stadium, so we had to walk almost all the way around to the entrance gate. I had no idea where the tickets came from but, this time, I did not pay. I slightly separated myself from the three in front and followed them, looking around, quietly pleased that I had an opportunity to come to a local baseball game, despite the reasons and circumstances for my being there. Although we had entered the grounds, it seemed the game would not start until much later, so after many 'Hola's and 'Como esta?'s, as well as slaps on the back, hugs and kisses on the cheek, we left and continued to Matanzas.

'OK, we go to my brother Karl's house, his wife has something to do in Havana, so she come with us.'

I turned to him saying, 'I want to make it very clear. I am not paying for anyone's food, accommodation or tickets to clubs or anywhere. I am not obliged to and I am not going to do it.'

He looked at me, shocked, and quietly nodded his head.

We picked up Karl's wife and there was animated and heated chatter between the three of them in the rear of the car but, in front, we barely spoke.

Arriving in Havana around 9 pm, earlier than expected, we found a small casa particular on Vigo Street, a narrow grimy dishevelled street, full of the traditional tall skinny buildings but, once inside, surprisingly spacious.

Celistina paid for a room on the ground floor for Alfonso and herself. Ours were on the top floor, with a large wide balcony, draped with various green creepers, sweating humidity into the air.

I looked around for Karl's wife but she had disappeared, maybe when we had stopped outside our new casa.

That time, we had two identical rooms, small and windowless, with a tiny shower cubicle and toilet, twin beds in each and a tiny chest of drawers. The air was musty through lack of an open window.

I was barely in the room, when he entered mine saying, 'Vale, we all go dancing now.'

His mood change was like a scene change.

Casa de la Musica, a well-known haunt, was our destination but, on the way, he suddenly mentioned that he had to stop off at a friend's house to collect something. I sat in the car and waited for over thirty minutes until the front door of another tall skinny building, much like the one we were staying in, opened and out walked Valeria wearing the shortest skirt possible and the highest heels possible, with her extension plaits piled even higher on top of her head, looking like several beehives, one on top of another. There was something quietly different about her that evening. A distance, a certain triumph. I must have been paranoid.

She opened the back door and casually said, 'Hola, Gina. OK?'

He jumped into the front with a large smile on his face and, without further words, we sped off, through streets awash with bright lights, to Casa de la Musica. I did not pay for the entrance fee for the three of us.

Towards the end of the evening, as we sat at our table, he turned to me and said that he felt very unwell, and had a pain on the right side of his stomach.

'I think I have a problem here,' he said, as he put his hand on his appendix.

I looked at him and asked if it was a new pain. He shook his head saying that it had started about two days ago but it was only a little pain.

Returning to our casa, he went to bed in my room and fell asleep instantly.

Morning arrived with a knock on the door and, opening it, I saw Vicente standing outside, with a big smile on his face, asking for Alex. On hearing his voice, he quickly dressed and walked out onto the balcony. It was about 10 am.

He returned to the room saying that Vicente had arranged for him to go to the military hospital for an examination and X-ray to check if his appendix had ruptured. To say that, by then, I was dazed by it all, would be a gross understatement.

I decided to accompany them as they got into the black Renault and drove down to the military hospital. The streets looked familiar and then I remembered that the house we went to the previous night, where Valeria was staying, was near the hospital.

I waited in the car for about an hour, as foreigners were not allowed to enter the military hospital. The sun was a burning globe in the sky, with the heat in the car continually oppressive so, unable to take the heat inside, I got out and sat on a narrow ledge of the nearside building, which had a wide lintel at the roof, giving some downward shade to the street.

They both returned, walking slowly down the street, arms around each others shoulders, smiling broadly. I slowly opened the passenger door letting out the steaming heat before sliding onto the hot seat. Vicente jumped into the back of the car, a quick dash of Spanish was spat out like a machine gun and then he said, in English, that Alex had to have an operation later that evening around 5 pm but would be allowed to leave after a few hours.

I put my hand over my face but, from the side, I took a peek at Alex's face, who by now was back in the driver's seat, his face wreathed in smiles.

'No problema, Gina, this small operation and then no pain.'

He pulled out his phone and showed me a picture of himself lying on a bed with ECG wires attached to his forehead and chest, with his shirt unbuttoned to his waist, and a smile on his face.

'Vale, we go have lunch now.'

'What?' I exclaimed. 'If you are going to have an operation this evening, you should not eat for a few hours before.'

'It's OK. We have time and we are both hungry,' announced Vicente.

'Alex, before we have lunch, there's a guy taking photographs in Jose Marti Square, and I would like one of the two of us.'

I had no idea why I wanted that photograph. He looked surprised but agreed and we left Vicente for a short time. He went off to have his hair trimmed and we agreed to meet in thirty minutes.

In front of the Jose Marti statue stood an elderly photographer, using an old-fashioned daguerreotype camera, with a black cloth over his head. We stood in front of him, with our backs against the statue. Within a few minutes, he produced two negatives of us standing upright in a military manner. I remember looking at them and thinking how "fated" those negatives looked. Ghostly, faded, our eyes like blank white sockets, so unreal, as this whole story seemed to have unfolded.

We all met up at a small and busy local café by the Trafalgar Hotel on the corner of Jose Marti Plaza. It was mainly filled with what looked like office workers, which was a crazy assumption. Men dressed in crisp white shirts and dark trousers. Entering a large rectangular room, we sat down at a round table in the middle of the restaurant. It was covered by a crisp white tablecloth, with glass salt and pepper pots sitting in the middle of it. Beams of sunlight poured in from the dusty dirty windows, their long rays dancing with particles of dust slowly drifting upwards. At that moment, I remembered one of the stories of Philip Pullman, The Northern Lights, in which dust particles were the souls of children, as I looked up at an effervescent Alex.

Lunchtime was, by then, well into the middle of the afternoon, and the restaurant atmosphere vibrated with healthy male laughter and camaraderie, heads bent over plates, laden with food, golden beer filling tall glasses, their bubbles tiny and frothy, kissing lips, or pouring down deep throats. Each patron already seemed to have one or two empty glasses by their plates.

Our food arrived on large white oval plates, piled with white steaming rice and Cuban shrimp (Enchilado de Camarones), delicate small shrimps in tomato, onion and green pepper sauce. I knew this was his favourite dish. He and Vicente tucked in, large forkfuls shovelled into their mouths, followed by Cristal beer, frothy, leaving a thin trail on their top lips, and their teeth gleaming beneath the frothy line.

I sat, fork in hand, looking at both of them, pretending to smile and laugh at their jollity, but wondering how he could be eating that heavy lunch when his operation was at 5 pm. What was really going on?

Gradually, the restaurant emptied and we were the last diners.

Pushing back the chairs, almost in unison, Vicente reminded him that it was time to go. He said he would drive to the hospital and would see me later. I left them at the restaurant and watched them leave, the sunlight still strong and, as they walked away, sunbeams seemed to be washing over them so that their bodies appeared to be semi-transparent. I stood awhile, unsure of what to do next as it was not yet on the verge of early evening. I walked from the restaurant towards Parque Central, then Hotel Inglaterra and the very word 'Inglaterra' connected me to home.

I was desolate, again feeling encapsulated in that vipers' pit. What should I do? Return to that small dark dismal room where I knew Celistina and Alfonso would be? I had a natural distrust of Celestina. Her bond with him was very strong and I could not decipher if they had been lovers, or just loved each other, and she had a natural protection towards him. I sensed that she disapproved of his relationship with me, and probably guessed the reason for it.

I knew that we had become trapped in a ridiculous relationship which I was trying to extricate myself from, knowing that I had made a gross mistake but also feeling sorry for him and his sense of entrapment in Cuba. He saw, in me, a way to leave that island paradise which held nothing for him at that stage in his life.

We had become victims of our initial attraction and desire, but I should have had more sense.

But what part, in all of that, was the appendix operation? How could he have had that ECG earlier, confirmed he had appendicitis, booked an operation, had a heavy meal, and then gone to the hospital? None of it made sense, particularly as his pains came on so quickly the night before. How was he going to benefit from all of that?

I found my stone bench in Parque Central, under a spreading dark leafy tree. August and hot, there were few tourists around, most probably sleeping away the afternoon heat. Only the regular elderly Cubans and tourist attraction women, with colourful flowers in their hair and protruding cigars from their red lips, sat on other stone benches. Large baskets at their feet, overflowing with white flowers to sell and one or two with tiny dogs, they were dressed in frilly collars and dresses lying amongst the flowers. I'd taken enough photos of them.

The heat wore on but gradually cooled as the sun set and twilight began to descend, along with a new and slower hustle and bustle of energy as the parque gradually filled up again with the evening crowd. Music began to play all around, streaming out of restaurants and solo guitar players in and around the plaza.

I awoke from my deep unconsciousness and looked around, unaware that I had fallen asleep. An elderly woman had been sitting next to me and, as I turned to her, she looked at me through her rheumy eyes and just reached out and put her rough warm hand on mine. I let it stay, resting for a few minutes. I withdrew my hand and, reaching into my purse, took out a 10 pesos note to give to her. She shook her head, refusing the note, and said, 'Cuidarse, take care of yourself.'

What expression on my face and body was I showing that so many people along the way in Cuba kept saying that to me? I guess they had heard too many stories and tried to warn the unsuspecting.

I left her and went in search of a café for something to eat. I had barely touched my Cuban shrimps at lunch, disliking seafood. I called Vicente, who immediately answered, and asked how he was and when he would return. He replied saying the operation was OK and he would return in the morning as he was sleeping then.

It was 8 pm and another long evening of wandering around the city centre lay ahead.

Just before I drifted off to sleep, I looked at those two negatives and felt a coldness seeping through my bones as I stared at them.


A gentle knocking on the wooden door awoke me at 8.30 am the next morning. He stood outside, bright-eyed, with the front buttons of his shirt undone to halfway down his chest. He smiled and kissed me on both cheeks.

As he entered and walked past me, he smelt heavily of the Hugo Boss aftershave I had bought him from an earlier trip, not of general anaesthetic as I would have assumed.

'Gina, I am so tired, I will sleep for a few hours.'

For an unguarded moment, I reached out and touched his stomach at which he flinched and, frowning, told me to be careful. He opened his shirt and I saw a clean square piece of white net gauze taped to his appendix area.

'It's a little sore,' he said and, kicking off his shoes, lay down on the bed fully clothed


It had been raining during the night, the streets glistening wet, the sky ominous with heavy black clouds, and the air languid and steamy. As I went down the stairs, Celistina emerged from her room followed by Alfonso, and handed me my phone charger. I had no idea that anyone had gone into my room to get it the previous evening. They both looked fresh and relaxed and did not ask about him which I thought odd but, on reflection, they already knew what had been going on.

The hours passed, doing nothing. With the constant drizzle and threats of rainfall, I found a small hole-in-the-wall café near Calle Vigo and read on my Kindle to pass the time while charging my phone.

Returning to the casa in the early afternoon, I saw him standing at the front door. Seeing me, he came out and gave me a light hug and kiss on the lips. I automatically stepped back to which he asked, 'Que?'

He then pointed to a turquoise blue painted house on the corner, saying one of his papa's friends lived there and rented out her house and made good money. He continued talking about the house I had bought next to Silvana and made plans on how we could turn it into a casa particular and make money from it when I was not visiting Cuba. He seemed to have woken in a paradoxical mood and continued to chat about some of his plans for a new business that he could do. He reminded me of a conversation we had had on an earlier trip about buying clothes from China and selling them in Cuba.

'Do you remember you told me you work in fashion in China and can get clothes? We could sell to all these guys here, designer jeans, trainers, t-shirts, jackets, belts, and jewellery. It's very good here for these clothes. Remember I tell you that these guys get lots of clothes from their family in Miami?'

I was no longer interested in playing that game but nodded and smiled and said, 'Yes. We could also go to the British Embassy in the morning, and you could apply for your visa to Inglaterra as you want. You could learn English and get a job there instead.'

He nodded his head, then said he was hungry and asked if I could buy some food as he had no money on him.

I'd passed a small café selling takeaway chicken and rice and leaving him on the doorstep, I retraced my steps through the wet sloshy back streets.

I ordered enough for four of us, assuming the other two would not have eaten, and waited outside looking at a 'bici' which was totally covered with a rain hood and the driver's silhouette, etched black against the misty plastic cover, had his head bent over a food container. I became captivated in this small cameo of time and a leaking memory of not paying for any further expenses came to mind.

The four of us ate in semi-silence in a room that looked prepared for Christmas, with red tablecloths, small plastic Christmas trees adorning the centre of the table, and gold tinsel hanging at the lace-curtained single window.

He seemed tired so we returned to our rooms, barely speaking, and there was still no acknowledgement of the money he had taken from me for the Chevrolet, still confirming the car was in Matanzas.

In total denial of everything.

Around 9 pm, he knocked on my door and stated we were going dancing. He phoned Celistina and told her to meet him downstairs in ten minutes.

I looked at him questioningly and he just mumbled that he was bored and had to get out of his room. I looked at him, about to say, 'But your operation?'

'It's OK, not painful. Vamos.'

I could not care whether he was in pain or not as I had begun to doubt that he had even had an operation and it was part of a plan that a lot of people knew about and had agreed to help him but for what purpose I still could not ascertain.

So, back to Casa de la Musica, where again I did not pay. Valeria had arrived with a tall Cuban man, who turned out to be her boyfriend. Paying for myself, I walked on ahead and, turning, saw that the boyfriend had paid for Valeria and himself.

While the others danced, we sat for about thirty minutes in silence until he stood up and, pulling me out of my chair, started to salsa with me by the side of the table.

'What, but you have had an operation yesterday and you can dance?'

'Si, it is only a small operation and no little pain. All OK, Gina. I know you like to dance.'

From Casa de la Musica we went to another venue where a group unknown to me was playing. The crowd there looked like Puerto Ricans and Miami Cubans, although they probably were not, but they were so painstakingly well-dressed. Men with thick gold chains around their bullish necks, oversized gold watches on their wrists, pants which showed every muscle of their legs, and feet encased in expensive-looking trainers. A uniform of white and gold wherever I turned to look.

The men walked around the heavily vegetated gardens, ringed fingers holding tall glasses of various coloured liquids or slim cigars between smiling lips. Those men were white cranes of sleekness, walking, strutting, heads slowly turning from side to side or bobbing up and down, while their women accompanied them on stork-high stiletto heels, their short skirts feathering and ruffling as they strutted.

All beautifully staged and crafted.

We sat outside, with the heat dripping and oppressive, and watched the theatre of music being played out on the stage in front.

He sat very still, head erect, profile carved out of soft stone, his face looked at peace and angelic and it was probably the last time I would see his face in such a profile. We stayed about an hour, and he did not move from that position until I gently nudged saying I was leaving. We all left as the early hours of dawn descended.

I'll never know what urged me to accompany him in the morning to the British Embassy to apply for his visa. We arrived there around 9.30 am, standing in a short queue for a while and then filling out the appropriate forms, handing them to the front desk and leaving to collect the other two from Vigo Street. I knew that I would have to send a letter of invitation and a few other formalities once I arrived back in England, but I left that thought behind.

Leaving Havana around 11 am, the four of us were in a quiet space, the two behind chatting softly, heads bent sideways together.

'We could stop off at Matanzas to look at the car?' I suggested.

'No time, you know it's far to Mayari. We have a long drive, and we go to Cienfuegos to give my brother Karl a gift from his wife, you remember she came with us to Havana.'

How could I forget. She must have met up with him sometime in the last couple of days.

'This is news to me.'

'Si.'

That was all he said.

We drove all day and through the evening. About three-quarters of the way we swopped so I could drive, and he could sleep. Approaching a long avenue of trees into a familiar town, it could have been Sibanicu, or Yurigua, too dark and tired to be sure, a stray dog shot out of the side of the road. The sound of a crunch and a faint whelp as the front of the car hit it and it disappeared under my car. I did not stop, the others did not react, and I felt a lump of sadness rise in my throat and my heart pounded with guilt for that poor animal.

I had never knocked a dog or any other animal down in my entire life of driving and the total disregard for that creature offended me but somehow, caught up in this environment, I continued to drive out of the town and back into the darkness of the motorway, leaving a dying soul and many unspoken and complex actions behind in Havana.

# 33

The day before I left, he asked if I would prepare a dinner for his family as it would be nice to have a last lunch together, as I had not spent much time with them on that trip.

I wondered why I was doing it. I told him I wanted the money returned. He appeared to not have a single peso on him and in Havana, Celistina was the one paying for all their drinks, food, and club entrances.

I asked Maria at Casa Carolina to prepare a special meal for eight of us, which she did. Delicious Cuban food which I did not know existed and had not sampled in any of the cafés or restaurants.

She and Tonio spent hours in the kitchen making small delicate pastries, Enchilado de Camarones, and a variety of other dishes. I stood by them, grabbing a pen and pad from my bag so that I would remember what they had made, as over time that meal became for me the last supper and the last big expense of that trip.

They spent all day preparing for the evening meal and I sat in the restaurant, reading and sipping several cool drinks or standing in the kitchen with my notebook, writing down all the different dishes they prepared. I did not care where he went in my car as I had decided that that was my last trip to Cuba and, the more graciously I behaved, I would leave feeling vindicated of all my trials.

From the kitchen came merry laughter and tinkling chatter with sweet, tantalising aromas wafting out into the afternoon air.

Costillitas - marinated baby back ribs, served with a mix of sour orange juice, lime juice, oregano, garlic, and olive oil - they taste sweet and tangy at the same time and are so delicious and I ate many.

Lomo Ahumado with rice - pork fillet, slowly smoked until the meat becomes full of flavour yet juicy. I had no idea how they smoked this, but I didn't eat it, thinking again of my first encounter with a pig feast.

Croquetas - delicious battered and fried balls of cheese stuffed with bits of ham. Tonio was very quick at stuffing those little balls into his mouth and I sampled a few.

Tostones - these are made across Caribbean countries and have different names. They are thickly cut plantains, fried, then pressed and refried. I remember the first time Ella and I ate these, then avoided them for the rest of the trip. They are like the dried banana slices we get in health food stores. I did eventually get to like them and ate quite a lot of these as munchies.

Churros - my favourite yet anathema to my waistline. Great street food and Maria's were as light as a feather. The dough is fried until crispy on the outside and soft on the inside, sprinkled in sugar and then dipped in a rich chocolate sauce. I remember eating these in Sevilla on many occasions, feeling my waist expanding and groaning.

Besides the churros, they made a flan, which is another superb dessert like that found in other countries in Latin America. Condensed milk, eggs and vanilla are cooked together over a delicious caramel. Oh, so sweet and tasty.

As well as the food they supplied a few bottles of Havana Club rum, cokes, beers, and lots of good cheer.

All the food was mouth-wateringly delicious and full of surprising tastes. Looking back over the food I had eaten on my several trips to Cuba, none had been as good or surprising as that last meal at Casa Carolina.

The family arrived, one by one, or in twos and threes, and they all looked as though they had made a special effort in dressing well. Papa had polished his black shoes and Laura, his wife, was in a frilly off-the-shoulder top and short skirt. Silvana had new, long hair extensions and her usual tight white pants and low-cut top. I think she was very proud of her bosoms. Norrie and his girlfriend were in matching white, Raul in his usual knee-length shorts and fresh white t-shirt, Valeria, back again in Mayari, in her short, emerald-green skirt and top, hair extensions with coloured beads woven through, hanging around her shoulders and, finally, Alex was in lilac chinos and shirt, and white sneakers. He spent the entire meal on his phone, like a teenager, quiet and distant. His family and I tried to engage him in conversation. We all chatted around him although, conversationally, it was a difficult meal for me not being able to converse with them.

The food carried all of us through to the end of the meal when finally, around 10 pm, they left with smiles on their faces, gracious gracias and many hugs and tear-filled eyes from Papa and Silvana, wishing me a safe journey home.

I wondered if they knew about the appendix fiasco in Havana. They most probably did.

As I lay in bed that night, thinking through the cameo of events which had surfaced and passed through my days there, I was glad that I had had an opportunity to sit with the family and have that last meal with them. As they ate and chatted amongst themselves, now and then looking at me and I at them, I felt overwhelmingly pleased to have shared so many moments with them in their simple homely surroundings, enjoying moments of everyday life and being welcomed into their homes and treated with respect. Alex was another being, separate from them. He had been tainted by avarice and a lifestyle that he was unable to reattain in Cuba and was therefore unable to live life back in his former home.

He had to drive me to the airport to return the hire car and we barely spoke, even though there was a pending visa application at the British Embassy in Havana. By then, I felt that we had nothing more to say to each other.

I was so glad when the plane's wheels touched down jerkily on the tarmac at Gatwick Airport. I exited the terminal, caught the train home, opened my front door and breathed in its home smells, promising myself that I would never return and that I would accept that everything that had happened, happened for a reason. Yet it was all a muddle and confusion, and the money lost was a painful acknowledgment of my vanity and a deep, narcissistic experience to be paid for as time transitioned to another era of my life.

# 34

I lived life in the slow lane for the next few weeks and ignored the texts and phone calls requesting Cubacell top-ups.

Messages from Vicente, missed calls from Silvana and Valeria, messages of 'Que pasa?' from him, asking about coming to Inglaterra, that he missed me, the car was OK but maybe he should sell it if he was coming to Inglaterra.

Seaside vacationing was still part of the summer season, buoyant by the coast, hundreds of visitors streaming out of the trains, onto the crowded platforms. Daytime picnickers with huge baskets stuffed with towels and unblown balls and life rings for children tripped off the train, down the platform and out onto the beach. Colour, chatter, laughter, and late summer joy filled the air from the station to the pebbly beach. The pier thronged with candyfloss people and the smell of smoke-grilled burgers hung densely in the air.

On some occasions, I would venture up to London, weaving in and out of passengers as I boarded the train to return to my longed-for tango milongas in Covent Garden and escape the holiday crowds.

When I did venture towards the beach, it was generally in the opposite direction, to the quiet of our Lifeboat Centre further down the coast where the waters were crystal-clear and the sunsets reminiscent of Cuba.

The business had slowed down in August but was gradually picking up, getting ready for autumn deliveries. We were immersed in ensuring that all our orders would be delivered on time and we could end the year in profit.

Sometimes I sat at the end of the day, on the warm stony beach, with my knees drawn up, burying my face between them looking at the myriad of pebbles, their colours, shapes and sizes and I wondered about their origins.

My family were quiet around me, knowing I was in a space that was not inviting their comments or conversation.

The mood at the office matched my home life.

As the days moved forward to the end of September, the weather changed from summer to the first cold drifts of autumn coming off the English Channel, bringing in the grey stormy skies in the early morning, and heavy winds throughout the day.

20th September was the start of a new week, a new morning, and a promise of change. My heart and head felt a little less foggy. The walk to the office took ten minutes and I was thinking of the phone call I had made around 5.30 pm the previous evening when he had sounded light-hearted for a few minutes before the phone died. I felt an unease, maybe it was nothing more than having been so intensely in touch with him for so many months, a habit I had stopped except for the previous evening.

I had made another call around 10 pm and again at midnight before I finally slept.

The staff were already at their desks, always on time at 9 am. Unlike me, who usually arrived around 9.30 am.

I went through my usual routine of clearing my desk, checking my diary, making a coffee, and greeting the staff. My son looked up at me and asked how I was, with a wry smile on his face, but clearing once I had acknowledged his comment.

I had about four different email addresses for various parts of my life. I checked the business mail and all seemed as expected, with the usual junk - delete, delete. Answers from buyers, a couple of new enquiries, world news, checking the latest fashion and business trends.

I switched to my personal mail, not expecting to see anything new.

The first one was in Spanish. I read through it, not comprehending what I was reading. A few words, 'accidente, malas, noticia de Alex' sent shivers through me, and I felt an instant numbness and the sound of rushing water through my head.

It was from Celistina his cousin and sent via a friend's email.

*'Hola, Gina, tengo malas noticias de Alex. Tuvo un accidente de transito esta madrugada y murio. Yo soy Celistina, la prima de el. Este correo es de una amiga. Mis saludos.'*

I had got the gist of it but google translated it to ensure I had fully understood it.

I raised my eyes slowly from my screen and looked at my son, in quiet shock. I heard my voice, as if from a distance, 'He's dead, he was killed in a motorbike accident.'

He looked at me, and the staff looked at me.

'Who's dead?' my son asked.

'Alejandro, he was killed in a motorbike accident last night.'

No one knew what to say. I was stunned, shocked and disbelieving. I reread the mail, remembered the time of my last phone call to him and then realised why I had not been able to get through to him. England was four hours ahead of Cuba. While I had been sleeping, around 4 am UK time, he had been killed. Where had he been the evening before?

My phone buzzed and it was Silvana, crying and asking me to come to Cuba.

I then received an email, which I think was from Celistina again, saying that the funeral would be at 4 pm Tuesday, 21st September and could I come. Tajo and Nestor would meet me at Holguin airport. She also sent me a photo of the accident and the bike.

A merry-go-round had started to whirl in my head, a carousel and its jangle spinning at comic speed.

I glanced momentarily at the photo on my desktop, not seeing it. I had to refocus and look again at the photo of him and his bike and relate it to the email I had just received. It didn't make any sense.

I had not agreed to return but felt under emotional pressure, some sort of obligation to take a flight back.

I picked up my bag and walked down to the seafront. I called my good friend, Elizabeta, and told her what had happened. The wind howled around me, and the waves were high. It seemed that Poseidon and Eurus were playing out a war over our coast. Our voices crackled through the speakers of the phone, but Elizabeta and I could barely hear each other. I was suddenly crying but did not fully know why. Was I in shock or relief? My last trip was still fresh in my mind, despite blocking out the events with layers of my heavy suppression of memories.

She asked me what I was going to do.

'The funeral is tomorrow afternoon, and I am here. How can I get there in twenty-four hours?'

She said, 'Don't go. You owe him nothing. The whole episode has scarred you, and he does not deserve for you to return there again.'

She was right but she did not know my character well enough. It was an episode which needed to be finished. I had not anticipated such an unexpected and tragic ending and walked slowly back to my home.

Opening the door, my daughter-in-law was just about to leave to pick up the children from playschool. I told her about the email. She was bent over, picking up something from the floor, with her long black hair skirting the ground. As she rose slowly, shock and disbelief registered on her face.

'How did it happen?' she asked gently. As I repeated the email, the full impact of the news began to settle over me.

'How can you get there by tomorrow?' she asked.

'I'll call Thomas Cook and find out if there are seats on tomorrow's flight. I doubt it as they are always fully booked far in advance and it's such short notice.'

My hands fell to my side, and I seemed to have gone into temporary paralysis.

Rousing myself, I called them and told them what had happened, saying that I had to be at my boyfriend's funeral at 4 pm (the first time I had referred to him as "my boyfriend") Cuba time the next day, as he had been killed in a motorbike accident during the night.

The lady at the other end did not ask me for evidence and calmly said that she would arrange my flight and charged me a compassionate fair of £1 to get there but the full price for the return journey. The whole fare cost about £270.

I walked into my bedroom, sat on the bed, and heard the front door bang. In numbed shock, I must have sat there for a while before I felt soft warm hands holding mine and, looking down, I saw the inquisitive face of my older grandson. He looked at me and, climbing on the bed, threw his tiny arms around my neck and hugged me.

Taking a deep breath, I picked him up and carried him back into our kitchen.

# 35

The night before I left, I called Silvana to ask her what I should wear to the funeral. She said that black would be fine, so I packed the only long-sleeved black cotton shirtwaister dress I possessed, hoping it would be appropriate for a Cuban funeral, bearing in mind that it would be above 30 degrees. I also wondered what I would do for the four days as, without him around, I did not need to be a tourist or visit any other part of Cuba. For some unexpected reason on that trip, there was a flight leaving Holguin for Gatwick on Friday of the same week, rather than the following Thursday, but the universe often maps out events not known to us.

Before boarding the train to the airport, I picked up a single red rose from a local newsagent to lay on his grave, a piece of Inglaterra that he would never see. I clutched it in my hand as I dragged my pull-along suitcase through to check-in, which on this occasion required my suitcase to be examined. As I rushed down the escalator to the departure gate, I realised that I had left the rose behind at Security. I ran back against the stream of passengers and, there, on the examining table, lay the red rose which was beginning to wilt. Clutching it again, back down the escalator, I heard a male voice say to me, 'He is a very lucky guy.'

Looking up, I stared into the face of a stranger smiling at me, and tears rolled down my cheeks. I remember saying to him, 'Not if you knew him,' and rushing down the stairs, reached the departure gate just as it was closing.

Nine and a half hours of flying time gave me plenty of time to think over the last few months. All the events, his duplicity, dishonesty, obsession for money and designer clothes, his longing to leave home in search of another life, all for nothing. He was gone.

I sat with my eyes closed, thinking of the many beautiful young men and celebrities who had died at an early age. Of course, James Dean came to mind.

I had difficulty opening my eyes, hiding behind them, hiding my continuing embarrassment of the whole episode. But I knew that I would see it out to the end, no matter what that end would be. I knew I would return once more after that trip. There was a need in me that I could not understand, and I wished I had someone around to explain it. When the wheels touched down, my head was filled with silence.

The plane landed around 2.45 pm local time, one and a quarter hours before the funeral. Tajo and Nestor were waiting for me outside the airport. They hugged me simultaneously. Sitting at the back of the car, Tajo kept looking at me and occasionally reached out and touched my wrist, his face drenched in tears.

As the car drew nearer, I recognised the place as we had stopped back in May, when he had dropped off his wedding picture at his mother's house although, at the time, I had not known it was his birth mother's house.

The car stopped on a grassy verge, outside the wooden fence, where it seemed that hundreds of people were gathered for the funeral. Motorbikes on their stands, their engines quietly idling, their riders astride, some leaning on the handlebars, others holding babies on the front.

Vicente came up to me and, taking my hand, led me down a stone path to a wooden house. I stopped for a moment at the gate, beginning to feel nervous as to what I would see inside, not having been given any further information as Tajo could not speak English, and Nestor was concentrating on driving.

I looked around. No one else was wearing black. Most people were in their usual clothes of tight camisoles, shorts or short skirts, and the men in long shorts or chinos, everyday clothes as if for an everyday event.

I continued walking up the short path in my black dress, high-heeled espadrilles, and black sunglasses to hide my tear-swollen eyes. As I neared the front door, a small overweight woman sat on a wooden chair to one side of the entrance and smiled at me. Vicente whispered that she was Alex's birth mother. As I walked down the path, I was aware of so many people quietly moving out of my path and staring at me. I wondered who they thought I was and why Silvana had insisted I come to the funeral. She had been anxious for me to be there.

I entered from the brilliant sunshine into a small stuffy room, the smell of death disguised with a heavy perfume of white flowers covering the coffin, trying to conceal that which could not be.

There, in front of me on a wooden tripod, lay a black coffin covered with large white lilies. I slowly approached, shaking slightly, holding my body close to me. The coffin was made from thick black cardboard, a pauper's coffin, once or twice seen in India. Towards the top, where his head would be, a cut-out square of plastic where his face could be seen. I was curious and at the same time became apprehensive as to what his face would look like.

Putting my hands on the side, I leaned over slightly looking down into the darkness of the inner coffin, his face covered in shadow. He looked the same, as though asleep, but I could see purple bruises, an indentation on his right cheek and something blue covering him from the neck down. I kept looking at him, my breath caught in my throat in disbelief. There was no feeling of love, more of sadness at the loss of his life, at some of the dreams he had shared with me, anger for what he had done, his stupidity, and for his papa, whom I had seen standing outside being held by his sister and daughter.

All around the house the sound of motorbikes opening their throttles sounded like distant thunder. Vicente gently touched my arm and whispered that we had to go and get to the crematorium on time.

I looked, one last time, at his silent face, bruised, purple, misshapen, and swollen.

Silvana stood outside, waiting for me by the front door. She grabbed my hand and almost pulled me down the path, through the gate, towards a gathering of people ahead. Within a few minutes, I turned to see the coffin being carried by Vicente, Tajo, Nestor, Papa, Norrie and some other men. They carried it to a small utility truck, slid the coffin into the back and closed the door. A crowd of people stood, with a few babies crying in the heat and teenagers chattering, all part of the funeral procession. I saw Celestina in the distance, dressed in shorts and a low-cut top, with large earrings dangling. I saw the whole scene as though I was an actor in a movie. It had to be a film that I was a player in. Why should he have been killed on his motorbike? What had led to the events of his death? Later I would discover, but now it was time to take him to a place that he could not have foreseen, as he rode his Kawasaki through the night and into an unimaginable place of darkness.

The procession of family, friends and neighbours walked slowly and reverently for a few more minutes, whispers of soft words caught in the air, as though flowing over our heads towards the coffin.

We all stopped, and I was almost pushed into the back of a car along with Silvana, Valeria and Laura, with Papa in the front passenger seat.

A cavalcade of motorbikes led the way, followed by the coffin and some other cars, with further motorbikes at the rear. Nestor looked at me in the rear-view mirror and said that it was normal for friends to ride their motorbikes, to pay respect. He seemed to have read my mind. I looked over at Valeria and saw that she had a white shirt in her lap, one of the shirts I had bought him on my second trip.

I remember turning to look behind and Silvana saying, 'Take a movie on phone.' I ignored her comment.

How could I be sitting in a funeral convoy in Cuba, nine months after my arrival? A crazy thought passed through my consciousness. A full term of pregnancy and, in hindsight, that episode had been like the full cycle of birth, life, and death, for quite a few players in that story.

As I sit here and write this story as it comes to the end of its nemesis, the events of the funeral cortege are so vivid. Travelling along the grey tarmac road, that Cuban family holding me with their closeness and possessiveness, the motorbikes with their raw roaring in front and behind, honouring him with their symbolism.

At the gates of the crematorium, a large sign in black read "Fenton Crematorium" and our car stopped outside. The truck carrying the coffin had already left and, stepping out of the car, Silvana was already at my door waiting for me. As my feet touched the ground, I looked towards the gate and noticed that most of the family, friends and neighbours had not travelled with the cortege. As we walked to the plot, I was flanked by Silvana and Laura holding me tight as if to prop me up so that I could barely walk. I had a crazy image in my head of a Haitian procession of white-faced ghosted people walking as though propped up, straight-backed. I tried to loosen their grip, but they held me closely.

As we walked through the lanes of graves, we approached his which was already surrounded by those people who had transportation, mobile phones high above their heads watching as his coffin was put into the ground. Coming up to the edge of the plot, I saw that it was not a deep six-foot hole in the ground but a shallow three-foot by six-foot-wide rectangular cemented trough. There was no priest, no last rites, no words of farewell, just a lot of people crowding around the coffin.

Silvana pushed me further to the edge, holding me by my waist and said, 'Gina, take movie.' The others were madly filming and I could not understand the bizarreness of that act. There was an air of fiasco around that crowded space.

I looked down at him as the lid had been removed and I saw his brother Karl, reach over the top of the coffin, his toes seeming to hang over the edge of the trough, and lay across his chest the unbuttoned white shirt which Valeria had been holding in the funeral car. The rest of his body was bound in blue bandages, wrapped around him tightly, like swaddling clothes. The duration of time in the coffin, probably from the early hours of the morning in Matanzas to Levisa, in the heat, had started the putrification of his body. His face had swollen, turning bruised and deep purple at the edges, the bruise on his face almost the colour of squashed purple aubergine. I could not look at his face and pushed myself back, pushing against soft bodies. I had to get away from that slightly demonic crowd, whom I thought would fall on top of the coffin, their toes gripping the edge or their bodies resting on those in front. They all seemed to want to get his death mask on video, their chatter like the chittering of cicadas before the coffin lid was replaced and cement poured over the opening of the trough.

Papa stood with Roberto, his brother, at the back of the small crowd, watching the scene in front, their fingers linked, their heads bowed, two people whom I knew loved him very much.

People gradually dispersed as though into the ether, the sound of the motorbikes silenced, the late afternoon sun cooled, and tiny twittering birds warbled in the trees which shaded the cement graves without crosses.

His cardboard coffin brought a clear realisation of just how poor those people were. In death, most people or their relatives strive to get a wooden coffin made from solid expensive wood with brass handles, a so-called fitting send-off for their dearly beloved. But this pauper's coffin of cardboard, with a piece of plastic for a window, was what could be afforded. Or maybe it didn't matter what type of coffin one was buried in, as underground who would see it? Only the worms and bacteria would relish what the body offered them.

I walked away towards the perimeter wall, feeling as though I had been physically beaten up. Turning around to face the rows of graves, I saw Vicente standing alone, watching me. He asked how I was doing, and I shrugged my shoulders.

We stayed a while longer and then walked back to the covered grave, with all signs of that former life gone.

Silvana walked around other graves and said to me that we should get an iron fence around his to make it look nice. I heard another voice saying that he deserved a marble headstone as he deserved nice things and turning, saw Celistina behind me, her eyes hard, hostile and full of what looked like venom.

Vicente came to me and quietly said, 'Let's go, Gina. All finished now.'

'Really?' I thought to myself. Even then I could still feel the master puppeteer pulling his strings.

Nestor drove us back at speed. Vicente was next to him, with Silvana, Celestina, and I in the back of the car. We arrived at the house of his birth mother, which piqued my curiosity,

When she saw me, she was full of smiles and took my hand, pulling me out through the small lounge where his coffin had been not more than a few hours earlier, through to the kitchen and out to the back garden which was planted with roses of all colours. It was early dusk, with the hazy sun hanging in a layered pastel sky and a faint perfume of roses drifting through the evening air.

A warm breeze blowing through all the open windows and doors seemed to have freshened the house, eradicating that heavy perfumed smell of death mixed with the heady sickening stench of those beautiful flowering white lilies. Death, which had pulled me back to this devilish island paradise, had now passed over this family. Its pall left a deep welt, a scar engraved into so many fragile psyches, its long sharp talons now filling us with unexpected memories. How long would I live with them?

She invited me to sit down at a small wooden garden table and brought out photos of him through various ages. I recognised the clothes he wore in some of the newer photos, and I found it difficult to look at them. She asked, in good English, if I wanted any of the photos, pushing them across the table towards me. I declined. She asked if I would like to stay the night there and sleep in his old bed. I gently declined and, turning to Vicente, asked if he could phone Casa Carolina to arrange a room for me.

I could not stay in that place any longer and as I walked back through the front garden, I noticed that it looked like an English country garden, with neat rows of rose bushes, trailing flowers along the garden fence, a prosperous-looking house, newly made with an outside water tap.

Her small ample frame filled the front door as I finally passed through the garden gate and out to the cracked footpath, bathed in the noisy silence of nature.

Nestor, who had appointed himself as my driver, drove us back to Silvana's house before going to Casa Carolina. As we drove back with Vicente, I asked him to tell me a little about his birth mother. It seemed she had been working in Venezuela as a nurse for a long time and had only arrived back in Cuba in the previous year. I did wonder about her house which looked newly built.

The sun had not quite set, and Silvana was sitting in the backyard, peeling yams. A small metal bowl lay on the ground at her feet, already filled with peeled garlic and cut red chillies. Her husband sat opposite on a small wooden chair, with his hat pulled down over his eyes as he whittled on a long stick.

I sat near her, with the ever-close Vicente on another small wooden stool and, while idly chatting with Vicente translating, I asked her what had happened to the house next door. What was the owner doing in the house? What happened to the £3000 paid for the house? I already knew but wanted some verification. She stopped, with her peeling knife held aloft in the air. She looked nervously at her husband and, while Vicente translated, she looked intently into my face. A glass of rum appeared in Norrie's hand which he pushed into mine.

'Gina, Alejandro came here on his bike, on his last trip, to see us and asked the owner to return the money for the house, saying that you did not want it and as the owner had not given any sale papers to him, he had to return the money. When we asked him what he would do with the money, he said he owed someone a lot for the Kawasaki. Back in July, he had ridden in the heat from Holguin, wearing his leather pants, jacket and boots and when he arrived at my house, he became very sick and had a fever. He stayed here for two days recovering and we were very worried. He seemed very anxious and nervous and then left.'

On reflection, that was when I had been in Maison Falon in Havana; the night I had reported him to the police and could not contact him.

# 36

'Tell me what happened last night.'

Vicente and I were back in the outside restaurant of Casa Carolina, with the small overhead lanterns throwing shadows across the ceiling and floor, the hot evening still and heavy. A bottle of beer, with frothy droplets fizzing over its top, stood on the table in front of him, and a fruit juice for me.

He started very slowly, his English reasonable.

'First, I am sorry that you lost the money for the house and the motorbike. It's too much money he had. He had become a little bit crazy over money.'

'Now it doesn't matter. What good was that money to him? He has lost his life. But tell me what happened on the night of his death.'

His head had been bowed but he slowly raised it, saying, 'I don't know all the details, but it seemed he had been in a strange mood. He was staying with friends in Matanzas and had gone to sleep at 10 pm that evening. One of the young friends he was staying with wanted to go to a salsa party in a nearby town and woke him up. He did not want to go but reluctantly agreed. They left on the bike and returned to

Matanzas at about midnight. He was driving very fast. Everywhere he went he drove fast, sometimes at 160 km/h. His friend sat pillion. The road did not have many streetlights and, ahead of him, a large yellow bus was slowly crossing an intersection from the opposite side to cross over to the bus station. It seemed that the bus driver did not see him coming and did not stop. At the speed he was travelling, he could not stop and rode straight into the side of the bus, sliding under it and was killed outright. I don't know how, but the young boy on the back was decapitated. The bus driver braked, got out, and a few people from the bus station, hearing the crash, came to help. There was another young friend close by who phoned his friends in Matanzas. They called Silvana in Santa Rita. He was taken to the hospital. Some friends went there and arranged for his body to be returned overnight to Levisa. Another one of his friends called me and I drove through the night. Here in Cuba, we must work very quickly when someone dies and bury them quickly, within twenty-four hours. Today, you felt its heat. So, all of this was a big rush.'

He paused, quiet for some time.

'Thank you for coming, Gina. I know that Papa and Silvana are very glad you came, you are very kind to them.'

I remembered the photos Celistina had sent me. One of him after the accident and one photo of his bike. He lay face down on the ground, his helmeted head to one side, wearing jogging pants and the Nike long-sleeved hoody I had bought him on a previous trip. I could not see his feet. His back arched upwards, arms twisted by his side. Almost the pose of a baby in its cot, bottom in the air, hands by its side. Content. Through the visor of his helmet, I saw a long trickle of dark blood trailing down his cheek. I had no idea how long after the accident this photo had been taken or who had taken it.

The bike was crumpled and twisted, beyond repair. It looked as though it had been crushed under the weight of the bus wheels.

There had been another photo of him, smiling, looking pleased and sitting tall on the bike, a black and white photo. It must have been taken recently.

I took a long breath, letting out a sigh that had been caught in my body for the past few hours.

'What was all this about, Vicente? He kept telling me that he still had the car, but he had sold it a long time ago and I had proof.'

'What will you do now, Gina? Will you ever return to Cuba?'

I thought that a strange question. What would I come back for?

'I still like Cuba. I did not expect to meet him and become fond of him. I did not come to buy anyone a car and if I had not given him the money for it and all the repairs, maybe … I think he became greedy. He did not want to work, did he? And all the money I gave him made it easy for him to continue the way he was.'

'When Alex returned from Switzerland after his divorce, he had a lot of money. I told him to buy a car and do business with it. He did not want to. Instead, he hired expensive cars and we drove everywhere. One night, we were returning from Levisa to Mayari, and he drove off the road into the side ditch. I was very badly hurt and had to go to hospital and have many stitches in my head. It took me about three months to recover. He was lucky, he had only a few cuts to his face and head. The car was destroyed and by then he had very little money left.'

I remembered seeing a photo of him with a bandaged head at his birth mother's house earlier in the evening.

'How long ago was this?'

'Back in early 2014.'

Suddenly Valeria and Papa arrived, and we sat quietly for a couple of hours drinking rum and beers, letting the warm evening breeze blow over us and through the sadness of the day.

Before they left, I asked where the nearest place was to get a headstone. Holguin was the only place, so we arranged to drive there in the morning and have a look, and order one for his grave. They said Nestor would drive us there the next morning.

Norrie, Valeria, Papa, and I were driven to Holguin, to a stonemason, a small yard in a backstreet. In its tiny stuffy office, a man stood covered in stone dust. We chose an open book with an angel perched on the top, made of white marble. They wanted me to choose the words to write in the book, but I could not do that. It was distressing to have to write words that, for me, would be a lie. They were his family, not mine. They looked at me tearfully, nodding their heads.

I stood aside from them until Norrie came to me saying it would cost about 50 pesos and would be ready by 10th December. As I gave him the money, our hands closed over each other and he gently pressed mine, leaning forwards to kiss my cheek.

On the way back, I thought of all the English funerals which I had been to and the after-gathering, the wake, of friends and relatives getting together to chat about and honour their loved one. There, it seemed, that would not happen. Maybe it was not the custom. I asked Norrie about it, and he said that Papa was too upset but maybe we could do something for him instead.

He suggested that we have something at the club in Nicaro, where we had danced a few times. We could make a video of all the photos I had taken of him, of which I had many on my camera and mobile, and play them on a screen, while we invited family and friends for some snacks and drinks in a private room at the club.

During the evening, Norrie, together with a few of his friends, converted the photos into a video with Alex's favourite music, then called various family members, inviting them to a gathering the following evening.

Vicente and I went to the club to arrange a room, time, and food for about 30 people, very close family, and friends. I was staggered at the cost that I was charged, took one final gasp, knowing there may still be another in reserve, and said I would pay them the next evening. The look on my face surprised him and he said he would talk to the manager about the cost.

I later found out that funerals in Cuba had no specific custom, being a mix of Catholicism and Santeria, based on the religion of Yoruba.

There had been no blessing at the graveside in the crematorium, just a crazy mayhem of photos taken. Like our funerals, it had generally been a sombre affair. I realised that I had not been to many funerals and those I had attended had been formal with eulogies and jokes spoken at the end of the church ceremony.

Maybe there had been a blessing at his mother's house before I had arrived in the late afternoon.

I had been told to wear black, and it seemed that it was the same tradition in Cuba, but out in the countryside all the attendees were dressed as though they had come from work or school or left their housework to attend his funeral. All done hurriedly. I had asked Vincente who had paid for the funeral and was told that it was state paid. Like so much else there.

The following evening, the club was full of local youth. Wednesday evening was party night, so it seemed as if those already there had nothing to do with the wake we had arranged.

I met a few of the family friends, who sat in a ring along the perimeter of the room, dressed for a party, but without smiles, all quiet, speaking in low tones. The music outside that special room was its usual thumping, highly charged self. Vicente acted as Master of Ceremonies and introduced me to each person, and I forgot the names as soon as I moved to the next one. As I passed from one to the other, I realised that possibly I had no right to suggest organising that event. It had not been his father's wish, as he was in deep mourning and shock. There I was, imposing my cultural requirements, for a person who had no affection for me, had duped me and, in the process, had died.

I remember leaving the room and walking outside into a dark blue, star filled evening, waves of pulsating cuban sounds, tapping gently into my soul, watching swaying bodies of youth, flowing hair, gyrating hips, and closely embraced bodies. A body I had last embraced, a final kiss, over six weeks earlier, was already slowly decomposing in a concrete pit.

Tilting my head back, I took in the void of blue darkness overhead and a flashback to the night sky of that bus ride from Holguin to Havana, that night of the first betrayal of a bonfire piled high, burning the vanities of my own making.

I heard light footsteps behind me and turned to see Vicente, with two full glasses of white rum.

'Come, there is a video on the screen of Alex, and a large crowd standing in silence watching.'

As I approached the screen, there were images of Norrie and him dancing salsa, a video I had taken on my second trip. His words repeated in my head, 'I want to be a famous salsa dancer, like Michael Fong.'

For a brief time, he was up on a screen, posthumously and locally famous.

That night, I too danced salsa and every other type of dance to every type of music that blasted out a trumpet of life.

To life here and gone.

# 37

One morning in late November, my phone rang. It was an unrecognised Cuban number. The voice spoke in perfect English, asking me to identify myself and if I knew Alejandro Rodriguez.

After a moment of silence, I heard myself confirming my name and that I had known him. The voice said it was from the British Embassy in Havana and they wanted to contact the family to return his passport.

I heard myself asking if he had been granted a visa to the UK, and the voice replied that he had not but asked who would come and collect his passport. I told him that Alejandro had died in September. I heard a soft intake of breath at that. I gave Silvana's number as she was his aunt and would arrange its collection.

The voice mumbled sympathy and said goodbye.

I felt the soft closing of another door.

# 38

I knew I would have to return for the setting of the headstone. It seemed that I had to walk that final path, to the very end which did not seem to have an ending.

I knew it would never end, there would forever be those thin arterial paths, various memories, and his relatives emailing, calling, seeing me as a living connection to him. I could not let go because of them. His actions did not reflect his family. I loved their warmth and their easy laughter; I understood their needs. I knew they had not been like him. They mourned him but he had eaten the proverbial forbidden fruit of a democratic and materialistic west, which had birthed a need beyond his ability to support himself. His charismatic character seemed to indulge in living off western women as an easy way to survive and this western woman, as naïve as they come, had fallen under his charm and perpetuated his needs.

I was there for five days, having decided to return via Manchester so I could return home earlier.

It was a perfect day to spend at a crematorium. The sun shone through the trees dappling little leaf shapes which trembled in the warm air. Papa and Roberto were already at the graveside.

The myriad birds sang lustful songs as I sat on a neighbouring tomb while Papa and Roberto began to set the marble book with its angel, at the head of his concrete box.

Over three months had passed since his death and Papa looked even more gaunt than before, his bony chest a little more sunken. When we met at Silvana's house on the day of my arrival, he greeted me with an affectionate hug and a bright smile, the same as the others. No sense of blame or animosity towards me. The loudspeakers were at full volume and Norrie was in the front, barbering. His girlfriend was almost due to give birth. The irony of life, one gone, another arriving.

Nestor had brought us in his car to Fenton Crematorium and then disappeared. Vicente arrived, having travelled from Havana the night before for the laying of the stone, the final earthly goodbye to his friend.

As I sat on one of the old worn graves, Roberto looked up at me and said, 'We must cement this headstone in very firmly or else it will be cut off and stolen by others. It is very good-looking so we must make this extra safe so no one can steal it.'

I was unaware until then that he spoke fluent English.

Vicente came and sat next to me while the cement foundation was laid, a small narrow ledge of wall built to house the base of the headstone. It took over three hours to build it. Buckets of sand and water were mixed, a small wall gradually built up to the required height to house the headstone. Idle chatter passed between the two brothers, a smile, a laugh, a tear wiped away from papa's cheek. I watched all of this from a faraway place, feeling a breeze on my bare shoulders and Vicente's soft breath on my cheek as he chatted to me in whispers, deeply respectful, sitting by Alejandro's grave.

Celistina turned up with Alfonso, looking like a tiny Vogue model, dressed in the shortest of shorts and low-cut top, belts and chains around her waist, tinted sunglasses masking her eyes, her mobile phone in one hand, long finger nails painted a bright pink. She stood a few feet from me, staring, burning brown eyes. I ignored her look, too disinterested in her relationship with him, which now meant nothing to me. She was there to pay her respects.

When the headstone was finally set, the top of the grave was cemented again and after a few hours, painted white. Another tiny cement box just below the headstone had been created to hold a bottle of flowers.

Silvana came later and we put candles around the edge of the grave, while Celistina played Divan's Alegria (joy) his favourite song and singer. He had met Divan backstage after a concert in Holguin, in August, and I stood watching as selfies were taken, His face was effused with happiness.

I had brought with me a large, black-framed photo, one which I had taken at the waterfall on my second return to Cuba when we were both enchanted with each other for all sorts of reasons. He had been dressed in white and stood on a rock in front of the waterfall. I propped up the photo against the newly laid book. To this day I cannot remember the words engraved on the stone written in Spanish.

The bird song quieted, and the sun beat hot through the trees as we all stood around his grave, candles gently flickering in the now almost still afternoon air. Music from

Celestina's phone played softly. Heads bowed; hands clasped in front. Silvana's arm was around my waist, tight as though I needed support. I gently had to disentangle myself from her grip and held her hand.

Papa could not speak as tears rolled down his cheeks, his brother standing close to him, one arm draped around his bent shoulders.

Only a few people at the final laying to rest. The white marble angel standing with hands clasped in prayer, atop an open book, paying homage to a man of importance, allowing his grave to have gravitas and be impressive amongst the other grey, bleak cement-covered graves, row upon row of what seemed forgotten peoples, as no names on the graves to mark a once living person. His plot number was 256.

'Vale, Gina. We go now, all finished, over.'

I stood at the foot of the grave; the birds had started singing. I had been unaware that they too, having noted the solemnity for a while, quietened, closing their beaks but now started their birdsong again. We had been there for almost six hours. I stared at the image of that once handsome face, a smile hovering around his lips, his eyes gentle, the short sleeves of his shirt showing off his muscular arms. The candles, the few remaining lit candles, had begun to flicker and some to die. No more thinking in my mind, the mental words had stopped, the recurring thoughts had stopped.

I turned on my espadrilled heels, the same ones I had worn on my second return to Cuba at the pig feast. What irony. Both had a violent death.

I had to leave then, I had to leave that place dappled in sunlight. Everything was normal, all those events were normal, birth, life, and death. Birth of a love affair, life of a love affair, and death of a love affair. I had been responsible for all the events that had taken place. I could have avoided them all, but I had created a life for all of it to happen and I would carry the burden of memories. Knowing the type of person I am, I would be unable to fully overcome the regret of my actions created on that paradise island.

# 39

We had returned from an overnight trip to Matanzas the day after the stone setting, to visit the site of his accident. Nestor and his wife, Clara, with Valeria, Papa and myself. Seeing Papa on the evening of my arrival, I impulsively asked if he would like to go to Matanzas to visit the site where his son had died. His eyes filled with tears, and he nodded his head, taking my hand and squeezing it gently.

Arriving late, we found a casa. Valeria and I shared a twin-bedded room, both a little shy of each other, as that would be the first time, we would be quite so intimate. She moved quietly about the room, sleeping a long quiet sleep. I was restless and felt like I had been awake all night. Papa stayed in the same casa, with Nestor and his wife next door to us.

We all breakfasted together and, after paying for all our accommodation, left by 10 am and drove to the highway intersection where he had been killed. It was a familiar route, being the main road down from Varadero to Matanzas.

Another hot day of blinding sun. My head felt as though drums were beating down into its core and, with the heat, my stomach constantly rose in waves of nausea.

There was barely any traffic and, parking the car, the four of them found a small stone wall at the edge of the same intersection where the bus had crossed on that tragic night. All was silent and still, with a few stray cars rolling down each side of the carriageway. Dry grass with a few white Michaelmas daisy-style flowers grew along the verge. I collected as many as I could, giving some to Papa and Valeria, and scattered the balance across the intersection.

Papa sat, legs crossed, clutching those small white flowers, which were gradually wilting in his hand. We all sat under the scorching sun, throats and skin drying, silent words murmured through closed lips, too stunned to utter any banalities, keeping our thoughts within our hearts.

I let Papa stay sitting for over two hours. He seemed to have become petrified in his solace, unable to move, just sitting and staring with eyes full of sadness, eyelashes wet. I did not allow myself to think about how he felt, or his sister and friends. Early afternoon finally dragged us from our somnambulance, and we left as silently as we had arrived.

I made the sign of the cross as we left, an age-old catholic habit of leaving a blessing of peace. We had paid our homage to that kind man's son and acknowledged the place of his death. I was hoping that through this act we could in some small way, close that door to Alejandro's past life. We had walked behind his coffin and now travelled back to the scene of his death. Maybe I could say goodbye, feeling I had repaid his family for my part in his death.

On an impulse, and before we got out of the car, I took off a thin gold bangle which I had worn on my right hand for over ten years and, turning around to Valeria sitting at the back, I took her slender hand and slipped it over her long fingers. She looked at me.

'It's real,' is all I said.

She reached over and stroked my hair.

# 40

What would I do for the next few days until my plane left? I had not hired a car, as I had been relying upon Nestor to taxi me around. There was nowhere that I wanted to visit. An obvious lethargy draped the air, and I had no desire to draw back that curtain. I wanted to go home, back to my own familiar space and people who had gradually realised the enormity of the events of this recent past.

I'd had breakfast and sat idly, only aware of the whirring overhead fan, my fingers clutching a glass of cold mango juice, lost in no thought. A movement made me look up and a stockily built Cuban man entered and sat at the adjoining table. He greeted me cheerily and looking up I caught his easy smile. He said he was waiting for his customer to drive him around Cuba. His next comment shocked me.

'I'm sorry to hear about the accident of your friend, but he was always very reckless and all in Mayari knew that one day something bad would happen to him. During the last few weeks, he came often through Mayari to Santa Rita on his bike, where I live. I know his Aunt Silvana. I am local here, so we all know what happens. I think I have seen you here in this casa before.'

I did not remember him.

His customer, a heavily built sun-tanned elderly American, joined him at the table and after a few beers and loud chatter, they left.

I looked over to the back of the restaurant, out towards the green field where I had stood and watched him play football, another eon away. A light cough made me look up and Vicente entered, walking across to my table. He had remained in Levisa after the funeral and for the next few days, as he had family there. His face was etched with deep lines of grief and his light brown eyes were filled with sorrow and kindness.

He asked me what I would like to do for the next couple of days and I suddenly remembered that I had not been to Baracoa on the eastern coast, having heard many stories about its heritage and cultural interest. There was no longer a need to be sad. I may never return to Cuba so decided to visit a new place. He seemed genuinely pleased to see me light up with life and sparkle, but I looked at him and wondered what he wanted, if he too wanted something from me, a leftover from his connection to Alejandro. Somehow though, stepping back for a moment, I saw his look of concern and a desire to do something for me to make up for all that had happened. I knew that they had been close for many years, and they talked about their lives intimately, their brotherhood.

He suddenly pointed his mobile at me and there, on the screen, was an image of what looked like a queue of people in an airport. I had to look closely at it as the image was not registering and then slowly realised it was an image of myself. I could not recognise that image of a shrunken, blank-faced woman.

'Is that me?'

'Yes, taken at Havana airport when you went to Miami back in July. I am Head of Security at the airport, and I was there that day and saw you standing in the queue.'

I remember passing my hands through my hair having been seen by unseen eyes and simply shaking my head from side to side. An unknown moment from the past.

We set off in a party mood at about 4 pm, cutting through the hilly region of de Humboldt National Park, a scenic route of densely covered verdant green hills and snaking roads.

Vicente, Valeria, and Clara, Nestor's wife, sat in the back, squashed, and merrily chatting, while I sat up front with Nestor driving confidently, and whistling to whatever music was blaring out on the radio. It was the taxi route, known as the cheapest route, to get to Baracoa from Levisa, about 165 km. We dropped down past Cayo Manubi, Sagua de Tanamo, and Moa (where Papa worked) along the upper east side of Cuba. An area steeped in the ecology of the island.

A mobile rang and Vicente answered, then spoke rapidly to Nestor. It seemed that an even shorter route would get us to Baracoa before too late in the evening. We turned off the main road, slipping through a narrow cut into the forest and came to a bridge which led onto an unmade road. We stopped and surveyed the road ahead which was without a surface and covered with small, jagged stones and sharp rock pieces.

I remained silent but wish I had not. That short road added over two painful hours onto our journey. Instead of driving at about 60 kph, we dropped to between 5 to 10 kph as the deeper we travelled that shorter route, the slower we had to go so as not to rip the tyres to shreds.

That strange route took us deeper into the forest, past small wooden houses almost built into the trees on one side and, on the other, a sheer ravine. I had no idea where we were, nor did the others. Silence settled in the car, as though we were all holding our breath in fear of hearing the burst of one or all the tyres.

We could not now go back as it was impossible to turn around on that narrow track, so we continued, finally coming out onto the main road, and continuing our journey to the coast.

I ruefully smiled to myself, as that short torturous journey reminded me of the past few months.

*'Within the beauty of this island paradise, a snake lies coiled, flickering its tongue, tasting the air, seeking out opportunities to feed.'*

Both men were quiet. I knew that they had taken that route on information someone had given them to save time and had then realised their mistake but had no choice but to continue.

Darkness had fallen by the time we arrived, all slightly physically rattled by the tension from that rock-piercing journey. What were the car's tyres made of to survive that surface?

Our party mood returned during dinner, the usual chicken and rice washed down with beers and wine. Both men spoke capable English and neither spoke of Alejandro. I was conscious of his lack of presence, and it seemed out of place to not have him there. Because of him, we were together, and those four Cubans were extending an abundance of care towards me.

I accepted that I would have to pay for that whole trip for all of us, as the total of their monthly income would have barely covered the cost of the meal and accommodation. I had resigned myself to this, knowing that in just a few more days I would be gone and probably never see them again.

In those last few hours, I surrendered myself to enjoying another side of Cuban life, with friends who were open and honest as their culture had nurtured in them.

Once again, I shared a room with Valeria but had no idea where the others slept.

The morning sun filled me with fresh happiness. We breakfasted, walked around the town, and meandered through some of the oldest colonial buildings in Cuba. Vicente was very knowledgeable about Baracoa and told me that its other name was Nuestra Senora de la Asuncion de Baracoa. We strolled to the top of an old fortress, El Castillo Baracoa, overlooking an exquisite turquoise and lapis lazuli blue sea, a true Caribbean blue, white pearls of froth lacing the top of the waves as they flicked headlong with the current to the white sandy bay.

In the afternoon, we drove down to Playa de Miel (Honey Beach), stripped off to our swimsuits and swam in those soft warm syrupy waves, washing my skin and my mind of all the betrayal, hurt, vanities, and any regrets of those past months.

Their playful laughter and the soft cadence of their voices created a dreamscape for the next few hours.

I bought fresh fish from a passing fisherman, his feet leaving deep indents in the soft sand and as he carried his sack of fish across one sloping shoulder. I took it over to the beach kitchen, where 30 minutes later, a waiter brought over a plate with the grilled fish, topped with lime and a salsa sauce and a huge bowl of steaming rice, A small square rickety table was set up under a tree, plastic chairs wobbled on the sand as we sat around the table, and I knew he was in all our minds. His death had brought us to a place where I had so often hoped he and I would have spent time together.

We sat, all of us gradually letting the effects of the beer drown out any further sorrows or concerns in that trap of time. Silence slowly descended upon us, comforting us, and locking away any tears until another time. That day was a celebration of a life that only being with those people could offer. The magic of Honey Beach, the magic of the white sand, and the ever-blowing softness of the Caribbean breeze wrapped its ageless arms around us.

A man came along with a huge bag packed with wooden salad spoons. I fingered the smooth polished wood and bought a pair, now lying in my kitchen drawer, bringing back memories each time I pull open that drawer. I did not feel the need to haggle with him over his price.

Vicente left the table and slid down the sloping sand and crouched in the sand, stick in hand, drawing enormous hearts filled with oversized flowers The words Gina and Alejandro at the centre of the heart. Gently cascading waves crept up behind him and, like a sleepy afternoon cat, licked away the words. I watched him, impressed by his love for his friend and at the sentiment he had drawn, knowing the falsity of it but not caring. What had been their dreams?

But I cared for the well-being of the people I was with. They had shown me friendship and concern. Whether they knew how I felt about their brother, friend or relative, mattered very little, only that I was on my own there and needed to be looked after.

Valeria, with her long-plaited extensions, piled high on her head, and wearing a tiny string bikini, caught the attention of a large Italian woman who ran towards her with her camera, insisting on taking her photo. The protective tigress in me arose and I told the woman she had to first ask and then pay her if she wanted to take photos. Her fury at that shouted out words of accusation at me and my jealousy of the young, a stream of spit dribbling from her lips. A laughing Valeria put her arm around me, hugging my shoulders.

These soft golden moments began to slip as the sun melted low over the distant horizon and we drove back to Mayari, in deep silence. Nestor dropping all of us at our various homes,

The next day before leaving, I phoned Vicente and asked him to ask his birth mother for the silver ring which I had given to him on that last day of leaving Havana at Hotel Beltran. I had a feeling that she would have it. Maybe the silver ring, silver which I valued in many ways over gold, symbolised breaking this ill-fated connection. I assumed that whatever jewellery he had worn on the night of the accident would have been removed. Within a couple of hours of asking, he told me that his birth mother had all his possessions, but she was at work in the hospital in Moa. He would phone and ask her if she could ask Celistina to give it to me as she lived near Santa Rita.

Just before leaving for the airport the next morning, Nestor drove me to his birth mother's apartment (it seemed she owned a house and apartment). I entered feeling apprehensive and slightly ashamed to be asking for the ring to be returned.

Four young women were sitting in the lounge, chatting and smoking, and became silent as I entered. Celistina walked out of a room, looking like she had just showered. She asked me to follow her to another room, a bedroom, and walked to a white wooden dressing table, opened a drawer, took out the ring, and handed it to me. She said she was staying there for a few days; I was unsure why she told me that. Her demeanour was cool as usual.

As I turned to leave the room, I looked at her again and noticed that she had the gold chain around her neck, the chain which I had given to him the last time I had seen him alive in Havana. The gold chain that I knew he had been wearing on the night of his accident as I had seen it around his neck in one of the other photos sent. That black and white photo of him sitting on the motorbike, presumably a couple of nights prior to the accident.

Tajo, Valeria, and Nestor drove me to the airport. We all hugged closely, Valeria with tears in her eyes, fingering the gold bracelet I had gifted her. Tajo standing awkwardly to one side. I knew he had no job, so I emptied my wallet and gave him about 64 pesos, as well as giving pesos to Nestor for fuel for his return home.

I stood and watched, as the three of them walked towards the exit and out through those glass doors I had so often exited.

My feet stood rooted while the tannoy for departure blared. No thoughts filled my body. I was numb and bereft of all emotion.

# 41

The years have passed now but the haunting of those memories linger.

I have not lost that sense of embarrassment or foolishness, but I've acknowledged the futility and the heartache of so many of those involved in this story.

A story that is repeated countless times, no matter how many people experience the same or similar. I guess many of us walk into those pages open-eyed but blind-sided by wanton longing and adventure; for the titillations of those moments, knowing the outcome, but unable to resist. It's entrancing and thrilling, and can we blame ourselves for the events we set in motion, in making that first moment of contact, a touch of the hand, a turn of the head, a frivolous smile, that innocent kiss? A fateful touch of lips to skin that drags us to ecstasy and remorse.

My life was altered. I forgave myself but could not forget the faces of the other innocents.

Sometimes a shadow nudges my thoughts. There were fragments of time when I did wonder just how innocent all the players in this story were. The moments when I caught those quick looks and glimpses between them, an erring on complicity. All that happened would have needed acquiescence from each of the players, for the something each got from those events which took place.

Could I bury those memories as the last candle flickered, as I stood by his grave? Would I ever forgive myself or somewhere in a future moment be drawn back into that same void of longing and wanting?

Christmas, New Year, Easter, and birthdays, those who had travelled with me to Baracoa still send messages of love and good wishes for my happiness and health and write, 'When will you return to Cuba? We miss you.'

*Will they ever let me go?*

# REFLECTIONS ON A KISS
## AUTHOR'S NOTE

In writing this story I have spent a lot of time thinking about the kiss.

I thought about that first tentative and gentle kiss that Gina gave Alejandro in that bici, on the ride back to her hotel during her final few hours in Cuba. She was being playful, a little bit of the vixen in her had to come out.

I remember reading a quote a long time ago which said that if you wanted to capture a particular look or feeling while taking a portrait photo, you should ask your sitter to think of something they especially liked. Gina could not ask that of Alejandro, as they had only just met and she felt he would not understand the meaning so, instead, she leant over and kissed him on the cheek, withdrawing very quickly and unaware of the consequences.

As she captured the look on his face which became suffused and wrapped in smiles, it reminded me of another quote by Aaron Siskind, photographer.

*"Photography is a way of feeling, of touching, of loving. What you have caught on film is captured forever … it remembers little things, long after you have forgotten everything."*

It seemed to have been important for Gina to catch the look she had seen on his face. I wonder if she ever regretted it.

A kiss is so multi-layered, and its meanings are so varied and complex. The evocation of feelings provoked by a kiss can be like tumbleweed through a deserted and dusty town. We went in with so much hope and were left barren in the face of desertion.

We sometimes give away our kisses like whispers in a breeze, like the 'Miu Miu kiss' that became so trendy a few years ago. Those air kisses of affectation and fun. Those casual kisses between friends, acknowledging and recognising friendship, longevity, secrets shared, bonds created and held close to the heart, never to be given away. Those hurried family kisses of hello and goodbye, sometimes almost obligatory, those stiff-lipped kisses of hardened familial love.

Then that shy, first-time kiss, of young blossoming love, so sweet, so exploratory, the unknown touch of the meeting of lips and that further unknown sensation that asks, "Will there be another?"

The Judas kiss of ultimate betrayal or the kiss that betrays our feelings for another.

As I wrote about that kiss on his cheek in the early stages of the story, I sensed that it was a kiss of betrayal. Gina not only betrayed her feelings, but she betrayed her hardened rule of not engaging with men while travelling. Yet on an impulse, and a vanity of emotion, she altered more than two people's lives as she travelled on a cosmic journey where every star was misaligned, and every further event became a mishap.

But a kiss, an embrace of lips, is as important as breathing.

It's the connection and the acknowledgement of one to the other, embracing their essence.

We breathe life into each other by that touch; lips to cheek, the softness of a baby's wet kiss, or the slow coiling of our bodies, entwining our breath, arms, chest to chest, stomach to stomach, and the total wrapping around of feelings.

As Alejandro thanked Gina for that light and hurried kiss, to Gina it was an affected action, but to Alejandro it was an opportunity to act.

# TRANSLATION

## Spanish words and phrases used in this story

| | |
|---|---|
| *a Habana* | *to Havana* |
| *abrazo lujurioso* | *lustful arms/lustful hugs* |
| *accidente* | *accident* |
| *ahora* | *now* |
| *amigas (f)* | *friends* |
| *besame mucho* | *kiss me a lot* |
| *bici* | *cycle rickshaw / bicycle rickshaw* |
| *carina (f)* | *darling* |
| *como estas?* | *how are you?* |
| *con leche* | *with milk* |
| *cuchillos* | *knives* |
| *cuidate* | *take care of yourself* |
| *costumbrismo* | *associated with Spain in the late 18th and 19th century (ref. Wikipedia explanation) – is the literary or pictorial interpretation of local everyday life, mannerisms and customs* |
| *demasiado, Senora* | *too much, Lady (I couldn't work out if she meant too much makeup or slow down)* |
| *estrano embrujado* | *bewitched stranger* |
| *extranjeros* | *foreign/strangers* |
| *hola* | *hello* |
| *joven* | *young* |

| | |
|---|---|
| *lo siento* | *I'm sorry* |
| *malos* | *bad* |
| *Mariposa* | *butterfly - national flower of Cuba - also known as white ginger* |
| *muchos difficile* | *many difficulties* |
| *no es seguro* | *it's not safe* |
| *no nos dice nada de su negocio* | *he doesn't tell us anything about his business* |
| *no problema* | *no problem* |
| *no se* | *I don't know* |
| *pero* | *but* |
| *Plaza Vieja* | *Old Square* |
| *Policía* | *Police* |
| *porque?* | *why?* |
| *que?* | *what?* |
| *que pasa con?* | *what's happening with? / what's going on with?* |
| *que pasa?* | *what's up?* |
| *que tal?* | *how's it going?* |
| *si* | *yes* |
| *siempre peleas* | *always fighting* |
| *sine leche* | *without milk* |
| *te amo* | *I love you* |
| *te quiero* | *I want you / I desire you* |
| *una mas* | *one more* |
| *vale* | *OK* |
| *vale, vamos a Habana ahora* | *OK, let's go to Havana now* |
| *vamos* | *let's go* |

**Noticia de Alex**

*Tengo malas noticias de Alex. Tuvo un accidente de transito esta madrugada y murio. Yo soy Celistina, la prima de el. Este correo es de una amiga. Mis saludos.*

**News of Alex**

*I have bad news of Alex. He had a traffic accident this morning and died. I am Celistina, his cousin.*
*This email is from a friend. My greetings.*

*Cuban Names – The Cubans have a great love of unique names, male and female. It is thought that it is a form of rebellion, that they were trying to forget their past as a Spanish colony and not giving their children names listed by the Catholic Church. Many names are of Greek origin as well as influenced by the Soviet Union.*

MARIPOSA

# ACKNOWLEDGEMENTS

## IN GRATITUDE

I began scribbling my novel, yet unknown to me, on my 1st trip to Cuba. I wrote about all I saw and felt, as I always did when I travelled. The experiences and peoples I encountered and the places I passed through were like no other. I had walked into a new culture, beguiling, and mesmerising. To the many Cubans I met I am eternally grateful for their warmth and generosity of selves, for allowing me into their private and intimate lives, with laughter and dance. I learned bittersweet lessons and immense humility in the course of time I spent with them.

A few years after my many trips to Cuba, an email popped into my inbox from Evolution Brighton, offering a creative writing course for memoir writers, run by Dorothy Max Prior. I immediately enrolled and for over one year, with her guidance and tutelage, my debut novel was born.

So, a big Thank You to Max for helping me to develop the art of writing, who opened my mind to the power and love of words and pushed me headlong into this wonderful dimension of memoir writing.

To Hannah Chapman, Isabelle Rushforth, Eddie Glebocki, Allan Winter, Helen Aguirre, and Anna Castleton, Thank You to these lovely people, part of the same Evolution Brighton memoir writing group, who patiently listened to and commented on my fledgling writing every week for almost one year. I hope that by now they too are published authors.

A special Thank You to another brilliant group of authors, whom I met through Michael Heppell's "Write That Book Masterclass 2021". Many of them selflessly gave off their time to advise and encourage me when I felt less than brilliant. They helped me keep my writing momentum almost at optimum level, not an easy feat.

So, thank you Richard Thomas, Alexis Scott, Ian Pilbeam, Roger Wilson-Crane, Matthew J Bird, Alan Rafferty, Elaine Allen.

Thank you, Michael Heppell, for your insights and opportunities given, to meet so many people, all eager to write. You helped so many of us.

And a special Thank You to Matthew J Bird, who has done the typesetting for my book, but not just the typesetting, the time spent on zoom answering so many questions not related to typesetting, but about the process of printing and publishing my book.

A very special Thank You to Hannah Powell, author of "The Cactus Surgeon", who has been my mentor and guide over the past couple of months, pointing me in so many right directions to help me get my book in front of key social media people.

To the many people like Hannah, who have helped me for no other reason than a generosity of self.

I cannot forget Christine Beech, my editor, who proofread my book and helped it to be the best it could be and her patience in correcting my many "wonderings" and "wanderings". Thank You Christine.

Designing the cover for a book is not as straightforward as I thought. So, Thank You to my good friend Kerry Lang, Artist and Jenn Garside, Illustrator & Graphic Designer.

To my dearest friend Laurel Sheridan, down under in Australia, who would chat to me just before she fell sleep, who read my novel three times, checking my thought processes, my reasons for including and then excluding certain parts; constantly making me question and consider almost every word I wrote. And she wants to read it again. Thank you, Laurel.

To those who will read this book, and those whom I will never meet, who will have experienced similar experiences to mine, that they will be gentle and non-judgemental on themselves.

To Gianni Zappas, thank you for the many hours you have given while I sat and wrote the final chapters, constantly being a sounding board and an inspiration for my creative soul. Your gentle presence has been curative.

To all those readers who will take the time to read my debut novel, Thank You.

My final gratitude to my son and his family who watched me travel along a stony path and never criticised or condemned my actions but were there with open arms and hugs when I needed them.

**Website**

www.bethjordanwriterphotographer.life

**Email**

thisisitamwriting@gmail.com

# ABOUT THE AUTHOR

I have always felt a misfit with a burning rebellious soul and a thirst for knowledge of global cultures, especially the cross-cultural peoples of the world.

I was born in India of Anglo Indian/Eurasian parents, residing in old colonial railway colonies. We lived a charmed but borrowed european lifestyle, attending catholic convents, far from home and being taught by narrow-minded nuns. I escaped my early cloistered life through my parents' immigration to the UK. Barely here I landed back in the arms of more nuns, until a further escape at sixteen to a teenage life of college.

I followed in the footsteps of family into careers in nursing, teaching, and then breaking free by setting up my own business in design and textiles, manufacturing out of China and India.

Love, marriage and a child came along to divert the course of my life but I continued studying, particularly anthropology, which further fired my passion for travel and cultures similar to my own. I wrote down their stories, kept copious notes, and gradually melded them with my own heritage. Diary keeping and photography became an obsession and soon, I became a scribbler, until my scribbles became my debut novel - **Thank you for the Kiss.**